HUNTING WITH RICHTHOFEN

THE BODENSCHATZ DIARIES: SIXTEEN MONTHS OF BATTLE WITH JG FREIHERR VON RICHTHOFEN NO.I

FOREWORD BY HERMAN GÖRING

TRANSLATED BY JAN HAYZLETT

GRUB STREET · LONDON

Published by
Grub Street
The Basement
10 Chivalry Road
London SW11 1HT

Copyright © 1996 Grub Street, London
Text copyright © Jan Hayzlett

British Library Cataloguing in Publication Data
Bodenschatz, Karl
Hunting with Richthofen: the Bodenschatz diaries: sixteen months of battle with
JG Freiherr von Richthofen No.I
1. Bodenschatz, Karl – Diaries   2. Richthofen, Manfred, Freiherr von
3. World War, 1914-1918 – Aerial operations, German
4. World War, 1914-1918 – Personal narratives, German
I. Title
940.4'4'943'092

ISBN 1 898697 46 9

Edited by Daniel Balado-Lopez
Typeset by Pearl Graphics, Hemel Hempstead
Printed and bound in Great Britain by
Biddles Ltd, Guildford and King's Lynn

This book was originally published in old German script as *Jadg in Flanderns Himmel*

And He who in sacred battle
A hero's death has found,
Though in foreign soil, also rests
In the Fatherland's beloved ground.

Loosely translated from a German soldier's handbook circa 1915

ABOUT THE AUTHOR

Karl Bodenschatz was born in Rehau, Germany on December 10, 1890. Upon the outbreak of hostilities in August 1914, he saw active duty with the 8th Bavarian Infantry, taking part in the Battle of Verdun. In October of 1916, having been wounded four times, he accepted the position of squadron adjutant for Jasta 2, headed by his former classmate, Hauptmann Oswald Boelcke, then the leading ace of the German Air Service. Boelcke died in a mid-air collision the same day that Bodenschatz reported for duty. After accompanying Boelcke's body home for burial in Dessau, Germany, Bodenschatz returned to Jasta 2, where he assumed acting command of the unit for a short time.

In July 1917, at the personal invitation of Baron Manfred von Richthofen, he joined the newly-formed Jagdgeschwader No.I as squadron adjutant, a post he would occupy for the duration of the war, serving under all three commanders. Following the armistice, Bodenschatz went on to serve in the Reichswehr. In 1919 he married Maria Walter and together they had one son, whom they named Manfred. In 1933 he joined his former commander, Herman Göring, in Berlin where he served as Göring's liaison officer to Adolf Hitler, eventually rising to the rank of General of Aviation.

His military career ended on July 20, 1944 with the injuries he suffered during the assassination attempt on Hitler's life. Bodenschatz surrendered to the American forces at the end of WWII, and was interned as a POW until July 1947, during which time he testified on Göring's behalf at the Nuremburg trials.

Following the death of his first wife in 1960, he married Frau Erna Dziuba in 1966. This exciting and eventful life came to a quiet end in August 1979 at the age of 89. His ashes are interred in the Bodenschatz family plot in the Waldfriedhof cemetery, Munich.

CONTENTS

FOREWORD

As the last commander of the Jagdgeschwader Richthofen, I have little in the way of words to add to these pages which tell of heroic deeds. In November of 1918, German aviation crashed to earth, struck by a fatal blow. It was with a bleeding heart there in Aschaffenburg that I discharged the officers of my Geschwader, the proudest and most victorious unit that has ever existed, for all time, among all nations. The heroic deeds of a *Nibelungenlied*[1] itself pale in relation to this symphony of heroism, passion, courage, and contempt for death. In fearful storms of steel, the Geschwader climbed victoriously towards the sun, bringing death and destruction wherever it encountered the enemy. All of this devotion, all of this courage in the face of death, all of this readiness to sacrifice now seemed in vain. The Front, which had stood for four years in a wall of smoke, fire and iron, seemed to have been cheated of its sacrifices and its meaning. That is how we felt as we disbanded there in Aschaffenburg and bade farewell to a unit that meant the world to us.

And yet, in the midst of the darkest night, there sprang up the first spark of a new faith, a faith founded on a blind trust in the German people, a trust that had just brought a miracle to achievement. From this spark came a torch, from the torch came a beacon, and from the beacon there came an ocean of fire in which the German people were refined and forged into a new greatness.

Today we have once more found the connection to the Front. Today, the sacrifice of the blood that was spilled has again regained its meaning, and like a phoenix, German aviation, the German Air Force, arose from the ashes of the former Jagdgeschwader Richthofen. But like an inalienable law, within this German Air Force the Jagdgeschwader Richthofen had to arise anew.

Bold pilots once more trace their circles in the German sky, led by the iron men of the Front, and all of them filled with that spirit which the immortal Rittmeister once gave us. This spirit guarantees that the new Geschwader, in sacred duty to the name it bears, will be ready at any hour to risk its life for the freedom and honor of the nation.

And with that, we have come full circle.

Reichs Minister of Aviation, Hermann Göring
General of Aviation, Berlin, 1 June 1935

---

[1] A Middle High German epic poem, dating from about AD 1200, in which the hero, Siegfried, performs many heroic deeds. Richard Wagner's opera cycle, *Der Ring des Nibelungen*, is the most famous adaptation of this work.

TRANSLATOR'S NOTES

Jagd in Flanderns Himmel by Karl Bodenschatz has long been considered a classic in the field of World War I aviation books. First appearing in Germany in 1935, its publication coincided with the re-establishment of the Jagdgeschwader Richthofen in that same year, with later editions appearing in 1938, 1941 and 1942.

On reading the original book, several facts become readily apparent. First, it is obvious that General Bodenschatz relied heavily on the original squadron log in writing the book. Many pages have been lifted directly from the log and expanded only slightly within the text. In other instances, the log served to spark vivid, personal recollections for General Bodenschatz who then narrated these episodes in abundant detail. The result is a text marked with frequent tense changes, often within the same paragraph and, in some instances, even within the same sentence. For the most part, these abrupt changes of tense, as disconcerting as they may be to the modern reader, have been left as written. In a few instances, however, when a sudden change of tense occurred in the telling of a specific incident, this was changed to correspond with the predominant tense of that particular account, in order to preserve the smooth flow of the story.

Secondly, it is obvious that the original book was rushed into publication with little or no proofreading. Certain obvious typographical mistakes have been corrected, for example where men were noted in the log book as being in 'Jasta 1', the last digit having been dropped, or where victories were listed as having occurred at 1.30 a.m. instead of p.m., etc. In most instances, however, suspected typographical errors have been left as they appeared in the original and footnoted.

The spelling of names, both of individuals and locations, varied widely throughout the text and log book. Every effort has been made to use the currently accepted names of the towns and villages mentioned, but a number of these have resisted positive identification. Those place names which could not be identified with certainty appear here just as they appear in the original book.

Names of various members of the Jagdgeschwader also presented difficulties. The names of several lesser-known members were spelled differently each time they appeared. Wherever possible, names are given as they appeared in the casualty list, *Verlustliste der deutschen Luftstreitkräfte im Weltkriege*, Verlag C. A. Weller, Berlin, 1930.

Much new knowledge has emerged in the last 75 years, and it is now known that many of the airplanes listed as victories in the squadron log were misidentified in the heat of battle. The discrepancies between General

Bodenschatz's records and recent findings were far too numerous to be dealt with adequately here, and therefore, the reader is strongly urged to consult the many excellent reference sources now available for the latest theories and information regarding the various victories mentioned herein and the types of aircraft involved. Among these reference works are *Cross and Cockade* magazine, *Over The Front*, the Journal of the League of World War I Aero Historians, and *Above The Lines*, Grub St, London, 1993, by Norman L. R. Franks, Frank Bailey and Russell Guest.

I worked mainly from the 1935 edition, incorporating a few changes from later editions. A revised account of Manfred von Richthofen's death which appeared in the 1938 and later editions has been included as an appendix. Only one significant change has been made from the original. A short chapter at the end of the book, entitled 'Spring 1935', which deals briefly with Hermann Göring's first exposure to and adoption of the tenets of National Socialism and with the re-establishment of the Jagdgeschwader Richthofen by Adolf Hitler, appears here in an abbreviated form. Adolf Hitler's decree, which re-established the unit and which may be of historical interest to some readers, appears in its entirety. However, the remainder of the chapter was devoted to the strident nationalistic rhetoric that characterized so many German publications of the 1930s, and after much deliberation, I have decided to omit it from this translation. This was done out of respect for the feelings of the Bodenschatz family who have been most gracious in lending their approval to an English translation, and for a later generation of Germans who are striving to put the Nazi nightmare behind them. Moreover, the brave men whose stories are told in this book fought and died long before Adolf Hitler cast his long shadow over Germany, and they do not deserve to have their names unfairly darkened by the ghastly events of later years.

Some trace of this strident rhetoric does remain within the main text, but it is my sincere hope that readers of this translation will pass over it, and read this work for what General Bodenschatz originally intended it to be: a loving tribute to those dear comrades and brave deeds that were already fading from memory into history in that spring of 1935.

I would like to thank the many wonderful people who have been so generous with their time, knowledge, encouragement, and support, among them: Norman Franks, John Davies, Howard Fisher, Neal O'Connor, George H. Williams, and his son, Scott Williams, Marianne Bodenschatz, and Johanna Kondratieff.

I am also deeply indebted to several people in particular for many of the photographs for this book: Lucrèce Falepin of the Courtrai Visitors' Bureau for the photos from the Courtrai Historical Society, George H. Williams for photographs from both his private collection and from the

Bodenschatz family album, Kenneth Greenfield for sharing his impressive collection of Imperial German postcards, and Sue Hayes Fisher for the rare, old photographs of the Richthofen museum in Schweidnitz from her Richthofen collection.

Lastly, many thanks are also due to my brother, Dennis Hayzlett, for his photographic skills, to my mother, Charlotte Hayzlett, for endless hours of babysitting and, of course, to my two patient and understanding boys.

Jan Hayzlett
Fort Collins, Colorado
1996

DEDICATION

TO THE FALLEN COMRADES OF
JAGDGESCHWADER FREIHERR VON RICHTHOFEN NO. I

As the former adjutant of Baron von Richthofen, I witnessed at first hand the life, struggles, and death of the glorious Jagdgeschwader Richthofen from the day of its formation till the day of its dissolution. My records make note of every hour and have been scrupulously kept. In the dark days of the Revolution, I succeeded in rescuing them from burning at the hands of the Communist criminals.

This record deals with an élite unit of the Field Army, a unit of very young men, whose youngest member was nineteen years old and wore the order *Pour le Mérite*; whose commander at the time of his death was twenty-five years old, had eighty air victories behind him, and was regarded as the most glorious fighter pilot who ever lived. Just as the noble name of the first commander entered into German history, someday the name of the last commander will go into history: Richthofen and Göring.

In the sixteen months of its existence, the Jagdgeschwader Richthofen fought a magnificent battle against an overwhelming force that grew with every day. Almost hour after hour, it dispersed the enemy squadrons that darkened the sky. Countless times it seized control of the air over crucial sectors of the Front. Countless times it provided relief to the struggling infantry. In sixteen months, it destroyed more than six hundred enemy aircraft. Jagdgeschwader Richthofen remains an immortal example of fighting and dying for the Fatherland.

Bodenschatz

GLOSSARY OF GERMAN TERMS AND ABBREVIATIONS

Armee Flug Park: Army aviation supply depot.

Assistant Arzt: Medical Officer.

Flieger Abteilung (Fl Abt): Aviation section or unit; an 'A' following this denotes a unit assigned to artillery cooperation duties.

Flieger Beobachter Schule: German Air Service school for training observers.

Flieger Ersatz Abteilung (FEA): Aviation replacement section or unit.

Fliegertruppe: The Air Service.

Freifrau: German title for a Baroness by marriage.

Freiherr (Frhr): German title of Baron.

Freiin: German title for a Baroness by birth.

Geschwader: Squadron. See also *Jagdgeschwader.*

Gitterrumpf: An airplane with an open lattice-work fuselage, seen in British 'pusher' type aircraft.

Graf: German title of Count.

Führer: Literally 'leader' as in Staffelführer. Can also mean the pilot of an airplane.

Inspekteur der Fliegertruppen (Id Flieg): Inspector of Aviation Troops or Air Service.

Jagdgeschwader (JG): Literally hunting squadron or fighter wing. A permanent grouping of four *Jagdstaffeln* under a single commander.

Jagdgruppe: A temporary grouping of several *Jagdstaffeln* under a single commander for deployment as a large unit during large-scale offensives.

Jagdstaffel (Jasta): A pursuit flight unit or echelon, usually consisting of nine to 12 aircraft.

Jastaschule: German Air Service school for the training of fighter pilots.

Kampfgeschwader der Obersten Heeresleitung (Kagohl): Bomber squadrons of the Army High Command.

Kampfstaffel (Kasta): A combat flight unit or echelon.

Kommandeur der Flieger (Kofl): The officer in command of the aviation units assigned to a particular army.

Kommandierender General der Luftstreitkräfte (Kogenluft): Commanding General of the German Air Service.

Luftwaffe: The German Air Force of the Third Reich.

Reich: Empire.

Rumpfdoppeldecker (RDD): A biplane with a solid fuselage.

Schlachtstaffel (Schlasta): An attack or ground support unit.

Staffel: A flight unit, used here interchangeably with *Jasta* and *Jagdstaffel.*

Uhlan: Member of a lancer regiment.

Wehrmacht: The German Armed Forces of the Third Reich.

German ranks with their approximate equivalents and abbreviations:

Feldwebel (Fw): Sergeant.

Feldwebel Leutnant (Fw Lt): Warrant Officer.

Flieger (Fl): Private in the Air Service.

Gefreiter (Gefr): Private First Class.

General der Flieger: General of Aviation.

Generalleutnant (Gen Lt): Lieutenant General.

Hauptmann (Hptm): Captain.

Leutnant (Lt): Second Lieutenant.

Leutnant der Landwehr (Lt d. L.): Lieutenant in the reserves, ages 35 to 45. *Landwehr I:* trained reserves; *Landwehr II:* untrained reserves.

Leutnant der Reserve (Lt d. R.): Lieutenant of the Reserves.

Oberleutnant (Oblt): First Lieutenant.

Oberst: Colonel.

Oberstleutnant: Lieutenant Colonel.

Offizier Stellvertreter (Offz Stellv): Acting Officer.

Rittmeister (Rittm): Cavalry Captain.

Schirrmeister: Maintenance Technical Sergeant.

Unteroffizier (Uffz): Corporal. Also the generic term for a non-commissioned officer.

Vizefeldwebel (Vfw): Vice Sergeant Major.

Werkmeister: Workshop superintendent; foreman.

CHAPTER ONE

THE SIXTEEN MONTHS OF COMBAT

I   SUMMER AND FALL 1917 IN FLANDERS

At the end of June 1917, in a castle in the vicinity of Cambrai, an orderly burst in excitedly, just as the soup was placed on the table in front of the men of Jagdstaffel Boelcke.[1]

'Take it easy!' said the adjutant disapprovingly. 'What's the matter?'

'Oberleutnant Bodenschatz is wanted on the telephone by Rittmeister von Richthofen,' the orderly bellowed solemnly into the room.

'Me?' asked the adjutant, surprised. He pushed his chair back and, to the inquisitive silence of the men, he left the room.

'Good morning, Bodenschatz!' he heard on the phone. 'Richthofen here. I have just been appointed commander of a Jagdgeschwader. I need an adjutant. Do you want the job?'

'Of course. I'll be there tomorrow morning. Where is it?'

'I'm glad, Bodenschatz. Marckebeke near Courtrai. Goodbye.'

The adjutant wandered slowly down the long corridor. He didn't go right back to the meal, but stopped at a window and stared out. That was one of the nicest telephone conversations he'd held in his conversation-rich, adjutant's life. He found it kind of Richthofen, not to have forgotten him.

Bodenschatz remembered back to the time, a year ago, when he had been appointed adjutant to Hauptmann Boelcke. He assumed this appointment under tragic circumstances at that time. When he arrived at the airfield, he was greeted by the news that Boelcke had fallen that same morning.[2] And the new adjutant's first job was to accompany his fallen Staffel leader home. Following his return to the Staffel, there was little time to brood over this irreparable loss, for a strong wind blew and the heroic

---

[1] On 17 December 1916, Jasta 2 was renamed Jasta Boelcke in honor of its first commander, Hauptmann Oswald Boelcke, who died in a mid-air collision on 28 October 1916. Boelcke had been von Richthofen's commanding officer and mentor.

[2] Hauptmann Boelcke's fatal crash occurred at approximately 5.00 p.m. on 28 October 1916.

spirit of the fallen leader burned on in the young pilots of his Staffel. There were fighter pilots with famous names: Böhme, Kirmaier, Müller, and a young Uhlan Leutnant, Manfred Freiherr von Richthofen. The adjutant very soon made friends with the Uhlan and, when Richthofen received command of Jasta 11 in the autumn of 1916,[1] Oberleutnant Bodenschatz felt the separation from him keenly.

It was grand of Richthofen, this call now, and the adjutant made his way to the table to pass the news on to his comrades. He already had his hand on the door handle when he hesitated once again. *Damn, there was still one catch!* Within seconds, a meeting he'd had a few days earlier ran through his mind like a movie. In Douai, he had run into Hauptmann Götz, battalion commander of the 8th Bavarian Infantry Regiment, in which Bodenschatz had been active. The Hauptmann had looked bad, and was very depressed.

And he had some reason for that. He came out of a region near Arras and, at that time, anyone returning from that district uninjured could count himself lucky, for he came from one of the bitterest of battles.[2] Except for his own weary and exhausted body, Hauptmann Götz had brought back few of those who had moved into battle with him; the entire regiment had been almost completely wiped out.

'Bodenschatz,' the captain had cried out, happily, 'that I should run into you! Listen! You won't leave me in the lurch, will you? The regiment must be put back on its feet. Number one, therefore, is we need a regimental adjutant. That's you!'

And because there was not one active officer in the German Army who did not remain utterly faithful to his old regiment, the adjutant of Jasta Boelcke had not hesitated a moment to become an infantryman again. He gave the Hauptmann his promise to be at his disposal, when the regiment was ready.

This meeting went through Bodenschatz's head as he held the door handle in his hand but, after a couple of seconds, he pushed the door handle down resolutely and entered the room. After all, someone else could be the regiment's adjutant, but to be the adjutant of a Jagdgeschwader, of a totally new kind of unit, that called for an officer who had been specially trained for such a job. As the higher duty, he mustn't leave Richthofen in the lurch.

To the questioning looks of his comrades, the Oberleutnant answered, 'Tomorrow morning, I'm gone from here. Adjutant to Richthofen.'

A congratulatory cheer roared across the table. And everyone understood completely when the Oberleutnant didn't spend any more time eating, but disappeared with murmured apologies after a couple of bites.

---

[1] Manfred von Richthofen was actually given command of Jasta 11 on 14 January 1917.
[2] Battle of Arras, 9 April to 16 May 1917, in which the Germans lost over 100,000 men.

'Andreas!' The shout raced through the castle and was passed along through all the corridors, halls and rooms. Andreas Seitz from Swabia, his batman from his Leutnant days of long-forgotten peacetime, immediately presented himself before the Oberleutnant. After a few words from his master, Andreas whizzed like an arrow to pack the trunks, and no Oberleutnant's batman had ever been happier than this Andreas who, in all cases and in all circumstances, always preferred the airmen to the infantry.

The next morning at the crack of dawn, a field-grey car left Cambrai in the direction of Courtrai, and around noon on this day, 2 July 1917, the new adjutant of Jagdgeschwader I arrived at Marckebeke airfield near Courtrai, in Flanders. He found his commander standing next to his airplane in the company of several men. And the officer who heartily shook Oberleutnant Bodenschatz's hand was no longer the little-known Uhlan Leutnant of the past, but was Rittmeister von Richthofen, victor of fifty-six air combats, Commander of the Geschwader, Knight of the Order *Pour le Mérite*, and the most renowned airman of the German Army.

It was just after 10.00 in the morning, and a wonderful summer day. And this beautiful day seemed to have found its reflection in the red airplane standing there, in the faces of the officers, and in the clear features of the commander himself. Everyone was in high spirits, and the best of moods. The Rittmeister, the thick-knobbed cane called the *Geschwaderstock*[1] in his hand, was playing around with his ever-rowdy Great Dane, Moritz, and he gestured to the sky in the direction of the Front.

'A paradise for pilots!' he informed the adjutant. And one of the gentlemen standing behind the commander said, 'Fifty-seven!' Richthofen had just returned from his fifty-seventh victory.

Bodenschatz secretly contemplated the Baron's face. Strictly speaking, it had scarcely changed since he had seen him last. Perhaps, it had become a little more stern. It was the face of someone who was a decent person down to the last corner of his soul. Within his face lay a resilient energy, an energy without restraint, without nervousness, the wonderful energy of youth. Under the amiable mouth sat the strong chin, and the look from his clear, sincere eyes was the look of a man at peace with himself, with the world, and with everything in his past.

As his gaze wandered further over the airfield, the new adjutant immediately got the picture; there was a great deal to do here. The Geschwader had arrived only yesterday. It had to be organized. In general, the reason for the establishment of the Geschwader and what it was to do were known. The order of the Commanding General of the Air Service left

---

[1] This 'squadron walking-stick' was carved for von Richthofen by his mechanic, Holzapfel, and became a symbol of the commander of Jagdgeschwader I.

nothing to be desired in its brevity and absolute clarity.

Supreme Headquarters, 26 June 1917

By order of the Chief of the General Staff of the Field Army, dated 23 June 1917 (Ic No. 58341 op.), Jagdgeschwader I is formed from Jagdstaffeln Nos. 4, 6, 10, 11. The Geschwader is a closed unit. It is appointed for the purpose of fighting for and securing aerial superiority in crucial combat sectors.

Chief of the General Staff
(signed) Thomsen[1]

With these three succinct sentences, everyone on the Marckebeke airfield was completely in the picture. Certainly, everywhere on the Front, in every dugout, in every trench, in every hut, in every bunker, they were fighting hard. But here, from out of Marckebeke, they were to fight harder than hard. It was necessary. The best material from the entire world was rolling incessantly toward France, in monstrous quantities. If ten airplanes were produced in poor Germany, at the same time a hundred would be unloaded on the French coast. Everyone in Marckebeke understood that.

On this day, according to regulations, the Rittmeister's report of the downing of his fifty-seventh enemy airplane went to the Commanding General of the Air Service. These reports, containing the most daring feats which took place high in the sky, on the brink of life and death, and which the pilots had to turn in written in their own words, were of an ultimate, military conciseness. The Rittmeister's report read as follows:

2 June 1917
Deulemont, between the lines,
10.20 a.m.

I attacked the foremost aircraft of an enemy squadron. The observer collapsed with the first shots. The pilot was fatally hit shortly thereafter. The RE reared up. I fired on the rearing aircraft from a distance of 50 meters with a few more shots, until flames shot out of the machine and the opponent crashed, burning.

von Richthofen,
Rittmeister and Commander
of Jagdgeschwader I

---

[1] Major Hermann von der Lieth Thomsen.

Just as short and blunt were the testimonies of the witnesses which had to be sent with the report of a victory, testimonies from the air and from the ground:

> After a short air combat, the enemy airplane crashed, burning.
>
> Bockelmann, Lt

> 10.25 a.m. An RE, in the direction of Deulemont, shot down in flames by an Albatros. Two occupants jumped out during the crash.
>
> Hauptmann Kuhlmann
> Anti-aircraft Artillery Group 21

> 10.25 a.m. In the direction of Hollebeke, an RE shot down in flames by a red Albatros.
>
> Lt Mann,
> Observation Post, Observer

> 10.20 a.m. An RE crashed in flames, shot down by a red Albatros in the direction of Warneton.
>
> Lt Schröder,[1]
> Air Defense Officer
> Army Group Wytschaete

The acknowledgement of the Commanding General of the Air Service is no wordier:

> Supreme Headquarters, 14 July 1917

> To Rittmeister Freiherr von Richthofen, Commander of Jagdge-schwader I, the downing of an RE aircraft on 2 July 1917 is acknowledged as his fifty-seventh victorious air combat.
>
> Chief of the General Staff
> (signed) Thomsen

The Baron leads the first Geschwader established by the Army. Up to this time, there were only Staffeln. Now four Staffeln have been combined. They are situated here at Château Marckebeke, and in the immediate neighborhood. In the château itself and in the convent buildings are Staffeln 11 and 4. Richthofen brought along Staffel 11; he had been its

---

[1] When von Richthofen was wounded four days later, Lt Hans Schröder was the first person on the scene as recounted in his book, *An Airman Remembers*, John Hamilton, Ltd, 1935.

leader and it remains his regular Staffel. He flies with it, lives with it, dines with it. They are his old comrades; he knows every one of them by heart. Jasta 6 is located at Bisseghem, Jasta 10 at Marcke.

When the Staffeln are lined up all together at one time on the airfield, behind each Staffel leader stand twelve machines. There are only two types of aircraft on hand, either an Albatros DV, or a Pfalz DIII. The assembled Geschwader appears extremely colorful. Staffel 11, with which Richthofen flies, has its machines painted red; Staffel 10 yellow; Staffel 6 has black and white zebra stripes; and Staffel 4 carries a black wavy line on the natural-colored fuselage. It isn't necessary to explain the purpose of this joyous color at length; with it they can distinguish between the Staffeln in the air. And since each pilot has placed another special insignia on his machine as well, it is possible to know immediately who is sitting in this or that airplane.

On the evening of 2 July, the commander invites the leaders of the Jagdstaffeln to a conference in his room on the second floor. Everything is still bare and cheerless. Moreover, not all of the rooms of the château are available, because the Count,[1] who is the master of the château here, would like nothing better than to blow up this entire bunch of pilots. Because this is not possible for him, at the very least he blasts each courteous contact with his surly unfriendliness and keeps as many rooms closed as possible. The Rittmeister, for his part, watched this inhospitable business patiently for a few days, then it was changed.

While outside in the corridors the orderlies and batmen rush incessantly up and down to bring order to the confusion of moving in, inside the room the conference begins. It is crucial to the work of the first Jagdgeschwader of the Field Army.

The four Staffel leaders stand before the commander and his adjutant.

Jasta 4: Oberleutnant Kurt von Döring, 17th Dragoons from Ludwigslust in Mecklenburg, a tested Staffel leader, who has a number of victories behind him. Obliging, amiable, correct.

Jasta 6: Oberleutnant Eduard Dostler, Bavarian Pioneer, an old Military Academy comrade of Adjutant Bodenschatz, stocky, solid, broad-shouldered, with the firm but merry handshake of the service.

Jasta 10: Oberleutnant Ernst Freiherr von Althaus, who wears the order *Pour le Mérite*, cavalryman (combat flying is teeming with cavalrymen), somewhat taciturn this evening. His Staffel has bad days behind it. It has been terribly weakened, and has had bitter casualties.

Jasta 11: Leutnant Kurt Wolff. At first glance, you could only say 'delicate little flower'. A slender, thin, little figure, a very young face,

---

[1] Although Bodenschatz used the German word for 'Count' here, the correct title of the owner of Château Marckebeke was the Baron de Béthune.

whose entire manner is one of extreme shyness. He looks as if you could tip him over backwards with one harsh word. But below this friendly school-boy's face dangles the order *Pour le Mérite*. And so far, these modest-looking eyes have taken thirty enemy airplanes from the sky over the open sights of his machine guns, set them afire, and made them smash to pieces on the ground. This slender youth was already one of the best men of the old Richthofen Staffel 11. That he is now its leader goes without saying . . .

The commander gives his instructions in clear succession. First, he no longer wants to chance receiving take-off orders indirectly, via the various command posts. He would rather be closely guided by the enemy air activity in his sector. Therefore, he orders direct communications to be established immediately with the forwardmost Front. He also requires a circular telephone link to his four Staffeln so that, when he lifts the receiver, all four answer simultaneously.

That is number one.

In addition, the Rittmeister apprises them of the ground positions, and these are not pleasant to hear. The enemy's breakthrough attempts are being repeated again and again with a tenacity never yet experienced, and each new attack is more brutal and more bitter than the one before. The troops who have to endure these insane pushes are suffering terribly under a heavy barrage that never ends. And if, by some miracle, a break in the fire does occur, then infantry-support planes come roaring over right above the trenches and dugouts. And high above the infantry-support planes, whole clusters of bombing squadrons swing into the hinterland.

That's how things look on the ground, and from that comes Jagdge-schwader I's assignment in the air: destruction of the infantry-support planes, destruction of the single-seater fighters, destruction of the bombing squadrons.

The commander has spoken.

Among the men, there are no further questions. The situation can hardly seem clearer. Oberleutnant von Althaus just requests that the best people be assigned to him, as he has lost his best men. The commander promises him good replacements.

The conference is over.

The Rittmeister and his adjutant go to supper with Staffel 11. Ober-leutnant Bodenschatz meets the gentlemen of Staffel 11. With few exceptions, they are new faces to him, and, one after another, he shakes the hands of the pilots:

Leutnant Stapenhorst, Uhlan from Saarbrücken, very young, the immortal, fresh, 'Leutnant-type'; Leutnant Joachim Wolff, the 'Sonny Boy' of the Staffel, the left corner of his mouth always pulled down ready to grin, always exuberant; Leutnant Meyer, also a cavalryman, brown face,

black hair, like a portrait of a boy from the brush of a Spanish painter;
Leutnant von Schönebeck, the technical genius of his Staffel, dark-
haired, a hard, molded face; the lanky Leutnant Groos, Uhlan, ready at
any time to have sporting fun or a serious conversation; Leutnant
Bockelmann, Army Corps student,[1] with the scarred nose from a tough
sabre match; Oberleutnant Reinhard, from the Foot Artillery, with the
same total, composed calm of these powerful weapons; Leutnant Müller,
from a Cuirassier regiment, reserved, very correct, and very well-
groomed; Leutnant Niederhoff, with the stern look and the cold energy
in his features and bearing; Leutnant Mohnicke, very young, lively, rest-
less, and fun-loving; Leutnant Brauneck, with the bold aquiline nose;
the taciturn Leutnant Busch; Oberleutnant Scheffer, with his calm
eyes and high-brushed hair; and the stocky, blond Vizefeldwebel
Lautenschlager.

The new adjutant's first impression of Staffel 11 is rather vague. 'This was
just a fleeting impression,' he thinks, 'and I will become closer acquainted
with all of them in time.'

But even if later on this first impression should give way to revisions, this
was the basic type of young German fighter pilot. Had the war not come
and brought them together, who knows where they would be now . . . in
universities, in military academies, in business firms or in hospitals, in
laboratories or in schoolrooms at the professor's lectern, in foresters'
houses or factories. They would be young men like a thousand others their
age; they would have had their high spirits or their earnestness, the one like
this and the other like that, each after his own fashion and according to his
own nature, talents, character, ambition or indifference. But within each of
them lurked some common element, something inexplicable, and even
they themselves did not know what it was. It merely oppressed them and
made them uneasy. It had something to do with their high spirits, their
excess energy and their wish for adventure.

When the war broke out, they blazed up with all the lofty, unspent
strength of their youth and with the purity of their souls. They came
running, as fast as their hearts and legs could carry them, and threw
themselves at Germany with such a vehemence that Germany fairly reeled
for joy at these youths. And what had been unclear within them now
became clear. Of course they belonged there, where the men of their nation
were; they belonged in the war, that was obvious. But, because they were
quite a special breed of young men, they went where the war appeared
romantic. They went to the airfields. And there in the field, when they had

---

[1] A student dueling society or fraternity, each having its own distinctive colors and
emblems.

gazed into the cold, cruel eye of this romanticism, they were in agreement with each other as never before.

They were in the right place.

They found themselves in a splendid group of their contemporaries, in all of the Jagdstaffeln of the Field Army. Together, they were an élite. They learned to fight in a manner unheard of, and they learned to die in a manner unprecedented.

They were between twenty and twenty-two years old.

The morning of 6 July dawns; it will be an almost cloudless, beautiful summer day. And today, bright and early, just like every other day, there is already a heightened readiness for take-off.

In earlier times, the bureaucrats ordered, for example: Staffel so-and-so will fly from eight to nine o'clock. The commander hates these bureaucrats like the plague; he puts his Staffeln into action when necessary, but then at a hellish pace. The machines are lined up, the pilots fully dressed next to them, the mechanics ready to swing the propellers at any second. If the take-off order comes, the Staffel can roar off inside of a minute.

And the order does come: outside of Ypres, brisk activity by enemy artillery spotters. Curt commands, the mechanics throw themselves at the propellers, the engines' tumultuous song thunders along the row, then the airplanes seesaw over the field and rise gently from the ground. Jasta 4 has taken off.

Jasta 4 soon returns. The artillery spotters have hastily disappeared. But around 10.30 a.m., the air defense officer's report comes in: infantry-support planes! This time, the red machines are standing on the starting line. Jasta 11 flies to the Front with the commander.

First of all, before he deals with the infantry-support planes, the Rittmeister discovers a squadron of Vickers aircraft. These are bombers with two- to three-man crews.[1] And they are just the kind of wasps that Richthofen loves; they arrive at exactly the right time. With his Staffel, he turns wide aside in order to let them past just this one time. He does nothing to them yet. They are to proceed peacefully into the hinterland; he doesn't bother them. The Englishmen drone on, comfortably and neatly aligned, into the German hinterland until they suddenly discover a bright-red glimmer between them and their way home. The way back has been cut off to them.[2]

And the dance begins, an evil dance at an altitude of 3,000 meters.

---

[1] Although Vickers did produce one bomber, the Vimy, which carried a crew of three, these aircraft were not operating on the Western Front in 1917.

[2] A flight of FE2ds from 20 Squadron, RFC.

The Rittmeister closes in on the hindmost airplane, sets himself on the same invisible track along which the other airplane is soaring. He has time to consider how the attack is to be done this time, since he is still over 300 meters away. He doesn't even need to arm his machine guns yet. He sees the Englishman change course and the observer begin to fire. But that doesn't make much of an impression on him for, from this distance, the observer certainly can't . . . and, at this moment, he receives a hammer blow to the head. Within a second, his whole body becomes immobile, numb, as if touched by an electric shock. He no longer feels anything . . . no arms . . . no legs . . . nothing. He is suspended in a terrible, incomprehensible void. At the same time, it grows dark all around him, a terrible, incomprehensible darkness. He can see nothing more; he has been blinded. The shot has disturbed his optic nerve.

And with that, it is all over. Rittmeister von Richthofen needs do nothing more in this world. But he does, nevertheless. First of all, with every bit of concentrated, inner strength that he has at his disposal, he overcomes the catastrophic effects, the paralysis and the sudden blinding, which the unexpected shot has caused in him. With concerted energy, he overcomes the shock. And after an eternity, he again feels his fingers and hands, gropes around, switches off the gas and the ignition, tears the goggles from his eyes, forces his lids open as far as he can. But he sees nothing, not even the sun.

On the other hand, he is conscious of how the machine is plunging, catching itself, plunging again. There is nothing to be done. He forces himself to consider how low he can already have plunged, and he estimates that he has descended to 2,000 meters. He cannot see that Staffel 11 is watching the strange antics of its commander, somewhat surprised and then a little alarmed, and that two airplanes of the Staffel, Leutnants Niederhoff and Brauneck, are going down with him and staying near him.

The worst part is this blindness . . . there is simply nothing to see . . . but, all at once, black and white dots begin to dance before his eyes and he pulls his lids up again. It is getting better. He can already look into the sun. Directly into the sun. He sees the shining star as if through dark glasses. That is enough for him. He forces his eyes to see more clearly. With a dreadful effort, he forces them to obey him . . . they must see, see, see! They obey.

He can now read off the altimeter. Still eight hundred meters. He can catch the machine. He goes down in a glide. So far, his eyes are again in good-enough shape that he can look over the terrain. It is a unique, cratered landscape of shell holes and he cannot think about landing. His head is so dog-tired that it would be a release for him now to simply go to sleep.

He stares at the area. From the shape of a bit of forest, he recognizes that he is inside the German front. And then, for a few seconds, he ponders why the Englishman who wounded him did not come after him; it would have been a trivial matter to shoot down the wounded German. The Rittmeister cannot know that the two machines of Niederhoff and Brauneck are staying close by him; they have protected and covered him. And now he could indeed land. He goes down to 50 meters.

Landing is not possible — there is shell hole after shell hole. And the half-paralysed, half-blind man gives it the gas one more time, and flies on towards the east, very low. This goes well, too, for a good while until he notices that the darkness is again creeping over his brow, and a weakness which he can no longer overcome is moving through his limbs.

It is high time to land. A few meters above the ground, he knocks down some telephone lines and poles, and then this wonderful pilot sets his machine on the ground as gently and as lightly as a butterfly.

It is done. He stands up and wants to climb out, but he falls out of the seat. He wants to stand up again, but he had better remain lying down. The other two machines have landed next to him. The two Leutnants jump out, rush over, and the gentle curses they are uttering are curses of thanks, so to speak, if there is such a thing. The commander has only a hard, glancing shot to the head. Sacrament of Heaven . . . Thank God . . . Damn it again! A bandage, telephone for the ambulance . . .

On the airfield in Marckebeke, several men are standing at the stereo telescope at the time when the Staffel is to return from its flight.

'There they are,' says the adjutant, 'one, two, three, four . . . six . . .' He then stops counting and is silent.

'Why six?' murmurs another. Yes, why six? Nine flew off. Where are the other three?

'Is the commander with them?' asks someone.

He receives no answer. And no one inquires further but, as the first machine sets down, they rush over. It is Leutnant Wolff, who witnessed the whole incident from above. He reports quickly. They stare at him.

'Niederhoff and Brauneck are with him,' he concludes. Oberleutnant Bodenschatz hurries to the telephone. He has no sooner reached the phone when Niederhoff calls and reports that the Rittmeister has been taken away, he doesn't know where.

At 12.00 p.m. Field Hospital No. 76, St Nicholas, calls from Courtrai. The Rittmeister has been admitted there. In the afternoon Bodenschatz, Dostler, Döring, and Wolff squeeze themselves into a car and drive over.

'You cannot speak to the Herr Rittmeister,' says the nurse.

'Why not?' all four of them cry, almost in unison, and they grow worried.

'Because he needs rest,' answers the nurse, impatiently.

'I see!' says Oberleutnant Bodenschatz, relieved. 'Well then, we can certainly go in for a moment.'

Sister Kate stares angrily at the foolish visitors then goes inside. When she returns, the four are allowed in. The Rittmeister receives them, rather dejectedly, a thick, snow-white bandage around his head.

'I am so sorry,' he says, 'to stay away now, right in the middle of everything, but I'll come back soon, very soon.'

He has a wound ten centimeters long on his head. The doctors had been able to stitch it together, but later, in one place in his hair, one always saw the bare, white skullbone gleaming out.

But . . . everything is going well. Richthofen's father, who is the local commandant in the Lille area, is notified and his mother, as well. Oberleutnant von Döring assumes command of the Geschwader.

On the airfield of Jasta 11 in Marckebeke, the German gentlemen sit crowded together, like doves. They have squeezed in around the adjutant, and they press him from all sides. They want to know exactly how the commander looks, what he said, what kind of a mood he's in, whether he has to lie in bed or if he may sit in a chair, and whether he has a good doctor, or at least a pretty nurse, how long his convalescence is expected to last, et cetera, et cetera.

When they have heard everything, and the adjutant has worn himself out from all the questioning, they sit together for a long time yet. That evening, in the officers' messes of the four Jagdstaffeln, there wasn't much talk of 'revenge' or 'we'll pay them back for this', but no one drank a toast 'to the day', either.

But in all of their faces there lay a certain pensive tension, and in their eyes was a certain concentrated hardness. Everyone held their chin just a centimeter higher than usual. The adjutant had noted it well. For his part, he sent an urgent evening prayer heavenward.

'May there be the finest weather tomorrow,' he thought fervently.

And the seventh of July dawned with an almost cloudless sky.

Early in the morning, the reports from the Front bring nothing exciting. But no sooner has the sun climbed a little higher when the acting Geschwader commander, Oberleutnant von Döring, receives the crucial message. As always, it reads monotonously: 'Brisk activity by enemy artillery-spotters in the Ypres salient.'

But with this monotonous report, Hell has enveloped one part of the Front. If, at this hour, the infantry is lying in a hurricane of shrapnel and in the midst of a forest of fountains spouting earth, and is being pursued from hole to hole; if, at this hour, heavy-caliber shells are smashing into the rest positions, munitions dumps are going up, and the advance routes are being pounded unmercifully; then, at the same time, the enemy observation planes are circling, at not too great an altitude, and directing their gun batteries. They range their guns until it becomes too risky for them. And when it gets too risky for them, then they clear out and fly for home. They really don't need to worry about being bothered for, high above them, their own pursuit squadrons of single-seater fighters are poised, ready to swoop down in a second to their defense.

The Geschwader commander gives the take-off order for Staffeln 11, 4 and 6. And with that, a rough day has begun.

At 11.00 a.m., Leutnant Wolff, the 'delicate little flower' shoots down a triplane near Comines. It is his thirty-third victory. Five minutes later, near Wervicq, Leutnant Krüger brings down the first enemy airplane of his life, a triplane. At 11.10 a.m., near Bousbecque, Leutnant Niederhoff destroys a triplane as well, air victory number four for him. At 11.35 a.m., Vizefeld-webel Krebs shoots an RE down in flames near Zillebeke, his sixth air victory. At the stroke of noon, Oberleutnant Dostler drives a Sopwith into the craterfield between the lines near Deulemont, his fourteenth victory. At 2.30 p.m., Vizefeldwebel Clausnitzer brings a Nieuport down in the Gheluvelt sector, his third air victory. At 6.07 p.m., Leutnant Klein shoots a Sopwith down over Houthem. It represents his fourteenth air victory. Three minutes later, near Wytschaete, Vizefeldwebel Lautenschlager heaves himself from his seat with joy. For the first time, he has destroyed an airplane, a Sopwith that crashed burning. Just as delighted is Leutnant Anders who, at 6.20 p.m. near Hollebeke, likewise destroys the first airplane of his life.

Nine enemy machines have been brought down on this day. In contrast with these nine machines stands not one casualty of their own. The Geschwader's first answer to the wounding of its commander is successful.

On the next day, it rains.

On the day after that, low-lying clouds and rain.

On the next day after that, a heavy layer of clouds and incessant rain.

On the fourth day, it is not much better, but the time has come to take a look at the Front again from close quarters. Moreover, during the night around 3.00 a.m., a thunderstorm broke over the airfield of Jasta 6. Like all thunderstorms, it consisted of lightning and thunder, but this one was orchestrated by an English bombing squadron making a morning visit. Three tent hangars and two machines were damaged somewhat, but the bombs didn't touch a hair of a single living being.

As first Staffel, Jasta 11 takes off and the airplanes have scarcely disappeared into the grey sky when one of them returns. It is Leutnant Wolff who clambers out rather laboriously, holding his left hand out in front of him. Blood drips down; the 'delicate little flower' has taken a bullet through the hand. They immediately stuff him into a car and transport him to St Nicholas Hospital in Courtrai, where the commander receives him, in the highest of spirits due to the unexpected, pleasant company.

The 'delicate little flower' writes a resigned letter to his fiancée:

> Since my leave, I have become a great gadabout. I didn't last long at Jasta 11 either,[1] and have moved on. Now I am lying in bed in a hospital, in the same room as Richthofen.
>
> Early yesterday, you see, I had my hand out right where an Englishman was shooting. And since my hand made just as little effort to turn aside as the bullet did, the bullet, being the harder component, went through the hand. Consequently, I have a clean shot through the left hand. The wrist bone was shot clean through, and this whole affair will be over with in a few weeks, without any after-effects. I believe I have to be in the hospital another three days. When I can get up, I will return to the Staffel, even if I cannot fly for the time being.
>
> I received my bullet wound when I attacked a squadron of fifteen Englishmen, a little east of Ypres. Afterwards, I still flew home, and landed smoothly on my field.

Meanwhile, after having satisfactorily contemplated the grey sky, which is very suitable for playing hide-and-seek, two gentlemen of Jasta 4 have decided: captive balloons. Attacking captive balloons is always an extraordinarily risky affair and always a dangerous game. The attacker must go down very low and he invariably comes under fire from the 3.5 cm anti-aircraft guns, the 'Quick Spitters', a rather mild name for these superb and feared guns which use a phosphorus shell every fifth shot. At the same time, the attacker may rest assured that he will have to bluster around in the midst of bursts of fire from the heavy anti-aircraft guns. If he succeeds in shooting down a balloon, he won't get away scot-free for long. Because it is, unfortunately, impossible for him to immediately climb straight up, he must first withdraw at a fairly low altitude and can only gradually spiral upwards, until he has finally reached his own lines and is relatively safe. However, during the time in which he must fly low, he is always within range of the machine guns.

Balloon-busting became an art for them. There were men who specialized in it, who developed their own tricks and who had their established methods: to swoop down unexpectedly from a single scrap of

---

[1] Lt Wolff was transferred to Jasta 29 as leader on 6 May 1917, transferred back to Jasta 11 as Staffel leader on 2 July, and was then wounded on 11 July.

cloud, or to put the sun at their backs, et cetera.

On this day, they don't make it too difficult for the observers crouching in the French and English captive balloons and diligently telephoning below to swing themselves overboard and jump out. They have no time at all to think it over. They jump.

At 3.05 p.m., Leutnant Klein races away, right over the captive balloon situated in map quadrant Q50. He sees the observer stagger over the rim of the basket and jump out with outstretched limbs. From out of the gasbag, there then comes a thin cloud of smoke, then a flame flares up. Leutnant Klein races on. In map quadrant Q53 stands the next balloon. At 3.07 p.m., he puts a burst into it. The observer is already floating halfway to earth, and above him smoke and flames drift out. In two minutes, Leutnant Klein has put his fifteenth and sixteenth victories behind him.

There is also an uproar in map quadrant Q56. Vizefeldwebel Wüsthoff suddenly appears over the balloon and brings it down, his third air victory. During the evening take-off, Leutnant Mohnicke shoots a triplane down near Comines, at 9.15 p.m., his third air victory. At 9.45 p.m., already dusk, Vizefeldwebel Patermann sends a Spad into the shell holes, his second victory. Vizefeldwebel Patermann is unable to increase his list, for on the next day, 12 July, the Geschwader's first casualty bears his name. He is shot down at 11.00 a.m. in air combat near Gheluvelt.

For that, the Geschwader reaps a rich harvest. In the same minute in which Vizefeldwebel Patermann gave up his life, Oberleutnant Dostler shoots down his fifteenth opponent near Houthem.

As if the death of this brave man had to be immediately avenged, at that exact same time Leutnant Deilmann shoots a Nieuport down in map quadrant C45, his fourth opponent. At 6.35 p.m., Leutnant Adam destroys a Sopwith near Dickebusch; Leutnant Küppers, a Sopwith, as well, at 7.40 p.m. near Wytschaete; Vizefeldwebel Marquardt, again a Sopwith at 9.05 p.m.; a quarter of an hour later, Leutnant Hübner, a triplane near Zuidschote; and on this rough day, Oberleutnant Dostler, who had begun the morning with a victory, ends the harvest with a second victory. He brings a Sopwith down near Zillebeke, his sixteenth air victory.

These are breathless days. One after another, the take-offs. One after another, the victories. One after another, the reports to the Commanding General of the Air Service.

13 July. Good flying weather. At 11.30 a.m., Leutnant Klein is wounded in air combat near Gistel. He manages, however, to land behind his own lines. At 11.35 a.m., Oberleutnant Dostler shoots his seventeenth opponent down south of Becelaere and, fifteen minutes later, his eighteenth north of Zonnebeke. Vizefeldwebel Krebs adds to his victory list of air combats at the same murderous tempo: the first Sopwith at 11.30

a.m. near Polygon Wood, and the second at 11.35 a.m. near Zonnebeke. At 11.30 a.m., Leutnant Adam shoots a Nieuport down east of Ypres, and Leutnant Deilmann downs a Sopwith east of Zandvoorde at 11.20 a.m.

In three days, eighteen enemy aircraft have been destroyed along with their passengers. The tempo is maintained.

On 16 July, brave Vizefeldwebel Clausnitzer attempts an attack on a captive balloon. He is last seen at 5.30 p.m., then he vanishes. He does not return.

He fell into captivity. He now gives an account of it:

> Shortly before I reached the English balloons, I was attacked by three English Spads. I immediately attacked the leader's machine but, after the first rounds, both my machine guns jammed; the left one by a broken cartridge case, the right by the edge of an advancing cartridge. I didn't succeed in clearing the jams because both bolts were stuck fast. In spite of all attempts to escape, I was gradually forced ever lower and, at an altitude of 50 meters, took a hit in the engine. The engine stopped and I went down in a glide into the fields. I was welcomed by some London artillerymen with a sound thrashing, removed by some officers, and in the evening I was handed over to the airmen with whom I spent four days altogether as their guest.

On this day, Vizefeldwebel Krebs, who shot down two airplanes within five minutes three days ago, is shot down in air combat north-east of Zonnebeke at 7.45 p.m. Vizefeldwebel Wüsthoff brings down a balloon near Kemmel at 6.15 p.m., and Leutnant Adam gets a Sopwith near Zonnebeke at 8.05 p.m.

On the next day, 17 July, Leutnant Meyer is wounded in air combat near Ypres, but he is able to land at the airfield and remains with his Staffel. In the meantime, Leutnant Krüger is seriously wounded at 1.15 p.m. near Comines, and dies that night in the hospital.

The great battle of Flanders rages on at the same tempo, on the ground and in the air. The diaries of all the combat troops report the outcomes with just a few sentences and, for those who know and understand, there are always examples of immeasurable bravery, contempt for death, and loyalty included within these few sentences.

The Jagdgeschwader is fighting against a tremendously superior force. On 17 July, the acting Geschwader commander issues an order:

> Jagdgeschwader I:
>
> After the experiences of the last few days, it has been shown that the Staffeln flying individually are not in the position to successfully

combat the strong English squadrons appearing mainly in the evenings. Simultaneous deployment of the Geschwader's Staffeln is therefore necessary, and will ensue from now on by existing order of the Geschwader. The Staffeln must appear at the Front at the same time, at high altitude (4,000–5,000 meters) and carry out the attack on strong English squadrons as close to the same time as possible. The Staffeln must endeavor to fly so that they are able to mutually support each other. For the time being, deployment of the entire Geschwader shall be limited to the evening hours.

During combat patrols of the individual Staffeln during the course of the day, attacking mainly those artillery-spotting and reconnaissance aircraft flying at low altitude is recommended, as the function of these aircraft is tactically most important, and is most unpleasant for the troops.

von Döring

Behind this sober order is written: We know that they are as numerous as hounds after hares. But we are not hares, and will allow ourselves to be neither baffled nor intimidated. For them, the factories of the world are working day and night. In the harbors of France, hundreds and hundreds of airplanes are being unloaded daily, airplanes made of the best material, gentlemen! We cannot count on our poor, surrounded homeland likewise sending us hundreds and hundreds of airplanes daily. We also cannot count on the material of our machines getting ever better and better. On the contrary, raw materials are becoming more and more scarce. Their superior power is becoming ever mightier, on land, on the sea, and in the air. We have nothing of equal worth with which to oppose them, nothing of equal worth, gentlemen, but something greater: our fervent love for our beleaguered homeland, our bravery, our cold-bloodedness, our determination, and our rage.

Their superior officers also know how things stand. On 19 July 1917, the Commanding General issues a general order:

In the last few days, enemy fighter pilots have appeared in overwhelmingly superior strength, against which our Jagdstaffeln have been unable to act. On the other hand, the results of air combats reported at the same time show that the ratio of enemy casualties to our losses is extremely good. We know that, in the coming days, we will also have a strong, numerically-superior force against us on the Fourth Army Front. I have confidence in the entire German Air Service and in this: that the airmen of the Fourth Army, above all the Jagdgeschwader and the Jagdstaffeln, will thin the ranks of the enemy squadrons and

defeat them. I beseech the flying units of the Army to bring this to
expression.

The Commanding General of the Air Service,
Generalleutnant von Hoeppner

The Commander-in-Chief of the Fourth Army, General of the Infantry,
Sixt von Armin, has yet another great worry. His troops are suffering to an
extraordinary degree, scarcely known till now, under the heavy artillery
fire. This hellish bombardment is being directed by captive balloons,
airplanes, and ground observers. The enemy captive balloons have become
particularly numerous in the last few days. The ugly gasbags stand in rows
far behind the lines, and the telephone conversations that are conducted
from their baskets have devastating results on the German positions.

On 18 July, the Commander-in-Chief issues the following order:

Combating the enemy captive balloons, upon which the enemy bases a
large part of his artillery observation, has become very necessary, and
is to be carried out primarily by means of the Army Groups. Aerial
attacks require extensive artillery support to suppress the very strong
defense from the ground. When the individual pilot proceeds to the
attack, the enemy ascension sites and the anti-aircraft guns and
machine guns positioned in their vicinity are to be attacked by brisk
harassing fire.

Batteries of the Combat Group 'Schwertes Flachfeuer des AOK'[1]
can be requested at any time by the Commander of Fourth Army
Aviation, for amplification of this harassing fire.

Jagdgeschwader I is equally at their disposal to keep the attack zone
free of enemy aircraft.

The individual Staffeln have to undertake the immediate protection
of their attacking aircraft. Preparations for attacks on captive balloons
are to be made very carefully in order to avoid unnecessary losses in the
way of aircraft.

The Commander-in-Chief,
Sixt von Armin

Thus, everyone from mechanic to commander-in-chief knows that this
superior force is to be met with their combined resources, and with the
greatest skill and care.

In St Nicholas Hospital in Courtrai, two officers sit together and listen to

---

[1] Heavy Flat-Trajectory Fire of the Army High Command.

the incessant rumbling of the Front. The Rittmeister, with his thickly bandaged head and the impatient wish that his nasty headaches might finally subside for once, and next to him, the 'delicate little flower', his left arm in a sling, with the same sort of impatient wish: to soon be able to put his healed fingers around a joystick. St Nicholas Hospital in Courtrai is not exactly comparable to a convalescent home. Peaceful tranquillity is out of the question. Troop columns clatter through the little town during the day, and night after night the English squadrons' heavy bombs roar into this important communications center. Baron von Richthofen and Leutnant Wolff don't make much of these bombs. They worry incessantly about their Geschwader instead. Every day, the adjutant comes rushing in and brings the reports.

It is obvious from these reports that Jagdgeschwader I is having difficult days, but glorious days as well. There is truly no need for the Rittmeister to write inspiring letters to his men. They know what they have to do. They take off and they fight. They have become accustomed to the fact that an unparalleled superior force may be set right in front of their noses at any time. They take note of this. They don't make a big fuss about it, but when the order comes, they take off, and they fight, and they die. But the reports tell in terse terms how, before one of the Jagdgeschwader dies, several others on the opposing side must always go down and burn amidst the shell holes.

On 20 July, at 7.40 a.m., Leutnant Adam shoots his seventh opponent down south-west of Ypres. At 8.40 a.m., Leutnant Walter Stock brings an RE down near Armentières, his first opponent. Twenty minutes later, north-west of Ten Brielen, a Sopwith flutters to earth with its burning occupants, the first air victory of Leutnant von Boenigk. Ten minutes later, the same picture again: a flaming trail of smoke, a Sopwith, shot down by Leutnant Niederhoff; and ten minutes later near Becelaere, once again another Sopwith smashes into the craters of Flanders, brought down by Vizefeldwebel Wüsthoff.[1]

These days, the Rittmeister's patience is at an end. He doesn't need long to persuade the 'delicate little flower'. Both of them are fed up. Last night, like every night, English airmen visited the little town and, in the morning, it is once again suggested to Baron von Richthofen that it would be better in the long run for him to go to Germany — home to Schweidnitz in Silesia. First of all, it would, of course, be very nice to be home and secondly, no enemy bombs have fallen on Schweidnitz to date, and presumably none would fall in the foreseeable future either. Besides, it would be quite good

---

[1] These two victories are listed in the squadron log as occurring at 9.10 p.m. and 9.20 p.m. respectively, and not in the morning as stated here.

for his poor, mistreated head to have a little peace for once.

That is quite clear to the Rittmeister as well. He looks at the doctors and nurses with his little smile. Naturally, he then supposes that even a little change would be absolutely nothing to sneer at. And so his mind is made up. He wants to visit his Geschwader in Marckebeke.

And so the next day, right after lunch, the adjutant comes to pick them up. In the meantime, Richthofen's father has arrived, and the whole group drives out to Marckebeke. The nurse comes along too, and she doesn't really care that the Rittmeister is making a face. To show up at the airfield with a nurse is not at all to his taste, but he is banging his head against a brick wall. If the Rittmeister is already undertaking such nonsense with his unhealed head, then she is going to be close by, the nurse explains grimly.[1]

The whole carload starts off. The car travels slowly and carefully. They sit close together: Richthofen, Leutnant Wolff, Major Richthofen, Ober-leutnant Bodenschatz, and the nurse. The entire trip takes just fifteen minutes, but in this quarter of an hour, they are constantly in the midst of marching troops and traveling columns. The first were coming out of battle, and the others were heading in. The Rittmeister's snow-white head bandage was visible a long way off. The first infantrymen to catch sight of them stared curiously and wearily into the car. Then suddenly they raise their faces higher, discover the *Pour le Mérite* at the young Uhlan officer's throat, and they look a little more closely at his face.

'Richthofen!!!' The name suddenly roars along down the long columns. A storm of fervent gratitude rushes through the infantry. Thin hands rise up and wave, weapons are brandished, steel helmets are raised high, and pale, exhausted faces tighten up. The car is surrounded by officers and men.

The infantry knows what this wounded young officer is worth. When they cowered in their wet dugouts, cramped together and defenseless, in the most deadly peril, and a hurricane of dirt clods and shrapnel howled away above them; when they swallowed their rage; when no rifle, no hand grenade, no pistol, no amount of bravery could be of any use to them in the hellish artillery fire . . . then it had always been an infinitely comforting sight for them when, high above them, the red machines came into view and the enemy infantry-support planes began to pitch nervously and cleared out, or when the artillery-spotting aircraft, which hung over them like ugly wasps and let shot after shot rain down upon them, suddenly roared off for home.

'Richthofen!!!'

This name rushes up and down through the companies. The drivers on the guns and wagons rise boisterously from their seats, wave, and shout. It

---

[1] Nurse Käte Wienstroth.

is an endless lane of love and respect through which the Rittmeister travels. He is overjoyed as the airfield appears at last.

Oberleutnant von Döring reports. The commander shakes hands. He really doesn't say much, but his clear eyes say so much more. He sees the familiar faces and the simple rooms again. He has a look at the machines, frequently shot-up and frequently patched, walks around them for a long time, and now he says, almost fiercely: 'You are getting new Fokker triplanes. They climb like monkeys and they're as maneuverable as the devil.' Then they sit out on the terrace, garland Richthofen's chair with flowers, group themselves as artistically as possible, and allow themselves to be photographed. Then they have coffee.

As he takes his leave from them again, he doesn't say when he will at last be coming back, but he doesn't need to. They all see it in him — in how he looked, how he moved about the airfield, and what little he did express. He'll be coming back to them very soon.

On 21 July, Leutnant Mohnicke and Feldwebel Leutnant Schubert exchange shots with a Spad, and when it is swept away and dispatched in flames, there is doubt, as there unavoidably will be on occasion, as to who should get credit for the airplane. Five days later, Richthofen decides it: Feldwebel Leutnant Schubert gets awarded the Spad as his second air victory.[1]

On 22 July, at 10.40 a.m., Oberleutnant von Döring shoots down his fourth opponent near Mangelaar. At the same time, Vizefeldwebel Heldmann begins his victory list with a Sopwith near Deulemont. At 11.25 a.m., a Sopwith slams into the muddy landscape near Kortewilde, dispatched by Leutnant Brauneck, his seventh victory. Five minutes later, visible for a long distance, a Sopwith burns in the shelled terrain south-east of Zonnebeke, shot down by Leutnant Niederhoff. In the evening, Oberleutnant von Döring gets his second victory of the day over the front lines near Oosttaverne, and Oberleutnant Reinhard begins his victory list with a Sopwith near Warneton.

Not only do they shoot anything that comes before their propellers, not only are they daring for daring's sake, but they precisely observe and record anything noticeable about the enemy. Each modification of his machines, each modification of his combat tactics, almost down to each practical new glove the enemy introduces over there, is noted.

On 24 July, Jasta 6 submits an important observation:

The enemy appears to have already recognized the regularity of our

---

[1] Unlike the British, French and later the Americans, German pilots did not share victories.

joint evening appearance, and is adapting himself to our flight times, so that his reconnaissance flights are made at those times during which we must be ready for Geschwader flights.

Fighter squadrons strive to be aloft prior to our appearance, and are constantly over us with their highest squadrons. Combat activity is mostly without result because, during an attack, everyone flies to the combat area, and friend and foe get so entangled with each other that generally only short, ineffectual combats are possible.

The enemy appears to have already recognized our numerical strength because he adapts himself perfectly in the ratio of forces, and is therefore also in the position to hold a superior force in readiness for crucial situations.

That is to say, it amounts to the same old story all over again. Let us start ten airplanes and over there, three times that number go aloft.

And as if someone in the hospital of St Nicholas in Courtrai had perceived this tricky situation, on 25 July, Rittmeister von Richthofen turns up again at the Marckebeke airfield. Not just to visit this time, but with bag and baggage. He resumes command of his Geschwader.

On 26 July, Leutnant Brauneck does not return. He fell at 8.45 p.m. in air combat south of Zonnebeke.

On 27 July, Vizefeldwebel Wüsthoff pursues a Sopwith at which he had been firing, in vain, with his guns. As nothing at all seems to be of any use, he pushes his opponent down, chases him behind the German lines, and forces him to land near Dadizeele. Leutnant von Schönebeck shoots a triplane down in flames near Beythem.

On 28 July, it continues at the same pace. As far as the number of their machines is concerned, they are always inferior and, as far as the number of their victories in proportion to their losses is concerned, they are always superior. At 12.10 p.m., Leutnant Adam finishes off his ninth opponent north of Terhand. At 5.20 p.m., Leutnant Bockelmann shoots a 'lattice-tail' down near Merckem.[1] At exactly this same minute, Leutnant Czermak enters his name in the honor roll of the Geschwader with his first victory near Meulebeke.[2] Near Oostrozebeke, Leutnant Adam dispatches yet another opponent on this day, and shortly thereafter, just before 7.00 p.m., Leutnant Tüxen shoots his second opponent down east of Ingelmunster.

At this time, an English bombing squadron of six two-seater aircraft

---

[1] This victory is identified by N. Franks as a French Caudron which was downed at 9.20 p.m. and which was unconfirmed.
[2] Lt Czermak's victory was scored at 6.50 p.m., the same time that Oblt Dostler achieved his 19th victory north-east of Courtrai, not at the time that Lt Bockelmann is listed as downing his opponent.

comes flying over the Front. Oberleutnant Dostler, with his Jasta 6, totally destroys this squadron. Not one enemy machine was able to escape. None of the passengers ever saw their home field again, and none of the heavy bombs they carried with them touched the life of even one German soldier.

Leutnant Niederhoff does not return. He was shot down at 12.00 noon in air combat west of Terhand.

During the night following this trying day, one half-hour after midnight, the English break through over the Front and drop bombs on the Marckebeke airfield. The report dictated by the Rittmeister the next day was short: 'A few houses were unroofed. Windows in the vicinity were shattered. No one was injured.'

On 29 July, Vizefeldwebels Heldmann and Wüsthoff both get the same wildly shooting Sopwith in front of their machine guns and, at 7.55 a.m., the airplane flutters down into the crater field, enveloped in smoke and flames. After investigating the matter, the commander awards the victory to Vizefeldwebel Heldmann.

Around 11.00 a.m. on this day, the officers and men of the Geschwader stand in St Joseph's Church in Courtrai to say the Lord's Prayer at the coffin of the fallen Leutnant Brauneck and then to accompany it to the railway station.

During the night of 30 July, around 1.00 a.m., the airfield's watch gets everybody out of bed. Over the airfield, they see an airplane's distress signal. Everyone knows what he has to do. First, the non-commissioned officers run out with all the flare pistols they can get hold of and shoot off rockets. Then the burning landing-cross is laid out. The officers have the glasses to their eyes and stare into the dark sky. But the airplane does not descend. A few particularly suspicious men prefer to proceed to the vicinity of the dugouts. One can't really know; after all, there is a war on, and there are bombers. A sly Englishman could also give off German distress signals, even though these signals are arranged in all secrecy . . . that's true enough. Everyone waits.

Nothing happens.

They then hear the airplane, with the distinct hum of a German engine, departing in a southerly direction.

'He has it, and he doesn't want it,' somebody shouts irritably. They return to bed.

The thirtieth of July is a good day for the Geschwader. Leutnant Voss arrives as the new Staffel leader of Jasta 10[1] and, with him, an 'ace' has once again arrived: very young, wiry, thirty-four victories behind him, and the order *Pour le Mérite*.

---

[1] Lt Voss replaced Oblt Freiherr von Althaus, who was transferred to Jastaschule II.

On 31 July, the usual pace of Jagdgeschwader I continues: 12.50 p.m., south of Zillebeke, a Bristol by Leutnant Hübner; 1.00 p.m., west of Deimlingseck, an RE by Leutnant Meyer; 1.10 p.m., near Frezenberg, an RE by Leutnant von Schönebeck; 2.05 p.m., west of Bellewaarde Lake, a Nieuport by Oberleutnant Dostler; 2.45 p.m., near Verbrandenmolen, a 'lattice-tail' by Vizefeldwebel Wüsthoff.[1]

At 3.00 p.m., the officers and men of the Geschwader once again stand in St Joseph's Church in Courtrai. The Lord's Prayer is prayed for the fallen Leutnant Niederhoff.

The first three days of August which now follow rage across the landscape with rain and gales that cannot be flown in. On 4 August, near Reninghe, Leutnant Hübner takes his third opponent out of the air. On 5 August, no longer Vizefeldwebel, but now Leutnant Wüsthoff[2] brings his eighth opponent down at 3.00 p.m., near Ypres. At 3.15 p.m., Leutnant von Boenigk brings down his third west of Staden. On 8 August, Jasta Boelcke is placed under tactical command of the Geschwader. On 9 August, over Houthulst Forest, Oberleutnant Dostler sees his twenty-second opponent crash in flames. On the same day, Jasta Boelcke departs again. Leutnant Voss, in the Geschwader formation for the first time, shoots down his thirty-fifth opponent.

During the night of 10 August they are shaken up once again. The ground roars, cracks, and splits. Five heavy bombs hit, quite unpleasantly this time. Two tent hangars are smashed to a pulp, and seven machines are heavily damaged.

The day began unpleasantly and it continues unpleasantly. At 10.15 a.m., an enemy squadron is reported by the air defense officers, but it is already over the German lines. At 10.20, take-off of all the Jastas ensues, but, at the last instant, the take-off is brusquely cancelled by the commander. The Rittmeister makes a report concerning this episode:

> It has once again been shown that taking off against a squadron which has already broken through is pointless.
>
> Reason: The English bombing and reconnaissance squadrons now fly over our lines at extremely high altitudes (4,500–5,000 meters). Our machines do not have sufficient climbing capability to reach the enemy in time. The possibility of approaching such a squadron would only exist if our ground observation reports the assembly of the same on the other side of the Front.

---

[1] Aircraft was an FE2b.
[2] Kurt Wüsthoff was commissioned on 1 August 1917.

During the evening, between 10.00 and 11.00 p.m., the men in the telephone exchange rush up from their equipment. A heavy bomb has struck so close to them that it literally takes their breath away for a while.

On 11 August, at 9.00 p.m., Leutnant Krefft of the Geschwader staff suffers engine failure in the vicinity of the airfield. He crashes, but is only slightly injured. The airplane's fuselage and wings are totally destroyed. On 12 August, three victories: Leutnant Stapenhorst, a Sopwith north of Bixschoote, at 8.50 a.m.; Oberleutnant Dostler, a Sopwith near Koelberg, at 3.55 p.m.; and Leutnant Adam, a fuselaged biplane in the area of Poperinghe, at 9.10 p.m.[1] On 13 August, at 9.20 a.m., Leutnant Bockelmann brings down a fuselaged biplane near Schellebeke. At 10.45 a.m., Oberleutnant Reinhard downs a Sopwith near Grotenmolen.

On 14 August, the monotonous list continues. It is written in Flanders' sky with letters of flame, smoke, and death: Leutnant Löwenhardt, 10.15 a.m., an RE near Zillebeke Lake; Oberleutnant Reinhard, 10.45 a.m., an RE near Boesinghe; Oberleutnant Reinhard, five minutes later, same place, a Spad; Oberleutnant Weigand, 10.45 a.m., a Sopwith south-west of Dixmude; Leutnant Müller, 5.35 p.m., a Sopwith north of Bixschoote; Leutnant Meyer, 6.40 p.m., a Sopwith near Wytschaete; Leutnant Adam, 7.30 p.m., a Sopwith over Houthulst Forest; Oberleutnant Dostler, 7.30 p.m., a Sopwith near St Julien.

At 7.20 p.m., Unteroffizier Brettel is wounded by a shot in the arm during air combat. He has to make an emergency landing near Moorslede, and goes to Field Hospital No. 34 in St Eloois Winkel. At 8.35 p.m., Leutnant Hübner is shot down in air combat near Moorslede, and Leutnant Wolff,[2] a namesake of the 'delicate little flower', is shot through the thigh in air combat over Zillebeke Lake. He goes to St Nicholas Hospital in Courtrai.

On 16 August, Rittmeister von Richthofen takes off once again. At 7.55 a.m., he sends his fifty-eighth opponent burning into the crater holes south-west of Houthulst Forest. There was seldom a time when his opponent was not shot down in flames. One of his first questions to his comrades during the victory reports was, 'In flames?' Eventually, the fighter pilots of his Geschwader were embarrassed if they had to answer this question in the negative. Richthofen's report concerning this victory read:

> About 7.55 a.m., in the company of four aircraft of Jasta 11, I pursued
> a small squadron of Nieuports. After a long pursuit, I attacked one of

---

[1] By this reference to a 'fuselaged' biplane, Bodenschatz is differentiating between a 'puller' machine with the engine in front and a solid fuselage, and a 'pusher' machine with the engine behind the nacelle and an open 'lattice-work' type of tail assembly.
[2] Leutnant Hans Joachim Wolff of Jasta 11.

the enemy, and after a short fight, shot up his engine and gas tank. The airplane went into a tailspin. I immediately followed it until just above the ground. In so doing, I got one more chance to shoot, so the airplane crashed south-west of Houthulst Forest and ran into the ground. Since I had followed him down to about 50 meters, I came into a gas cloud so that, for a brief moment, I became ill.

At 11.20 a.m. on the same day, Leutnant Groos shoots down his fourth at Zillebeke Lake; Leutnant Mohnicke, his fifth at 12.29 p.m. near Linselles; and at 9.00 p.m., Leutnant Voss, his thirty-seventh opponent in the region of St Julien. The English have not been idle and they attacked the Geschwader in its own wasps' nest. At 6.15 a.m., two bombs roared down between the railway embankment and the airfield, but no one was hurt. A quarter of an hour later, a better aimed bomb struck the airfield of Jasta 4, destroyed a tent hangar, and blew two machines to shreds. At 8.05 p.m., a bomb once again fell to earth in the vicinity of Jasta 11. It made a nice dust crater, as high as a house, and nothing else.

On 17 August, the monotonous, yet exciting carousel revolves again: Leutnant Groos, 7.25 a.m., an SE west of Passchendaele; Oberleutnant Dostler, 8.10 a.m., a Martinsyde north of Menin; Leutnant Ohlrau, 10.15 a.m., a Sopwith near Becelaere; Leutnant von der Osten, 8.55 p.m., a Sopwith near Staden.

In return for that, there was an intense bombing raid around noon. On the airfields of Jastas 11, 4, and 10, the earth sprayed high, the wings of two airplanes were damaged, and a non-commissioned officer was slightly injured.

In the evening, they sit together in the officers' mess, and the Rittmeister regards the Geschwader's new acquisition almost affectionately: the young, very young, Leutnant Voss, leader of Jasta 10, this 'Daredevil First Class', who is sliding around on his chair like a lively schoolboy. Suddenly, Richthofen stands up, goes over to a highly surprised Leutnant von der Osten, extends his hand to him, clasps it firmly. What is going on? Is it because Leutnant von der Osten has his first victory behind him? After a few words by the Rittmeister, there begins a loud cheer. Leutnant von der Osten has only achieved his first victory, to be sure, but, at the same time, it was the 200th victory of Richthofen's own Jasta 11. For that reason, Richthofen has also invited the other Jasta leaders this evening in order to celebrate properly. Döring has put in an appearance, Löwenhardt, Dostler, and Adam.

A very brief speech follows, a brief look back at Jasta 11's greatest days of success outside of Douai. The telegram to the Commanding General of the Air Service is just as brief: 'Today, after seven months of action, Jasta

11 destroyed its 200th opponent. In so doing, it has captured 121 airplanes and 196 machine guns.' But on the same evening, yet another report goes to the Commander of Fourth Army Aviation,[1] and this report is a little less friendly:

> The Geschwader is being broken up by deployment of individual Staffeln. On days of major combat, the deployment of several Staffeln at the same time and in the same area is necessary. The Staffeln which must provide cover for the Kampfstaffeln leave the Geschwader formation for the greater part of the day. A pilot who has already been called on for cover flights during long-range missions and bombing flights cannot, on the same day, fully and completely fulfill his duty as a fighter pilot, because, for successful execution of aerial combat, he must be unfatigued and completely fresh.

That means, therefore: 'Utilize us correctly, please, and don't exhaust us with assignments that others could carry out just as well. We are fighter pilots, you see.'

On 18 August, at 8.00 a.m., bombs again thunder down. They don't harm anyone. On this day, a telegram arrives from the Commanding General of the Air Service. The Rittmeister begins to read it with pride at first, and then he pensively lays it aside as he reads the final sentence. The telegram reads:

> From your report concerning the combats of 16 August, I have seen that relentless deployment of the units and the superior bravery of the crews have decided the air battle in our favor.
>
> The troops are indebted to their comrades in the air. To you, the Commander of the Geschwader, especially, but also to all of the pilots, I express my thanks and my warmest appreciation.
>
> I heartily congratulate Rittmeister von Richthofen on his fifty-eighth air victory, and I expect that he himself is cognizant of the responsibility of deploying his person, and that he will fly only if absolute necessity warrants it until he has overcome the last traces of his wound.

This last sentence is bitter. The second telegram to arrive is only an inadequate plaster:

> On 17 August, Jasta 11 defeated its 200th opponent in air combat since its first day of mobilization, 12 October 1916. These successes are a

---

[1] Hauptmann Helmuth Wilberg.

shining example for all fighter pilots, and the finest memorial to the
fallen comrades of Jasta 11. To Jasta 11, its leader, Leutnant Wolff, and
especially to its former leader, Rittmeister Freiherr von Richthofen, I
express my appreciation.

On 19 August, General Ludendorff comes to visit, to see for himself the
most daring airmen of the German Army, and to shake their hands. He also
has the opportunity to view the newly-arrived triplanes which every pilot
has been ardently awaiting, and which make an excellent impression.

After so many pleasant events, a hard blow strikes the Geschwader on 21
August. Oberleutnant Dostler does not return from a patrol. The valor and
joy-of-battle which were linked with this name can scarcely be expressed.
The Rittmeister is hit hard by this loss. He sends out flights to look for him.
Nothing is found. He must be lying somewhere between the lines in no-
man's-land. Finally, the following information comes:

> According to a telephone report by the Commander of Fourth Army
> Aviation, the English Royal Flying Corps has sent this information
> concerning Oberleutnant Dostler: that precise details concerning his
> fate cannot be provided. It is known only that on 21 August 1917, at
> 11.00 a.m. English time (12.00 p.m. German time), a German airplane
> was brought down in the vicinity of Frezenberg by an English pilot, and
> is probably lying in the forwardmost German lines.
>
> Time and location in accordance with the above-mentioned details
> correspond with Oberleutnant Dostler's air combat of that time.
> During the following night and the next morning, there was heavy
> English artillery fire over the site of the downed aircraft.

At those times when one of their comrades hasn't returned, it is always a
little quieter in the officers' mess that evening, but not for long. By
unspoken agreement, nothing much is said about their fallen comrade.
That only happens later, when the chance arises. This evening, it is quiet
longer than usual. Dostler had been neither quiet nor 'usual'. God knows,
he had not been that.

And as if, over in the enemy flying camps, they themselves felt that a
mighty piece of work had been accomplished with the downing of this man,
the enemy now took a break in the fighting. The Commander of Fourth
Army Aviation immediately sends an order:

> The enemy is obviously conserving his aviation forces. We must do the
> same, as far as possible, during the break in the fighting.
>   I refer to the Army Order of 12 August, Roman numeral II, and ask

to be notified, if need be, in case this point is not being satisfactorily taken into account.

Roman numeral II concerns Rittmeister von Richthofen and calls his attention to the fact that he is to fly only if an absolute necessity exists.

On 22 August, Leutnant Adam is appointed leader of the orphaned Jasta 6. On 23 August, at 7.50 a.m., Leutnant Groos shoots down a Sopwith south of Poelcapelle; at 9.05 a.m., Oberleutnant von Boenigk downs a triplane near Boesinghe; and at 10.10 a.m., Leutnant Voss shoots a Spad down south-west of Dixmude.

On 24 August, there comes some unexpected news: a captured Englishman is said to have stated that Oberleutnant Dostler was taken into English captivity, uninjured. Jagdgeschwader I is skeptical. The report proves erroneous.

On 26 August, the Rittmeister forgets Roman numeral II of the Army Order and takes off. At 7.30 a.m., he shoots a Spad down over the forwardmost lines between Poelcapelle and Langemarck. It is his fifty-ninth air victory, and his report concerning it is not without irritation:

> During a patrol with four gentleman of Jasta 11, flying at an altitude of 3,000 meters, I saw below me a single Spad above a solid cloud cover. The enemy was apparently hunting for low-flying artillery reconnaissance aircraft. I attacked him, coming out of the sun. He tried to escape by means of a dive, whereby I got a good shot at him, and he disappeared through a thin layer of clouds. Upon pursuit, I saw him, under the cloud cover, first plunge straight down and then explode in the air at an altitude of about 500 meters. Due to the new, very poor incendiary ammunition, my pressure line, intake-manifold, exhaust, etc., were again so damaged that I couldn't have pursued even a crippled opponent. As a result, he would have escaped, and I had to see that I glided as far from the Front as possible.

On 1 September, the Rittmeister goes up for air combat in one of the new triplanes for the first time. (Roman numeral II, Army Order of 12 August, doesn't worry him. It is totally forgotten and overlooked.) At 7.50 a.m., he shoots down his sixtieth opponent near Zonnebeke. The fight was brief.

> Flying the triplane for the first time, with four gentlemen of Jasta 11, I attacked a very boldly flown English artillery-spotting aircraft. I flew to within 50 meters of him, fired twenty rounds, whereupon my opponent plunged out of control and smashed to pieces on this side of the lines near Zonnebeke.

Apparently, my opponent had taken me for an English triplane, for the observer stood in the machine without making a move for his machine gun.

Forty-eight hours later, there is a fantastic day. The Rittmeister starts it off, despite Roman numeral II, and its corresponding orders concerning his person. At 7.35 a.m., he tangles with an exceptionally brave opponent:

> With five airplanes of Jasta 11 engaged in a fight with Sopwith single-seaters, I attacked one of our opponents at an altitude of 3,500 meters and, after a fairly long dogfight, forced him to land near Bousbecque. I was absolutely convinced I had a very skillful opponent in front of me, who, even at an altitude of 50 meters, still did not surrender, fired again, and opened fire on a troop column while flattening out, then deliberately taxied his machine into a tree. The Fokker Triplane FI 102/ 17 was absolutely superior to the English Sopwith.

That evening, the list is definite. Eleven aircraft downed: Leutnant Mohnicke, a Sopwith; Leutnant Wüsthoff, a Sopwith; Leutnant Voss, a Sopwith; Leutnant von Schönebeck, a triplane; Leutnant Stapenhorst, a triplane; Oberleutnant von Döring, an RE; Leutnant Wüsthoff, an RE, his second opponent of the day; Leutnant Adam, a Nieuport; Oberleutnant von Boenigk, a Sopwith, and a quarter of an hour later, yet another Sopwith. Leutnant Bockelmann took a shot through the lower leg and was delivered to Field Hospital No. 133 in Courtrai.

On 4 September, the old, familiar names appear again in the reports: Leutnant Wüsthoff dispatches his eleventh opponent; Leutnant Mohnicke, his seventh; Leutnant Stapenhorst, his third; and Leutnant Wüsthoff, his twelfth, three quarters of an hour later, during his second take-off of the day. Oberleutnant Reinhard is severely wounded over Houthulst Forest by the almost obligatory bullet in the thigh. He is deposited next to Leutnant Bockelmann in the same hospital.

On 5 September, tireless Leutnant Wüsthoff dispatches his thirteenth opponent; Leutnant Löwenhardt, his third; and Leutnant Voss, his fortieth and forty-first, one after the other. On 6 September, only one victory is submitted: the forty-second victory of Leutnant Voss. On this day, ignoring Roman numeral II in the Army Order of 12 August has rather strong repercussions: the Rittmeister 'voluntarily' begins a compulsory, four-week leave which had been vigorously pushed by everyone higher up.

On 9 September, Leutnant Löwenhardt goes for a captive balloon. At 8.55 p.m., he brings one down near Alveringhem and from then on, this officer becomes a specialist in the downing of captive balloons. In time he will receive the *Pour le Mérite* because of these ugly gasbags.

On 10 September, Leutnant Voss proves the undoing of three enemy airmen all at once. At 5.50 p.m., he circles over Langemarck and dispatches a Sopwith, the second Sopwith five minutes later, and twenty minutes later, in the same place, an FE. And comes back with victories forty-three, forty-four, and forty-five. Langemarck seems to be a lucky hunting region for him, because on the next day, he is there again, circling up and down, and he shoots down his forty-sixth opponent in the morning, and his forty-seventh in the afternoon.

On 12 September, a dispatch comes addressed to the 'delicate little flower':

> His Majesty, the Kaiser and King, has signified His pleasure to promote you to Oberleutnant, in recognition of your outstanding achievements as a fighter pilot. I am pleased to be able to inform you of this and I congratulate you on this renewed proof of the All Highest's recognition.
>
> The Commanding General

The 'delicate little flower' seems to have been more distressed than pleased by this promotion. Once again, he writes a resigned letter to his fiancée:

> I now come with a bit of good news. This morning I received a telegram ... therefore, one step closer to 'captain'. It just depresses me that I am receiving this distinction now without having shot one down. Because, so far, I've had bad luck. I have already fought it out with about twenty Englishmen and haven't gotten one down ...

And then the newly appointed Oberleutnant went all out.

Three days later, on 15 September, in his Silesian hometown of Schweidnitz, Rittmeister von Richthofen tears open a telegram.[1] It is from his Jagdgeschwader and reads, 'Oberleutnant Wolff has fallen in air combat north of Wervicq.'

First Dostler, now Wolff! How deeply this loss grieved Richthofen can be seen from the obituary he had published in two newspapers in Wolff's hometown of Memel, the *Kreuzzeitung*, and the *Militärwochenblatt*.[2]

On 15 September 1917, after fierce aerial combat, Royal Prussian

---

[1] Rittmeister von Richthofen was hunting in Thuringia as a guest of the Duke of Saxe-Coburg-Gotha on this date.

[2] *The Cross* and *The Military Weekly*.

Oberleutnant Kurt Wolff, Knight of the Order *Pour le Mérite*, died a hero's death for his Fatherland.

In deep pain, the Geschwader, together with the entire flying corps, stands at the all-too-early grave of a leader proven in valiant combat, who led his brave band from victory to victory. He offered up his young life not in forced defense, but rather in a ruthless attack of his own choosing.

With his friendly nature and his quiet modesty, he was one of the dearest and best of comrades to us all.

He will live on for all time in the history of the Geschwader as a model of soldierly virtue, as an example that is given only by the very finest.

It had hit him hard. The 'delicate little flower' who was such a crazy man[1] in combat had given his life away, and a man full of cheerfulness, kindness, and indescribable modesty had been extinguished.

The eighteenth of September is a gloomy day. At 11.00 a.m., the officers and men of the Geschwader are once again assembled in St Joseph's Church in Courtrai. What is lying there in the flower-covered coffin is the shattered body of a young man who was a true man and champion.

The kiss of Death hovers over those bowing their heads and saying the Lord's Prayer for their comrade, regardless of how carefree, young, and smooth their faces may be. They know it, but they do not speak of it. If they do speak of it, then it bursts forth lightly, in a word spoken in jest. It is likely — more than likely — that each one's turn will come sooner or later. Around noon they carry the fallen youth to the train station. In Memel, the 'delicate little flower' will be returned to his native earth.

With this death, the spirits seem to be stirred up once again. The twentieth of September is a day of aerial combat on a grand scale. On the ground, as well: a powerful attack by the enemy is in progress between Langemarck and the Canal.[2] It rained the night before. At 8.30 a.m., however, as soon as the day's first wisps of cloud disappeared, a strong enemy bombing squadron appeared over the airfields of the Jagdgeschwader. And this time it proved serious. The bombs screamed down on the huts and tents. An English two-seater had dropped some heavy bombs and the pilot then undertook a daring attack: he swooped down to eighty meters and emptied his machine guns. Five men collapsed dead, several more were severely wounded, and nine machines were damaged.

---

[1] Literally, a 'berserker', historically, one of a class of warriors in Norse folklore who were seized by a howling frenzy in battle, and who were believed invulnerable.
[2] The Battle of the Menin Road Bridge (20-25 September), near the Ypres–Yser Canal.

When the weather cleared up around 9.30 a.m., the Geschwader took off. Jasta 6 flew to Lys, south of Ypres, under the command of Leutnant Adam. Immediately following their arrival at the Front, three enemy aircraft were shot down.[1] The Jasta then flew out over the lines and pushed the enemy airmen back. Jasta 6 kept watch and, during the entire flight time of an hour and a half, not one other Englishman came across the lines in this sector. A few solitary enemy artillery-spotters and infantry-support planes soared far in the distance on the other side of the lines. Fighter aircraft were spotted too; they ventured no closer. Around noon, Jasta 4 took off. The cloud cover had now lifted somewhat. Jasta 4 flew out over the enemy lines and shot down two Spad single-seaters.[2] In the afternoon, the Jasta took off for a second time and brought down yet another Spad.[3] Jasta 6 dispatched yet another balloon and Leutnant Wüsthoff achieved his nineteenth victory.[4]

Jasta 10 took off only twice, with five airplanes each time. It had suffered heavy losses in the way of wounded pilots in the last few days. The Jasta's low flight led them through an enormous cloud of gas extending eastward from Polygon Wood up into the clouds. It caused only nausea, not serious health problems. On this hellish day, Jasta 11 took off four times.

On 21 September, Leutnant Löwenhardt shot down a captive balloon, and Leutnant Wüsthoff shot down his twentieth opponent. On 23 September, at 9.30 a.m., Leutnant Voss shot his forty-eighth opponent down in flames south of Roulers. At 6.05 p.m., he took off again with his Staffel.

In Schweidnitz, early on the morning of 24 September,[5] Rittmeister von Richthofen again tore open a telegram. It came from the Geschwader and read, 'Leutnant Voss did not return from a flight, probably fallen.'

Dostler, Wolff, Voss!

On 24 September, Leutnant Wendelmuth of Jasta 8 reports that Leutnant Voss had been shot down from behind during air combat with a Sopwith. His machine crashed north of Frezenberg just behind the enemy lines.

Fighter pilot Oberleutnant Waldhausen (of a neighboring Jasta[6]), who had been shot down while attacking a captive balloon and captured by the British, found the death of Leutnant Voss described in the memoirs of the

---

[1] Lt Adam was credited with two, and Lt K. Stock was credited with the other.
[2] Listed as victories by Lt Wüsthoff and Oblt von Döring.
[3] Credited to Lt Wüsthoff.
[4] Same victory mentioned above.
[5] Rittmeister von Richthofen was still hunting in Thuringia when this telegram arrived.
[6] Jasta 37.

English fighter pilot, James McCudden.[1] This description gives a vivid picture of the manner in which these young German men went up against a superior force.

The English officer writes:

> We were just about to engage six German Albatros scouts which were off to our right. Then, in the direction from which we had just come, we saw an English SE (a single-seater scout) making for the ground in a tight spiral. A silver-grey German triplane (it was Voss) was hard on his heels. Because the situation of the SE was obviously very serious, we changed our original decision to attack the six Albatros aircraft. We hurried to come to the aid of the unfortunate SE instead.
>
> The German triplane was lower than our formation, so we went into a dive and dove on him at great speed. I was to the right of my friend, Rhys Davids, and together we got behind the tail of the triplane. The German pilot spotted us right away and he made such a quick turn that we were all absolutely amazed. He didn't really climb, or fly an Immelmann turn, it was more of a flat half-spin. Now he was in the middle of our formation; we had him. His flying was so masterful, however, that we couldn't get over our deep astonishment. He seemed to be firing at all of us simultaneously. I succeeded in getting behind his tail once more but I couldn't stay there even a second, for the movements of his machine were of such an amazing quickness and dexterity that each one of us got him in our sights for just a fleeting moment.
>
> Then my prospects got better as he came at me from the front without seeing me. I was slightly higher than he was. I lowered both my guns. But I had no sooner begun to fire when he pointed the nose of his machine at me and I heard . . . rattatatatatatatata . . . next to me as his shots peppered my wings. I could clearly see the reddish-yellow fire coming from the muzzles of his two Spandau machine guns.
>
> In the meantime, another Albatros scout had arrived. It was painted red in front and it tried its best to bail out the silver-grey triplane. This machine was handled splendidly too. The formation of six Albatros scouts which we had originally intended to attack stayed high above us. They couldn't do anything to us, however, because they were being kept quite busy by a formation of Spads whose leader had grasped our tricky situation.
>
> It was an incredible picture: the German triplane was still circling in

---

[1] This is a translation of the account as it appeared in the German original, which was itself a translation. For Captain McCudden's exact account, please see his book, *Five Years in the Royal Flying Corps* (later entitled *Flying Fury*), The Aeroplane and General Publishing Co. Ltd, 1918.

the midst of our six SEs, who were all firing at him like crazy whenever the opportunity presented itself. At one time I could see that the triplane was in the midst of the cone of fire from at least five machines. And each machine had two machine guns!

The fight finally slacked off. The red-nosed Albatros that had come to the aid of his comrade went hurtling downwards to be seen no more, and so was no longer in the fight. The silver-grey triplane was still with us, however, and did not back off. I lost sight of him for a short time while I loaded a new cartridge drum. When I then caught sight of him again, he was still fighting, all alone. At a much lower altitude, he was now in combat with one of our machines marked with a roman 'I'; so it was Rhys Davids. Shortly thereafter, I noticed that the triplane's movements had suddenly become very erratic, and then I saw him hurtling downwards at a fairly steep angle. I watched the dive which ended only at the ground. There the machine disintegrated into a thousand pieces. It seemed to literally dissolve into dust.

Strange to say, I was the only pilot who had seen the triplane shatter on the ground. Even Rhys Davids, who had given him the final rounds, couldn't see the crash.

It was fairly late in the day, and so we now returned to our airfield.

As long as I live, I will always remember with admiration that German pilot who single-handedly fought seven of us for ten minutes, and inflicted some hits on all of our machines. His flying was wonderful and his courage amazing. In my opinion, he is the bravest German airman whom I have had the privilege to see fight.

We arrived at the mess, and at dinner the conversation revolved around that singular air battle. We all conjectured that the enemy pilot must be one of the enemy's best, and we debated as to whether we'd had Richthofen, Wolff, or Voss before us. The triplane had come to earth inside of our lines. The next morning we received the report that the fallen pilot had an order ribbon around his neck, like Boelcke wore in his day. It was the ribbon of the order *Pour le Mérite*. Its wearer was Werner Voss.

Rhys Davids received a flood of congratulations and he had truly earned them, but the good fellow said to me, 'I would have rather brought him down alive!' These words were in agreement with my own feelings.

In this way, they fight and they die, come and go, scarcely grown out of adolescence, hard as steel, of the same stature as the legendary heroes of antiquity.

On 25 September, Leutnant Lothar von Richthofen arrives at the Geschwader,[1] and of him there must be much discussion yet when speaking of the Jagdgeschwader Richthofen.

On the same day, a telegram arrives from the Commanding General of the Air Service:

> Since the available reports hardly allow us to still hope that Leutnant Voss will return to us, I am thinking of the Jagdgeschwader in heartfelt sympathy. What the Air Service has lost in him is shown by the number of his victories. A strong, sound will is needed of our fighter pilots in order to overcome the loss of our best, to the honor of our fallen comrades. The strength of their will and their abilities must live on for the victory of German air power.

The General knows this as well: just as surely as two times two equals four, in time, they are all going to buy it, every one of this whole élite group of young men. Anyone who is wounded up there at an altitude of 3,000 meters cannot crawl away, cannot be transported to a doctor. There are no stretcher-bearers close at hand. No one can carry him away, and what the bullet fails to destroy will be finished down below by the awful crash on the ground. The General knows that this cannot be changed.

Certain thoughts and worries do have him concerned, however. First of all, how do things stand as to enemy machines, and above all, how do things stand as to enemy tactics? He demands a precise report from each Staffel of Jagdgeschwader I. Immediately, of course.

Oberleutnant Freiherr von Boenigk, acting commander of Jasta 4, reports:

> According to the experiences of the Staffel on the local Front, the enemy is primarily using the following types:
>
> | Single-Seaters | Two-Seaters |
> | --- | --- |
> | Sopwith Camel | Bristol Fighter |
> | SE 5 | FE |
> | Spad Single-Seater | De Havilland |
> | Sopwith Triplane | RE |
> | Nieuport, new type | |
>
> Almost all of the single-seaters have a fixed machine gun. Recently, SEs have appeared with 200 hp Hispano–Suiza engines which possess very good climbing capabilities and speed.

---

[1] Lothar von Richthofen was returning to active duty for the first time since his wounding on 13 May 1917.

Promising the most success is an attack on a single-seater squadron from above and behind, during which you mustn't push out over the enemy machine. The best defense against an enemy single-seater attack from above and behind is to climb steeply in a sharp turn, but only if the enemy does not have machines too very superior to our own aircraft. In such a case, allowing yourself to go into a spin is the most advisable.

The attack on two-seaters best takes place from the front and above, or from behind and below. In a dogfight with a two-seater, always try not to climb above him, but rather stay below and behind him.

Leutnant Adam, the leader of Jasta 6, submits the following report:

1. Attacks on single-seater Sopwith Pups and Sopwith Camels, from above towards the rear, or from above obliquely towards the front, can be carried out almost without any counter-action. Technically, both are inferior to the Albatros 'D' machine.

2. SE 5. Attack as in paragraph one. Technically, about equal to the Albatros 'D' machine; superior to the average 'D' machine in dogfights at higher altitudes. They themselves frequently attack from behind, in a dogfight, as well.

3. Spad, 140 hp. Inferior to the Albatros 'D' machine. Spad, 200 hp: superior to the Albatros 'D' machine in climbing capability and maneuverability.

4. Triplane of more recent construction (same length wings) is very maneuverable, good in a dogfight, tolerates the steepest dives, is not better than the Albatros 'D'.

5. Nieuport single-seater, exceptionally maneuverable, always defends itself by diving, is otherwise inferior to our 'D' machines in every respect.

In general: Attacking from below advisable only if first burst of fire will hit for certain. When enemy single-seaters approach at a higher altitude, they are almost impossible to climb over, since during an attack, they usually don't push down low enough for us to dogfight and possibly climb above them. When the enemy single-seater attacks, many times he fires too early, so upon hearing the first shots, turning and flying under the attacker is still possible. If the attacker has a rotary engine, defense by means of a right-hand turn is advisable because machines with rotary engines perform poorly in right-hand turns, and less possibility of being hit exists.

Two-Seaters and Multi-Seaters: De Havilland 4. Attack from the rear and from the same altitude if you are close enough to be able to hit with the first burst of fire. Otherwise, do not close in any more. This type is just about as fast as an Albatros 'D' in a climb. If possible, attack first from in front and above and then from the rear immediately afterwards, in order to make the observer turn the gun in the gun turret. If the de Havilland is at the same altitude and must still be approached from further away, then the attack is almost always without hope of success. Usually operates at an altitude of over 5,000 meters.

Jasta 10 summed up its experiences most pragmatically and at the bottom of this report is the name of Leutnant Voss. It was the last thing he left behind: his own practical experiences.

All English single-seaters are superior to the German fighter aircraft in climb, handling, and dive capabilities, and most of them are also superior in speed. Only the Sopwith Pup is slower.

You should not, under any circumstances, attack formations of Sopwiths, which fly higher, on the other side of the enemy lines for you must then start the fight under unfavorable circumstances from the outset.

Of the two-seaters, the FEs can be particularly dangerous in air combat; they band together in a circle.

Vickers and FE squadrons respectively must be attacked together as a unit. Only then does the possibility of successfully dealing with them present itself.

Most fighter pilots do not like attacking the FE directly from the front, but this very method of attack is the most advantageous for us against the FE since the enemy has the least protection in front, while our fighter pilots have good protection because of the engine. With this last type of attack, it is absolutely essential for the fighter pilot to keep himself below the enemy airplane and not fly over the latter, under any circumstances.

Leutnant Groos, the acting commander of Jasta 11, says:

The combat method of the enemy single-seater is always the same and doesn't depend on the type itself. The enemy single-seaters swoop into German squadrons from overhead, usually coming out of the sun (even in the mornings). With the sun at their backs, they attack just as readily from the front or the rear. If the Englishman does not have visible success after the first attack, he then again climbs sharply, and after a short time, tries a renewed, surprise attack. The English flights do not usually attack together as a unit, so the few brave ones get caught up in a dogfight where they are then overcome by the numerical superiority of the German single-seaters. If the German single-seater has found an opportunity to attack the English single-seater from above, the latter then seeks to evade his attacker by continuous tailspins and turns. However, as soon as he notices that the German is close, he turns suddenly and attacks from the front and below, attempting thereby to climb over his opponent, which he often succeeds in doing, owing to his fine machines.

The General has read these reports through, over and over again. And he needn't ponder long to come to a clear conclusion. That's the way things are, all in all, and there is nothing in the world to be done about it: the English machines are superior to the German machines. (*But truly just the machines!* he thinks proudly.) This cannot be changed. And it is not even a reproach against the German aircraft builders. If the equipment produced at their hands is gradually getting worse because they are lacking the raw materials, how can they change it?

The General has grave worries. In the midst of these worries, however, the conviction shines through over and over again that he has other material that is not so easy to beat and which remains independent of any factory: his pilots. They are men he can depend on, regardless of how things might be. They put their youth — their steely, unspent, iron-nerved youth — up against the toughest circumstances, along with their fearlessness, their ability, and their daring.

Was there ever a finer illustration of such young heroes than the two Richthofen brothers? Lothar, the Dragoon Leutnant, at the side of Manfred, the Uhlan. In the winter of 1915, with urging from Manfred, Lothar had gone into aviation, first as an observer, and then as a pilot a year later. In March of 1917, he passed his third examination and went straight to his brother's Jagdstaffel.

The Rittmeister told how Lothar had still been a very young and inexperienced pilot who never dreamed of loops and similar skillful stunts, but who was satisfied if he could take off decently and land cleanly. He told how, after fourteen days, he had taken Lothar along against the enemy for the first time, and had asked Lothar to fly close behind him in order 'to just watch things closely the first time'. And how, on the third combat patrol, he watched as Lothar peeled off, dove on an Englishman, and shot him down.

Four weeks later, something astounding had happened: Lothar had shot down his twentieth Englishman! That was totally unprecedented in aviation. But then astounding things constantly happened with Lothar: his twenty-second opponent was England's best airman, the famous Captain

Ball. After a murderous battle, Lothar shot him down.[1]

Those days outside Douai were a heyday for Richthofen's Jagdstaffel. Names like Schäfer, Allmenröder, Wolff, and Vizefeldwebel Festner gave it a glory unequalled in the Army.

Lothar and Manfred . . . they were models of comradeship and chivalry, models of audacity and fearlessness, models in every sense.

September has become October, and the weather is getting worse. In the log, the same entry reappears regularly: hazy, poor visibility.

The Kaiser gives Richthofen a bronze bust of himself with the engraved dedication, 'To the illustrious fighter pilot Rittmeister Freiherr von Richthofen, His Grateful King.' Decorations arrive for him from all the princes of the different kingdoms.[2] On 23 October, after an absence of four weeks, he returns to his Geschwader and resumes command.

On 27 October, Leutnant Müller crashes during a test flight in the vicinity of the airfield. The machine is completely destroyed, and the officer is killed. During the night, around 9.30 p.m., the telephonists of the telephone exchange once again come rushing up, flames and thunderclaps right outside the door. Bomb fragments go whistling through the window, and one of these fragments lifts a telephonist bodily into the air. He collapses, dead. The telephone system is heavily damaged. At 2.00 a.m., another bomb fell on the airfield of Jasta 4, falling in a vacant area. On 29 October, Vizefeldwebel Lautenschlager dies in air combat north of Houthulst Forest.[3]

On the last day of October, with rainy weather and a heavily overcast sky, the Rittmeister is flying around with his regular Staffel, Jasta 11, looking for Englishmen in the wet, grey, desolate skies, when he notices that one machine of his Staffel is flying rather erratically. Is it breaking off? Breaking up? What is wrong? The machine is going down in a rather fast dive, and a sudden jolt goes through the Rittmeister. It is his brother, Lothar! Something seems to be wrong. And because he never leaves a comrade in the lurch in a precarious situation, he doesn't leave this comrade in the lurch either. In any case, he rushes down after him.

The airplane dives steeply and the Rittmeister soon gets the picture: his brother has to make an emergency landing, the Devil knows why. So he too

---

[1] Lothar von Richthofen was widely credited with downing Captain Ball who was flying an SE 5, despite his own claim that he had downed a triplane.
[2] Imperial Germany consisted of four separate kingdoms (Prussia, Saxony, Württemberg and Bavaria) in addition to five grand duchies, 12 duchies and the three 'free' cities of Hamburg, Lübeck and Bremen.
[3] Vizefeldwebel Lautenschlager was brought down by a German airplane, the victim of mistaken identification.

will make an emergency landing. In an area that is not exactly the best, the two of them set down, first Lothar, and then Manfred. Lothar makes an absolutely smooth, perfect landing. And that is the last thing the Rittmeister sees, for he himself falls victim to some kind of damn mischief. His machine sets down, cracking and bursting. It shatters into a number of large pieces and many small fragments, and is, to use the pilots' slang term, 'totalled'. The commander clambers out of this mess, uninjured and somewhat bewildered, and his brother watches him, equally bewildered. The Rittmeister doesn't say a word, and Lothar clears the matter up, somewhat timidly: his engine failed, failed completely, and as a result, he'd had to get down as fast as possible.

The list of Life and Death, of Fighting and Dying, continues monotonously on. Leutnant Wüsthoff sends his twenty-third Englishman into the shell holes. Leutnant Pastor crashes near Moorseele; they must dig his shattered body out of the wreckage.[1] On 5 November, Leutnant Wüsthoff continues his string of destruction: within a quarter of an hour, he shoots down his twenty-fourth opponent near Poelcapelle, and his twenty-fifth down near Staden. On 6 November, Leutnant Löwenhardt rushes to earth with a broken wing. He lands with a shattered machine and climbs out of the wreckage, uninjured. On 9 November, Leutnant Wüsthoff shoots down his twenty-sixth Englishman and Lothar von Richthofen, his twenty-fifth opponent.

On the evening of 15 November, the conversation in the officers' mess is somewhat strained and the faces are somewhat grim. At 9.20 a.m., the splendid Leutnant Adam, leader of Jasta 6, had been shot down in air combat north-west of Kortewilde. On 20 November, the comrades of the Geschwader stand in the fog in front of the Carmelite chapel in Courtrai to bring his coffin to the train. They all know the way to the train station in Courtrai quite well. Leutnant Adam traveled the route many a time as well, whenever a fallen comrade went home. Now he himself is going home, stilled for ever, and his coffin is smothered with such flowers and boughs as the late autumn could still offer.

Late autumn . . . The November sky seems to have fallen silent, free of exploding shells and chattering machine-gun bullets. The air and weather turn wintery . . .

---

[1] Killed 28 September 1917.

II ABOVE THE TANK BATTLE OF CAMBRAI

Down on the ground, the battle is roaring; a strange, ghostly battle which rattles noisily through the thick November fog near Cambrai. The battle has broken out unexpectedly. The English have smashed into the German lines with a huge number of tanks in the sector of the Second Army.[1]

The officers and men of Jagdgeschwader I can throw only a hurried glance at the train taking the deceased Leutnant Adam home, then they hurry back to their machines. The Jagdgeschwader is being hurled at the endangered Front, and they depart in frantic haste. The technical officer has already disappeared along with the advance detail to prepare the new airdrome, and the Staffeln will follow by air. Everyone else is to follow immediately by rail. *Immediately?* Cars and vehicles are scarcely to be had at all, and the railways are jammed full of troops from every branch of the service racing to the area of the breakthrough. It was to take until 25 November before all the Staffeln of the Geschwader had occupied their new airfields.

Airfields or no, the fighter pilots will not wait that long. They flew to the Jastaschule at Valenciennes for the time being; the other personnel are to follow as soon as they can. These few people from the Geschwader and the Jastaschule's mechanics grit their teeth and go without sleep. The English have broken through! And this time the English are also gnashing their teeth more fiercely than usual, on the ground and in the air as well. Hundreds and hundreds of their tanks rattle down below, and hundreds and hundreds of their airplanes buzz in the air overhead. And the airplanes are not seeking the higher altitudes this time, but are flying quite low, lower than they have ever flown before. Fine! Let them fly as low as they wish! At that low altitude, they will just be shot down.

Over Bourlon Wood, whole swarms of English squadrons are cruising around, close together in massed formations; single-seaters and multi-seaters, machines of all types.

On 23 November, at 2.00 p.m., Jagdgeschwader I intervenes in the Battle of Cambrai. The commander lets his machine guns rattle, and the first Englishman goes rushing downward out of the swarm. Leutnant Lothar von Richthofen and Leutnant Küppers each get one.

On 24 November, the word seems to have gotten around on the other side of the lines that the 'Baron's' red machines have arrived. There is hardly any other way to explain the fact that there are conspicuously few airmen visible on this day. Only a few solitary Englishmen are observed, far behind their own lines. In return, the Staffeln of the Geschwader have plenty of time to get themselves settled at their new airfields in the vicinity of Avesnes le Sec.[2]

---

[1] 20 November 1917.

[2] Jastas 4 and 6 at Lieu St Amand, Jasta 10 at Iwuy, and Jasta 11 at Avesnes le Sec.

On 25 November, everything is in order and in good shape again. On 26 November, it rains, and there are no flight operations. They can get some paperwork done. On 27 November, rain and heavy clouds again, and again the paperwork can get done. A telegram comes for Leutnant Wüsthoff from Supreme Headquarters. His Majesty has conferred the order *Pour le Mérite* upon him. The next day, even more paperwork gets done.

On 29 November, the ink and the typewriters are suddenly shoved aside. In the morning, numerous enemy reconnaissance aircraft come over the Front. Their return home is not without pain. At 9.45 a.m., Feldwebel Leutnant Schubert brings one of them down and, at 10.00 a.m., Leutnants Klein and Heldmann each get one. This is opponent number twenty-one for Leutnant Klein, and, presumably, the famous telegram from Supreme Headquarters will soon arrive for him.[1]

On the next day, the morning passes in absolute quiet. Only in the far distance on the other side of the Front, where the enemy captive balloons are standing, are there a couple of Englishmen moving about in the clouds. Leutnant Klein climbs into his machine, and hauls out without saying much. At 12.30 p.m., they see a trail of smoke and flame over across the lines; a balloon has been set on fire. Leutnant Klein has his twenty-second air victory behind him. And then begins the afternoon's dance of death. Five Englishmen are shot down, among them the commander's sixty-third victory. His blunt report:

> At 2.30 p.m., with Leutnant von Richthofen and Leutnant Gussmann, we attacked an enemy single-seater squadron of ten Englishmen just over the front positions. After I had fired on several different English-men, I fired from close range behind a single-seater which, after a hundred rounds, crashed in flames in the vicinity of little Quarry Wood.

In this afternoon's dance of death, two officers of the Geschwader are killed: Leutnant Schultze, who collided with one of our own airplanes, and Leutnant Demandt, who did not return from his combat patrol.[2] On this day also, Leutnant Klein opened his well-deserved telegram. His Majesty has conferred upon him the order *Pour le Mérite*.

Then, slowly, a stillness comes over the battlefield of Cambrai. Once again, the Brits have not succeeded, neither on the ground nor in the air. Richthofen, who never exaggerated under any circumstances, can state in his evening report for 30 November: 'Air supremacy was fully and completely in our hands the entire day.'

---

[1] It was usual, although not automatic, for the *Pour le Mérite* to be awarded after 20 aerial victories.
[2] Killed in action near Cambrai.

III   WINTER IN NORTHERN FRANCE

In Avesnes le Sec, it grows quiet. Of the English, little is heard and even less is seen. Winter has set in over all the fronts and there is no opposing it. Rain alternates with fog, and fog alternates with driving snow. More often than not, heavy ground haze lies over the entire landscape.

The Geschwader adjutant can now think about trying to make things a little more comfortable than had been possible earlier, during the rush. The Geschwader staff is situated in a sugar factory. They have pleasant rooms and even a real fireplace which they keep efficiently and continuously lit.

The evenings spent close to the blazing logs were unforgettable for them all. Memories awaken, far more powerful and intense than in the days of fighting. The commander himself becomes talkative. The faces of those no longer with them come alive once more in the stories told within that room . . . Dostler . . . Wolff . . . Voss . . . Adam . . . and the many others whose deaths, like the death of each one among them, were brought to a close with two lines in the log book, and who were inscribed still in the hearts of everyone who'd known them with much, much more than just two lines.

The adjutant prepares to undertake some little trips in order to procure provisions and maybe even nab something special somewhere. There is, of course, scarcely anything to be had in a wide radius, not for love nor money. Until one day he hits upon a miraculous remedy. And from then on, whenever he runs into someone with all sorts of good things to give away, but who shrugs his shoulders and spreads his hands with regret, the adjutant simply reaches into his tunic pocket and pulls out a postcard. On this postcard is pictured Rittmeister von Richthofen, in his finest uniform with all of his medals and his most winsome face, and what is more, under the photograph is Richthofen's autograph, written in his own hand. That works wonders and proves more precious, more valuable, and more effective than love or money. The adjutant never comes back from his little travels empty-handed any more.

As far as the beverages to go along with these provisions are concerned, in the long run, absolutely nothing more can happen to him, since that business there at the airfield and Château Marckebeke, where a delightful incident had taken place. One fine evening, his orderly, Andreas, had seemed extremely excited, animated, and in a very good humor, and had reported simply: 'Herr Oberleutnant, the infantrymen are drunk down there!' Incredulous, the adjutant had followed his orderly into the garden. How in the world was anyone supposed to get drunk in Marckebeke? Nevertheless, in the garden he saw that quite a few men in different positions had, in fact, indulged in considerable drinking. As the adjutant looked one of these men in the face rather inquisitively, and inspected the label on the bottle a little closer, it hit him: the man was drinking a first-rate white Bordeaux, so superior and so old that you could no longer see through the bottle. From where in Flanders had this wonder come?

Now, one of these valiant men had been pulling on one of the shrubs in the garden just for fun, when all at once he found himself holding the whole shrub in his hand. And although this shrub-puller had no forestry or agricultural knowledge, that seemed strange to him. He went and got a few of his comrades, a general shrub-pulling ensued, and lo: in one sharply defined corner of the garden, the shrubs were without roots. In view of these facts, no front-line soldier in any army of the world would have hesitated even a moment. They dug and dug. And they dug out two thousand bottles of the very finest wine, extremely old Burgundies and Bordeaux.

The commander, to whom this was immediately reported, fought briefly with himself. Should he send the wine to headquarters? He looked pensively around the circle of his dear comrades and thought, 'Just as surely as they are sitting there, one like the other, him, and him, and him over there, and I myself, each and every one of us . . . in the end, we're all going to be gone one day. Sooner or later, we're all going to be gone. That's as certain as an "amen" in church . . . The wine stays here.' On the strength of that reasoning, six hundred bottles were immediately distributed to the valiant mechanics and, with the remaining supply, the officers' mess of the Geschwader was set for the rest of the war. The adjutant had no further financial headaches about how the officers' mess was to be maintained: he sold each bottle at a price of one mark.

The winter goes on.

During clear weather, there are some isolated air combats. In the icy air of the winter sky, Death does not spare all those who sat in Avesnes le Sec on previous evenings. A few days after Christmas, on 27 December, Leutnant von Schweinitz crashes due to fuselage and wing failure and burns to death, along with his machine. On the same day, Vizefeldwebel Hecht does not return from a flight.[1] On 5 January 1918, Leutnant Löwenhardt again shoots down a captive balloon. On 13 January, Leutnant Stapenhorst also takes off after a captive balloon. He does not come back. On 19 January, the commander travels to Berlin-Adlershof where he has been ordered for a time.[2]

---

[1] Taken prisoner of war.
[2] Rittmeister von Richthofen had left Avesnes le Sec on 28 December 1917, with his brother, Lothar, to attend the peace conference in Brest–Litovsk. He returned to the Front at the end of January, 1918.

There can be no talk of total peace in the air. Time and time again, the air seethes with bursts of machine-gun fire; time and time again, the bold birds of prey soar in their turns.

On 19 February, upon his return from combat patrol, Leutnant Klein clambers out of his machine, badly upset: the index finger of his right hand was shot off during air combat and he has to go to Field Hospital No. 253.

And now, gradually, things are starting to become extremely uneasy in all of the staff headquarters. Preparations are being made for the big offensive in France. These vast preparations are proceeding with an unparalleled precision. There is considerable work being done at the Jagdgeschwader, as well. Work on an intermediate landing field is begun, and the necessary quarters are completed.

On 21 February, a most gratifying letter arrives from the Commander of Aviation, and this evening by the fireplace turns merry. The letter reads:

> The Württemberg Red Cross Society's Prisoner Information Office, Stuttgart, has been notified by English Headquarters that Leutnant Eberhardt Stapenhorst, home address Essen an der Ruhr, Semper Strasse 6, was taken prisoner near Cambrai on 13 January 1918, and was taken to England on 30 January 1918.

Such letters are very rare, and such a fate is very rare for a pilot. In air combat and especially during an attack on a captive balloon, there is hardly ever an interim solution and an interim fate between 'either/or'. So . . . Stapenhorst has been spared. A glass of the old Burgundy is raised in the direction of Great Britain. And when we look down the row of these young faces . . . let's have another look at the personnel roster!

In reality, how old are these young men, today, on 1 March 1918, shortly before the great offensive in France? Let us draw up the list:

Geschwader Staff

Rittm Frhr Manfred von Richthofen	25 years old
Oblt Bodenschatz, Karl (Adjutant)	27

Jasta 11

Lt Frhr von Richthofen, Lothar (Staffel Leader)	23 years old
Lt Steinhäuser, Werner	21
Lt von der Osten, Hans Georg	22
Lt Esser, Karl	24
Lt Mohnicke, Eberhardt	20
Lt Wolff, Hans Joachim	22

Lt von Conta	20
Lt Lübbert, Friedrich Wilhelm	20
Lt d. R. Just, Erich	20
Lt d. R. Gussmann, Siegfried	22
Lt d. R. Krefft, Konstantin (Technical Officer)	26
Lt d. R. Bahr, Erich	24

Jasta 10

Lt d. R. Klein, Hans (Staffel Leader)	27 years old
Lt Löwenhardt, Erich	20
Lt d. R. Kühn	23
Lt d. R. Heldmann, Alois	22
Lt d. R. Grassmann, Justus	21
Lt d. R. Bohlein, Franz	21
Lt d. R. Friedrichs, Fritz	23
Lt d. R. Bender, Julius	24
Offz Stellv Aue, Paul	26
Vfw Burggaller	21
Vfw Delang	22

Jasta 6[1]

Oblt Reinhard, Wilhelm (Staffel Leader)	26 years old
Lt d. R. Wenzel, Paul	30
Lt d. R. Tüxen, Robert	20
Lt von Breiten-Landenberg, Otto	21
Lt d. R. Wolff	22
Lt d. R. Janzen, Johann	21
Fw Lt Schubert, Fritz	30
Vfw d. R. Hemer, Franz	23
Vfw d. R. von Raffay, Leopold	20
Sgt Beschow	27

Jasta 4

Lt d. R. Wüsthoff, Kurt (Staffel Leader)	19 years old
Lt d. R. Rousselle, Oskar	24
Lt Frhr von Barnekow, Raven	20
Lt von Gluszewski, Heinz	22
Lt d. R. Koepsch, Egon	27
Lt d. R. Maushake, Heinrich	23

---

[1] Although not listed here, Oblt Kurt Lischke, Specialist Officer assigned to Jasta 6, was also on the Geschwader roster on the date of 1 March 1918.

Lt d. R. Joschkowitz	23
Lt d. R. Drekmann, Heinrich	21
Lt d. R. Meyer, Karl (Specialist Officer)	22
Lt d. R. Skauradzun	21
Sgt Schmutzler, Otto	28

These are the fighter pilots of Jagdgeschwader I, the best and the most famous Jagdgeschwader of the Army. The oldest one among them, a Feldwebel Leutnant, is thirty years old.[1] The fewest members of the Geschwader have come directly from the Flying Corps. The commander is an Uhlan; his brother is a Dragoon. The adjutant is a Bavarian infantryman. There are a few members of the Field Artillery, one man from the Foot Artillery, the others are Dragoons, Uhlans, Grenadiers, Fusiliers, Hussars, Heavy Cavalry, Infantry. The majority of them are not over twenty-five years old.[2] The youngest member is Leutnant d. R. Wüsthoff, leader of Jasta 4, with twenty-six victories, a Knight of the Order *Pour le Mérite* . . . nineteen years old.

The Rittmeister selects his people himself. During the winter, he traveled around to the various flight schools and Jastas and viewed the operations. He has long since stopped having his fighter pilots assigned through official channels. He is allowed to get them himself. And if anyone has an eye for faces and behavior, for shooting ability and flying ability, for daredevils and non-daredevils, it's him.

He has damned hot chestnuts to fetch from the fire.[3] For this kind of work, he needs men who are fast to act, men who fetched chestnuts out of the fire before they burned their fingers. Pilots who are 'timid', namely pilots who do not know the razor-sharp word 'onward!', are the kind of pilots the Geschwader cannot afford to have.

---

[1] Fw Lt Schubert of Jasta 6.
[2] Average age was 23 years.
[3] This is a colloquial saying, with the connotation of 'having dirty work to do'. Those pilots not meeting von Richthofen's strict requirements were soon posted out.

In such a frame of mind, the Baron moves into the great offensive in France with his Staffeln. Things happen the way they always happen for pilots: the battle in the air erupts long before the battle on the ground.

The English are very much aware that something is not quite right opposite them, that something is going on, but they don't know exactly what. Along the entire Western Front, the mood has grown uneasy. In countless places here and there, tensions are beginning to bubble up, and throats are being cleared nervously. The High Command intentionally allows the commotion to rumble from the sea all the way to Switzerland, in order to mask the planned breakthrough point.

It is obvious to the English that everybody on the other side of the Front is getting nervous. It is also obvious that the English themselves are growing uneasy. And since they can't very well stroll off across the trenches with their foot patrols and stick their noses into the German hinterland, they stroll across the Front at high altitude with their reconnaissance aircraft and fighter squadrons.

It is truly not a pleasant sight to see these gigantic squadrons arriving. The French and English have not been sitting with their hands in their laps since November of last year. They have been toiling in preparation for 1918, just as Germany has. Only they had it easier, for they possessed the vast materials with which the entire world was supplying them. The Germans could only make their preparations with such pitiful, meager resources as they were still able to wring from their exhausted land.

The enemy squadrons approaching the German front since 10 March 1918 were brand-new squadrons, with the newest and best machines with the newest and best equipment, with well-fed and well-cared-for crews, with countless replacement materials behind them, with fuel that never ran low, with all of the technological frills, large and small, that only the finest raw materials could produce. The German fighter pilots knew exactly what was in store for them. They didn't have much in the way of materials to oppose it with.

From 10 March 1918 on, the airspace overhead grew turbulent. Again and again, large squadrons approached the Front, wanting to get a glimpse behind the German lines, no matter what the cost. Baron von Richthofen and each of his pilots could have almost written the orders, word for word, that these squadrons had received along the way: 'Get the reconnaissance at any cost.'

There was only one way of preventing this mission: to put their own unified and massed squadrons up against the mass deployment of enemy squadrons; to breach the advancing columns, tear them apart and bring them down, machine by machine, until the rest of them were so shaken to the bone that they turned back.

It is obvious that the Geschwader is being overwhelmed with a veritable hurricane of orders which must be painstakingly heeded, lest the smallest gear in this terrible clockwork fail. Everything is prepared down to the smallest detail. The newly devised, secret wireless radio communication sends reports of enemy air operations to the airfield commanders. And when the receiver transmits the peculiar little word 'kuk'[1] it will mean 'come and fight'.

Countless orders are issued for 'Day X'. Above and beyond everything else, however, the fighter pilots are to see that the English are unable to put their 'eyes and ears' — i.e. their field glasses, their photographic equipment, and their wireless radio stations — into action, to say nothing of their bombs. With the visibility hazy, the air traffic mounts on both sides, with the machines growing ever more numerous. There is a great deal of flying at high altitude.

The eleventh of March passes with two aircraft downed.[2] On 12 March, the fighting is heavier. At 11.00 a.m., Leutnant Lothar von Richthofen shoots down two Bristols, the commander brings down his sixty-fourth, Leutnant Wüsthoff his twenty-seventh, and Leutnant Löwenhardt gets another captive balloon. Towards evening, Leutnant Franz Bohlein ventures upon a captive balloon. The balloon falls in flames as the first recognized air victory of his life. There are seven aircraft downed on this day.

On 13 March, Lothar von Richthofen singles out an opponent from an English squadron. He comes down in a dive, lets his machine guns play, and then hears a cracking noise in his machine. He'd been hit, and hit disastrously. His triplane had become a biplane. At an altitude of four thousand meters, a wing had broken off. He quickly lets the Englishman go. He is surprised that the Englishman doesn't shoot him down in a flash, and he is even more surprised that his own machine doesn't go rushing straight downwards. So he seizes on this prodigious piece of luck and attempts to get to the ground in a glide. Since his rudder controls are no longer working, he can only glide straight ahead.

By chance, he came upon a large, open space where he thought of landing, but at an altitude of fifteen hundred meters, he spotted a high-tension wire. Flying over it was no longer feasible, and flying under it was even less feasible, for there were troop columns moving there beneath it.

---

[1] 'Kuk' stood for 'Komme und kämpfe'.
[2] These were scored by Lt Lothar von Richthofen and Vfw Scholtz.

So, he risked a turn . . . and woke up in the hospital. He had crashed while attempting to make the turn, and had immediately lost consciousness. He had been hit in the head and in the legs.[1] When they went to lift him out, his hands were still on the controls. Everyone who had witnessed the crash was convinced they would find a dead man, but the Richthofens were made of extraordinary stuff.

On the same day, three aircraft are brought down, among them the commander's sixty-fifth. On 14 March, there is a little peace and quiet. On 15 March, Leutnant Löwenhardt once again gets a captive balloon. On 16 March, Leutnant Bohlein crashes to his death during an air combat. On 17 March, the Geschwader is inspected by the Commanding General of the Air Service.

Then comes the eighteenth of March, a day of glory for Jagdgeschwader I. Already early in the morning, far on the other side of the Front, strong squadrons of single-seaters and two-seaters were buzzing about in the spring sky. Jagdgeschwader I stood ready for take-off, but at first no Englishmen ventured over the Front.

Then, around 10.30 a.m., they came. At a great altitude, together as a unit, these heavily concentrated squadrons wound their way to carry out their orders, come hell or high water: to fly over the German front and finally get a glimpse of what was causing all the commotion back there; to ascertain the significance of the considerable, nightly clamor they were hearing; to find out what was really going on. Along the entire Front there in France, from the field marshal down to the last little *poilu*, the suspicious rumors had not ceased.

Now they were going to stop.

At an altitude of over 5,000 meters, the most powerful squadrons of the English Army move towards the German front.

The radio reports from the German air defense officers had arrived in Avesnes le Sec in good time. The commander took off with three Staffeln in a closed formation. It was a wonderful, yet solemn sight. Far out in front, the commander flew at the head of his Staffeln. Behind him to the left was Jasta 6, staggered 500 meters higher, and to the right was Jasta 10. There were thirty airplanes, piloted by the boldest and most famous pilots of the German Army.

At an altitude of 5,300 meters, the commander discovered several English squadrons which had just flown over the German lines in the direction of Le Cateau. The Baron turned his Geschwader sharply and followed the Englishmen. The last airplane of the squadron bringing up the

---

[1] From all available accounts, the facial injuries suffered by Lothar von Richthofen apparently resulted from the violent impact of the crash itself, not from enemy fire.

rear, a Bristol Fighter, broke up and crashed under the machine-gun fire of Richthofen and Leutnant Gussmann, who attacked it at the same time. With that, the commander had started to penetrate the main English formation. He reassembled his thirty airplanes, and raced after the two squadrons that had already broken through as far as Le Cateau. The English immediately turned off, in order to quickly get back behind their own front, but it was too late. Jagdgeschwader I attacked.

Within a few minutes, both English squadrons had been totally torn apart and dispersed. Opponents rattled around each other in numerous single combats and, within twenty-five minutes, the fight had been decided. At 11.00 a.m., Leutnant Gussmann had dispatched his opponent. At 11.05 a.m., Leutnant Kirschstein took his first Englishman out of the air, and with this victory, this as yet unknown officer began to compile a remarkable list within that of the Geschwader. At 11.10 a.m., Leutnant Löwenhardt shot a Bréguet to pieces. At the same minute, Oberleutnant Reinhard destroyed a Bristol Fighter which broke up in the air and fell into the devastated landscape in burning pieces. At 11.15 a.m., Leutnant Wolff, a namesake of two already renowned Wolffs, was engaged in the first victorious combat of his life.[1] He sent the single-seater to earth, where it disintegrated into dust. At this same minute, the commander dove on a Sopwith Camel that never even fired a shot, despite the respectable leader's streamers on its wings. It went rushing downwards and was forced to land near Molain. Five minutes later, Vizefeldwebel Scholtz shot down a Sopwith for his fourth victory. Two minutes later, at precisely 11.22, this same Vizefeldwebel Scholtz positioned himself behind the next Sopwith to come in front of his guns, and saw it crash in flames a few minutes later. At 11.25 a.m., another Sopwith broke up under Leutnant Friedrichs' fire.

When the thirty fighters looked around after these twenty-five heated minutes, they discovered first of all that the English had disappeared, and secondly they made a rough determination that no one from their own Geschwader was missing. A whole flock of English squadrons put to flight inside of a paltry half hour; nine aircraft shot down from the midst of this formation, and not a single man or machine of their own as casualties.

They still had something to offer in opposition to the superior materials and superior numbers against them, something that could not be bought with money — not with English money, or American money, or any money of the world: their wonderful ability, despite having few good machines, few good materials, and few well-nourished air crews, to fetch the hottest chestnuts from the fire with elegance.

---

[1] This victory was scored by Lt H.J. Wolff of Jasta 11, not by the lesser-known Lt Wolff of Jasta 6 as implied here.

On this day and in this battle, the commander's chivalrous camaraderie was once again given charming expression. What kind of gossip were the English and French airmen spreading about him? That, either by his own wish or by order from above, he would transfer his comrades' victories to his own list, in order to achieve the highest possible number of victories . . .

In the Rittmeister's report concerning his actions in the air battle of Le Cateau, it says, among other things:

> . . . and, together with Leutnant Gussmann, Jasta 11, I shot down my last opponent, a Bristol Fighter. He lost his wings and Leutnant Gussmann brought him down . . . the airplane flying closest to me, apparently either a Bréguet or a Bristol Fighter, was fired upon by me and by Leutnant Löwenhardt, whereupon our opponent's fuel tank was shot to pieces and I saw the airplane plunge straight down. Leutnant Löwenhardt brought him down . . .

To whom were these victories then credited? To Leutnants Gussmann and Löwenhardt, on the basis of the commander's testimony.

Jagdgeschwader I's mission had been carried out. The English squadrons' forced reconnaissance had been totally prevented. The great 'Day X' could go on to fulfillment, undisturbed, unhindered, and unobserved.

A man from the Field Recruit Depot of the 238th Infantry Division describes how this air battle looked, as seen from the ground:

> The eighteenth of March dawned with a steel-blue sky. In the morning, we moved out for drill. Not far from the village of Molain where we were quartered, we had our athletic field. On this beautiful day, the time flew by and we began the last hour of our morning duty. It was shortly before 11.00 a.m.
>
> Suddenly, we saw an absolutely huge squadron of airplanes appear on the horizon from the direction of St Quentin. There must have been about 30 to 40 machines. Flying very neatly in a large rectangle, they flew in the direction of Le Cateau at an altitude of 4,000 to 5,000 meters. They were coming ever closer to us, and the air vibrated slightly with the hum of the many engines. With their glasses, our officers soon ascertained that they were English aircraft. With the absolutely clear sky, this squadron looked quite splendid, moving quietly there in the sky. We racked our brains as to what the Englishmen had in mind with this large contingent of men. They couldn't very well be bombers, for those always came only at night, as we had learned only too well.
>
> While we were still talking about this, a new squadron suddenly

appeared from the direction of Cambrai. It flew just as quietly and just as neatly in the shape of a triangle. Upon its approaching closer, we detected the iron crosses on the wings showing they were German machines. It was simply incredible to watch how this triangle of German airplanes closed in on the English formation, and unswervingly drove itself into the English squadron, like an unstoppable wedge.

The Englishmen's neat rectangle was torn apart in no time, and everything suddenly dissolved into something resembling a swarm of gnats. We were already hearing the first machine-gun rounds rattle, and then we saw a bunch of small groups roaring around and firing on each other. In doing so, most of the airplanes were coming lower and lower, and we were able to follow the whole thing ever more closely. Suddenly, an Englishman broke away from the swarm, and crashed to earth west of our village. Overhead, though, there was still such confusion we didn't know where we should look first.

Another English machine came down, a long trail of smoke behind it, and right after that, it was engulfed in bright flames. With the next Englishman, we saw just the fuselage hit the ground. The wings came down slowly after it. Over Wassigny, another one now fell; again it was an Englishman. All this was taking place at an altitude of just 1,000 meters. An Englishman now appeared over us, and came gliding down with his engine switched off. A German machine circled over him, like a bird of prey. The Englishman set his machine down about 150 meters away from us. He climbed out, and we brought him into the village. He was a Canadian who had taken a hit in the propeller. Next to the enemy machine, the German airman now landed as well. He climbed out and cut the number from his opponent's wing. At the same time, he made us aware of a red machine circling just 100 meters above us, and from which someone was waving down at us. It was Rittmeister Manfred von Richthofen.

Meanwhile, still another couple of machines had crashed, quite a distance from us. We were unable to determine right away whether it was friend or foe lying there, demolished. To our great joy, however, we were able to establish one thing beyond a doubt: the huge squadron was pulling out. Spread over the whole sky, they were pulling out.

On the horizon, a solitary German pilot was constantly turning loops, no doubt for joy over one such victory.

We marched back to our quarters, extremely excited and deeply moved by this incident.

No other aircraft showed themselves in Jagdgeschwader I's sector on this day. Nor on the next day, 19 March. On the following day, 20 March, twenty-four hours before the big offensive, still no enemy aircraft were spotted in this sector. These forty-eight hours of total emptiness in the air space over their sector, this total lack of Englishmen . . . this was the most splendid proof that they had fulfilled their assigned mission.

The men who had remained behind on the airfields at the observation posts, in the huts, replacement depots, and orderly rooms during that air battle of Le Cateau knew, just as the men overhead in their single-seater scouts knew, that this time it was not just a hard fight, but a fight to the bitter end. And when the adjutant left the telescope for a quarter of an hour to do some necessary paperwork in the staff hut, more than once his gaze strayed pensively over to the iron safe. Behind its door, stuck in a corner, lay an official grey envelope addressed to him in the commander's hand-writing, and sealed with the Geschwader's official seal.

On 15 March, the Rittmeister had suddenly pressed this envelope into his adjutant's hand. 'If I do not return, open.' The commander knew as well that this time it was a fight to the bitter end. On this evening, however, the adjutant had not yet needed to open the Geschwader commander's will.

Not yet.

On the evening of 20 March, the German assault army takes a deep breath. During the night of 18 to 19 March, a radio message came in to the staffs of the front-line troops, an enigmatic group of letters. When the officers have deciphered the letters, they read:

> Xtertageinu ndzwanzigst erdritteryz eitvieruhrv ierzigvormi
> ttagsnullze itneunuhrvi erzigvormit tags[1]

This is the decisive order. The mysterious cipher 'X' has cast away its mask. The twenty-first of March is the day of attack.

The three armies of von Below, von der Marwitz, and von Hutier[2] are in their assault positions with 64 divisions, 950 field batteries, 701 medium batteries and 55 heavy batteries. The attack front is 70 kilometers wide.

Jagdgeschwader I has already fought its first battle. For the last eight days, they have been preparing an advance landing field at Awoingt, south-west of Cambrai. Night after night, the shovels fly, the trucks roll, and industrious, dark forms abound. When the first crack of dawn comes creeping over the spring landscape, every living thing disappears into the dugouts, into the shelters, and underneath the tarpaulins. Even the cur

---

[1] This reads 'X day the twenty-first, third month, time 4.40 a.m., zero hour 9.40 a.m.'
[2] Generals Otto von Below, Georg von der Marwitz and Oskar von Hutier.

sniffing around loose in the area is dragged into a hiding place and locked up.

When one inquisitive Englishman, a couple of thousand meters up, actually approached and looked down, he could see only an unoccupied airfield and nothing else: no machines, no men, nothing. And when he returned on the next day, nothing had changed. He couldn't know with what diligence they had toiled during the night. Over on the other side, they couldn't possibly suspect that every night, across an expanse of 70 kilometers, countless troop columns were advancing, countless guns were being put into place, and that, with flashlights which flashed furtively for mere seconds, an assault army was taking up its position.

They were nervous, however. They were waiting dully for something, but they didn't know what this something would look like, or whence it would come. Their attempts to open their eyes failed. Their squadrons returned from the region around Le Cateau mangled, battered, pursued home. Jagdgeschwader I had veiled the eyes of the enemy.

In the evening twilight of 20 March, the machines of the Jagdstaffeln suddenly appeared high over Awoingt, landed, and were shoved hurriedly into tent hangars, unseen, unheard, unlooked for by the English. During the night, the Rittmeister sends for his Staffel leaders. For days now, he has had the order of the Commander of Aviation of the Second Army in hand.[1] The order is clear, energetic, and confident. It reads:

1. Up until the start of the battle, the Jagdstaffeln had to guarantee concealment of our troop concentration, in addition to protecting our reconnaissance aircraft. With commencement of the battle, their activity over the battlefield will move far enough into enemy territory that enemy aerial reconnaissance (aircraft and captive balloons) is put out of action, so our own reconnaissance will have unrestricted observation at an altitude from which they can observe with their own eyes.

2. Confidence in the Jastas' fighter pilots is the basis for this. To assist with this assignment, the fighter pilots are hereby once again granted permission to take the action to the enemy.

3. The pursuit area is ordered by the above-mentioned orders. On the first day of the offensive, it is especially important that you fight to keep the region between Villers–Guislain, Nurlu, Bellicourt and Roisel completely free of the enemy. Pursuit Regions North and South[2] will overlap heavily in this region.

---

[1] Hauptmann Wilhelm Haehnelt.
[2] 'Pursuit Region North' was under command of Rittmeister von Richthofen, and 'Pursuit Region South' was under the command of Oberleutnant Hermann Kohze of Jagdgruppe 9. Oblt Kohze was also the commander of Jasta 3.

4. Patrol flights outside of the region directly over the battlefield are forbidden. As to pursuit of enemy squadrons that break through, bear in mind that the battlefield may not be stripped of fighter pilots.

5. Rittmeister von Richthofen and Oberleutnant Kohze will control the deployment of the fighter pilots according to the aforementioned orders.

6. From dawn until 9.45 a.m., only weak fighter forces are to be deployed. From 9.50 a.m. until 1.00 p.m., a stronger deployment must be guaranteed. During the time from daybreak until 9.45 a.m., it is important to create a clear path for our observation pilots, and to prevent the enemy spotters from advancing over our Front to reconnoiter our artillery and concentrated assault divisions. From the attack on, the enemy must be absolutely blind for three hours so he cannot institute any counter-measures.

7. The activity of our airmen must give the infantry and artillery absolute confidence in our victory.

8. Jasta Löwenhardt[1] will attack the captive balloons between 9.45 and 10.00 a.m. These attacks are to be repeated during the course of the day.

The commander of Jagdgeschwader I doesn't need to add much to this order. It is in keeping with his own view, and his Staffel leaders know him well enough to know what this view is: *Onward! Onward!* — the Prussian Army's curt, cold, harsh word of attack.

During the night, there is tremendous activity outside on the airfield. The mechanics are clambering around on the machines, pounding, hammering, and tightening screws. The enlisted men are filling in the last holes on the open field, gasoline cans are clanking softly, muffled shouts are flying about. There will be no sleep in Awoingt tonight. Besides Jagdgeschwader I, still another eight Staffeln have arrived: Jastas 5, 46, 16, 34, 3, 37, 54 and 56. These one hundred and fifty machines stand ready to inaugurate the great 'Day X' in perfect form. At 9.45 a.m.,[2] the onslaught of the German infantry is to begin. Three quarters of an hour before that, Richthofen will take off with Jasta 11. The time of the main battle, presumably the bitterest forty-five minutes of the day, he has reserved for himself.

As day breaks, the fighter pilots are standing dressed and ready on the airfield, non-plussed, disappointed, and furious, staring into a thick, grey, damp wall of fog.

---

[1] Jasta 10.
[2] German and Allied times were the same at this period.

It is impossible to fly.

'One man's owl is another man's nightingale!' says the Rittmeister. That hits it right on the head. The crazy ones among them swallow their long stream of curses and calm down. It is right on, for the exact same fog that is keeping them from taking off is providing the infantry with the possibility of an enormous, unexpected advance. So they stand around patiently, put their heads back, and allow the thundering hurricane of artillery fire being laid down by the German guns to howl away continuously over them.

They look at the clock, and when the hands show 9.45 a.m., from more than a dozen throats comes the hoarse cry, 'Now!' At this very minute, the tidal wave of the Germany infantry climbs out of the trenches and, in their first advance, they overrun the totally bewildered French and English fronts.

But they themselves? They have to stay home. It makes no sense to go flying around in the thick fog. Rather sullenly, they loiter around back and forth between the machines, smoking one cigarette after another, and consider themselves damned slackers.

A telephonist brings a note to Leutnant Löwenhardt. He reads the note together with Leutnant Friedrichs, then the two of them disappear to their machines. The note came at just the right time. It contained the report that there were captive balloons near both Ruyaulcourt and Fins. Finally, there is something they could do something about, fog or no fog. At precisely 1.00 p.m., both English balloons are lying like charred lumps on the ground. Löwenhardt got one, and Friedrichs the other.

Incidentally, those were the only reports that came into the telephone exchange. Of enemy airmen, there is nothing to be seen or heard, and that is no wonder in light of what was happening on the ground meanwhile. The infantry broke through with such an infernal force, with such an incredible leap, and at such an overpowering pace that it created a void in front of it, as if with a mighty scythe. And from out of this void, there came either long columns of prisoners stumbling towards the German hinterland, or confused swarms of steel-helmeted German soldiers racing in shock towards the enemy's hinterland.

The enemy airfields cleared out in a hurry as well, in so far as they succeeded in clearing out. Taking off for the German lines was out of the question during these hours. They were just glad they were able to escape. The shock left their knees shaking. On this day, not one English airman appeared over the assault waves of the German divisions, much less over the German hinterland.

On 22 March, the fog still hangs bleakly over Awoingt. Not one enemy airman appeared on this day either. Under the protective cover of the heavy ground haze, however, the infantry hurled into the wide expanse before it.

On 23 March, the fog persists; only quite gradually are there a few delicate, and faint rays of hope. In two minutes, the men of the Staffeln are sitting in their machines, and they roar off. They forage along the Front, and find nothing on which to bite. In an extensive circuit many kilometers wide, they fail to find so much as a gnat. Despite this, they come home extremely excited. The fog will lift tomorrow, they say.

And on 24 March, a clear day does indeed arch over the battlefield. Furthermore, the Englishmen's muddled heads have cleared somewhat, and they quickly set out to make up for what they missed. In Awoingt, they see the English vibrating along in a great many squadrons. They get what they've been yearning for. They get it in plenty. It seems as if the English airmen wanted to vindicate themselves in their own eyes, for the battles on this day are bitter indeed.

On the same day, 24 March, the commander shoots down his sixty-seventh opponent; on 25 March, his sixty-eighth; and on 26 March, his sixty-ninth and seventieth opponents. The Baron's terse reports concerning these English tragedies:

Number 67: During a protracted single-seater combat between about ten SEs and twenty-five machines of my Geschwader, I attacked an Englishman at an altitude of 2,500 meters. Under my machine-gun fire, both wings broke away from the airplane in the air. The pieces scattered in the vicinity of Combles.

Number 68: With five airplanes of Jasta 11, I attacked a couple of low-flying English single-seaters north-east of Albert. I came up to within 50 meters behind one of the Englishmen and, with a few rounds, shot him down in flames. The burning airplane crashed between Contal-maison and Albert, and continued to burn on the ground. The bombs which it was apparently carrying exploded a few minutes later.

Number 69: With five gentlemen of Jasta 11 at a low altitude, I encountered, with Leutnant Udet, a Sopwith single-seater at the Front. At first, my opponent tried to escape me by skillful flying. From an airplane's length, I shot him down in flames. The plane disintegrated into pieces during the crash. The fuselage fell into the small forest of Contalmaison.

Number 70: A quarter of an hour after downing the first airplane, in precisely the same place, I encountered an RE two-seater, at an altitude of about 700 meters. I went into a dive behind him, and shot him down in flames with about 100 rounds from close range. At first, the Englishman defended himself with the observer's machine gun. The airplane burned in the air until impact. Half an hour later, the airplane was still burning on the ground.

In one of these reports, the name of Leutnant Ernst Udet appears for the first time in the history of the glorious Geschwader. It was in those stressful days that he came to the Geschwader, a very cheerful, younger gentleman, who had the tender initials 'Lo' painted on his machine,[1] and who had, by that time, already taken twenty-one opponents out of the air.[2] Richthofen welcomed him with great warmth and absolute joy, for he knew who was arriving there, so pleased: a first-rate fighter pilot. Leutnant Udet was immediately given command of a Jagdstaffel.[3]

Meanwhile, like the embodiment of an ancient, heroic song, the German infantry had pushed forward. After more than three years of war, the infantry was no longer well-fed, no longer splendidly clothed, and no longer exceptionally well-equipped but, like a myth of destruction, hour after hour, it smashed a front which was being primed, supported, and replenished by the entire world. The steel-helmeted German soldiers poured out across Combles, Bapaume, and Peronne.

Awoingt no longer pleased Baron von Richthofen.

'Onward!' he said.

He is too impatient to wait for the observations of others. He finds it simpler to see for himself, with his own eyes, where he can assist the German infantry.

On 26 March, the airfield is shifted further forward to Lechelle, which had formerly been an English airfield. Five days earlier, however, the 'lords'[4] had jammed their machines under their elegant breeches, and had been forced to pull back.[5] With great anticipation, the Jagdgeschwader rushes up to Lechelle. They are said to have gone in for incredible luxuries, these 'lords'. The young German gentlemen are dripping with cutting remarks, however, when they get a closer look at things. It is a rather neglected airfield: wretched sheds, and crude, standard corrugated-iron huts. The English seem to have detested window glass and wood; instead, there are copious amounts of oil paper fastened over every opening. To make up for that, at least they turn up some first-rate blankets and some very fine fabric, of a quality they hadn't seen for a very long time. What's more, all of the machines are accommodated very nicely and comfortably in four large tent hangars, and that's worth something. For his part, the commander doesn't have the slightest objection to the Lechelle airfield.

---

[1] Udet's nickname for his fiancée, Eleonore Zink, whom he married on 25 February 1920. They later divorced.
[2] Udet's victory claim of a Camel downed on 9 March 1918, which would have put his score at 21 upon joining JG I, remained unconfirmed.
[3] Udet was acting commander of Jasta 11 from 23 March to 8 April 1918; he was then appointed leader of Jasta 4 on 21 May 1918.
[4] A nickname given to the British airmen by German pilots.
[5] 15 Squadron, RFC.

Quite the contrary: he thinks it is splendid that, from here, he can stand at the telescope himself and observe the battlefield.

Meanwhile, the enlisted men are filling in the numerous shell holes, and the adjutant is less than pleased with the meager 1,500 litres of English petrol he has found. He had counted on 15,000 litres, at the very least.

Now, the fight could begin again.

On 27 March, they came. They came *en masse*. Not at a great altitude, but there, where the commander had expected them, right over the lines of the German infantry. It is certain that Richthofen's heart leaped at this sight. Now he could show the infantry that he was there when they needed him. Shortly before 8.00 a.m., the hornets of Jagdgeschwader I were raising hell amongst the English infantry-support planes, and this day was to be terrible indeed for the red, white, and blue cockades.

Vizefeldwebel Hemer began the dance at 7.50 a.m. by shooting a Bristol down in flames. At this exact same minute, Leutnant Löwenhardt drove his fifteenth Englishman into a shell hole. The victory list of the Geschwader is being written at a furious pace with their machine guns. Leutnant Janzen gets his fourth opponent; Leutnant Friedrichs, his third; Hauptmann Reinhard,[1] his tenth; Leutnant Udet, his twenty-second; Vizefeldwebel Scholtz, his sixth; Leutnant Kirschstein, his second and third; and Jasta 6, its ninety-sixth victory. The commander himself finishes the day's list with the downing of his seventy-second and seventy-third opponents, after he had begun the morning with his seventy-first. The English lose thirteen machines, along with their crews; Jagdgeschwader I, not a single man or machine.

The commander's report of his seventy-third air victory tells of the drama which took place before his eyes, inside of a minute:

> Shortly after I had shot my seventy-second opponent down in flames, with the same men of the Staffel, I attacked again. I saw a Bristol Fighter attack one of my men, set myself behind him and shot him down in flames from a distance of 50 meters. In doing so, I noticed that there was only one passenger. The observer's seat was closed off and filled with bombs, I presume. First, I shot the pilot dead. The airplane was caught on the propeller. I gave it a few more rounds. The airplane then burned, and broke up in the air. The fuselage fell into a small forest, and continued to burn.

The infantry had experienced the fist that liberated the airspace above their heads.

---

[1] Promoted to Hauptmann on 23 March 1918.

That evening, two new officers arrive at the Geschwader: Leutnant Hans Weiss, a student from a technical college, and Leutnant Richard Wenzl. Richthofen had also selected these two himself. He knew why. He greeted Leutnant Wenzl with the whole program in just a few sentences. 'Well now, we've managed for you to get here, eh? You are transferred to Jasta 11. There you'll be joining a circle of comrades where you'll certainly feel at home. You'll be flying triplanes. There are enough machines, and there is no lack of ammunition, so you have your chance. I cultivate just a few aces.'

And with that, he turned to go to bed. Fighting, eating, and sleeping: those were the three basic instincts that comprised his life at the Front. Whoever said of him that he was a predator of the most magnificent kind was using a somewhat literary comparison, of course, but it was true in a certain, noble sense. Only men who had been molded both inwardly and outwardly in this way — without nerves or sentimentality — could be leaders of similarly molded men to such a superhuman degree.

On 28 March, he gets his seventy-fourth; Leutnant Weiss, his thirteenth; and Leutnant Udet, his twenty-third. For the commander, an era is again at an end. The Commanding General of the Air Service sends a radio message:

> I have expressed my congratulations and those of the Air Service to the father of Rittmeister Freiherr von Richthofen, upon the 100th air victory of the two brothers. I convey my sincere appreciation to Leutnants Udet and Löwenhardt, who, in quick succession and with an exemplary thirst for action, have continuously increased their number of victories. The twenty-seventh of March was once again a proud day for Jagdgeschwader I.

The miserable weather at the end of the month gives all of the troops a rest. The Geschwader adjutant is able to draft the activity report for the past month in peace. The contents of this report were less than pleasant for the English. In this activity report for March, Leutnant Löwenhardt, who had by that time shot down eight captive balloons, gives a report concerning his practical experiences during these risky attacks:

> During attacks on captive balloons on the English front, defense from the ground and by machine guns and anti-aircraft guns is very strong. The balloons are lowered very quickly so you must frequently go down to 300 meters. Attacks on English balloons when the sky is cloudy can get tricky, for you can easily be surprised by enemy single-seaters. In clear weather, you must remain behind our Front at the highest possible altitude, and wait until there are no more enemy airmen in the

vicinity of the balloon. The attack is then to be carried out by the shortest route and at the greatest speed. Fire only from close range (from 50 meters) and repeat the attack until the balloon burns. On your flight back, attempt to reach the Front quickly by means of continuous turns, depending on the strength of the enemy anti-aircraft fire. Most advantageous times: mornings and evenings. On the first day of the offensive, two English balloons were aloft, which were shot down. Since then, no enemy captive balloons have been sighted by the Second Army.

On 1 April, the weather is again clear. The English airmen, who obviously had a similar word to the old Prussian word 'onward' in their speech and way of thinking, never stayed on their airfields in clear weather, unless a thunderstorm like the one of 25 March had hurled them back. On the first day of the new month, the Geschwader shoots down five Englishmen. Then the commander no longer cares for Lechelle, either. In any case, he wants to follow the infantry which has already reached the western edge of the former Somme battlefield, but there are few airfields in this accursed and confounded wasteland of craters. The Rittmeister knows this. He reckons then that an advance landing field is just going to have to be conjured up somewhere; he doesn't care how. And so one is conjured up. On the old Roman road to Amiens, just six kilometers behind the forwardmost front, they find a vacant field, and if they were to dig for twenty-four hours, it could look like an airfield.

After Richthofen cremates his seventy-fifth opponent on 2 April, a couple of days of rain are enough to put the vacant field in Harbonnières to rights. From 6 April on, the red triplanes fly to Harbonnières in the mornings, set off from there on their flights against the enemy, and fly back to the Lechelle airfield again in the evenings. In this way, they are close to the struggling infantry and can be there with them in next to no time, should the need arise.

On the first day, the Geschwader immediately christens the new advance landing field by downing ten airplanes during their first take-off; among them, the commander's seventy-sixth, Leutnant Udet's twenty-third,[1] and Leutnant Weiss' fifteenth and sixteenth victories.

Supreme Headquarters is hard pressed to keep up with this pace in the manner it deserves. On the day of his seventy-sixth victory, a radio message comes for the Rittmeister:

---

[1] Lt Udet's victory of 28 March and this victory of 6 April are both listed in the squadron log as his twenty-third, indicating that his score had been adjusted in the meantime to reflect the unconfirmed victory of 9 March 1918.

His Majesty, the Emperor and King, has signified his pleasure to award you the Order of the Red Eagle, Third Class with Crown and Swords, on the occasion of the downing of your seventieth enemy airplane. It is once again a great joy for me to be able to express to you my congratulations on this lofty and rare decoration. Wear it as a symbol of the very highest recognition of your outstanding work as a pilot, which has been crowned by glittering successes proven in three years of war, and of the gratitude of your King for what you have accomplished in the mighty battles of the last two weeks at the head of your Geschwader, as the champion of German air power.

The Commanding General of the Air Service

On the next day, 7 April, between 11.30 a.m. and 12.00 noon, the Rittmeister adds to his victory list: numbers seventy-seven and seventy-eight. On 8 April, however, the Front solidifies. The powerful, headlong plunge by the three German armies succeeded, to be sure, but it met with a vast sea of the enemy which was not to be crossed.

Bad weather across the entire, dreary landscape.

The Jagdgeschwader searches for a new, permanent airfield. One is found near Cappy. To be sure, there is only one road here and nothing else, but once again, an airfield is conjured up. Huts are brought in from Rosières and set up, and on 12 April the Geschwader moves in.

Bad weather.

No sooner does the weather clear up somewhat than the Rittmeister rides against the enemy. On 20 April, he rounds off his list to seventy-nine and eighty. Upon this unparalleled number, however, the God of Battle now lays his terrible, devastating claw.

V   21 APRIL 1918

It is 21 April 1918.

Fog and grey ground haze hang over the Cappy airfield. The air smells of frost and spring at the same time. The officers of the Geschwader are standing together, dressed and ready. They are all in a marvelous mood. Again and again, their laughter sweeps across the airfield, carried by the east wind. They have every reason to be in a good mood: the splendid successes of recent days, the unreserved appreciation of their superiors, their speedy triplanes which have proven to be first-rate, the new airfield where they feel very much at home. Once again, everyone is in great shape, mentally and physically.

This time, the Rittmeister himself is boisterously leading this good mood. He suddenly tips over a stretcher on which Leutnant Wenzl has lain down for a proper nap, and as soon as another tired, equally-unsuspecting human lies down on the vacant stretcher for a proper nap, the Rittmeister tips this youngster into the spring mud as well. Wishing to truly avenge this personal infringement of their comrades' right to some sleep, in return, a couple of men fasten a wheel chock to the tail of Richthofen's Great Dane, Moritz, so the poor, aggrieved creature, utterly dejected, goes looking for some comfort and appreciation from his master.

Again and again, the Baron's laughter rings across the field. They have seldom seen him so downright, openly delighted, and they know that this hunter is actually extremely pleased about his eightieth kill which he bagged yesterday, even though he says little about it. Besides, in a few days, he will be taking off for the Black Forest with Leutnant Wolff,[1] to indulge in a milder form of hunting. The father of the fallen Leutnant Voss has invited him to his home. Two tickets already lie in the adjutant's office.

Everyone on the airfield is very much agreed that the commander should relax a little. If any of them were in line to climb into a sleeping car instead of a triplane, it was him. And outside the airfield, there are still others very much in agreement with this; the 'higher beings', so to speak, sitting in Supreme Headquarters. There at Supreme Headquarters, they were following, with great respect and admiration, the pace at which Richthofen was writing his victory list. At the same time, however, they were unable to free themselves of a certain apprehension. The names Boelcke and Immelmann were harsh examples of where the path of the best must ultimately lead, simply because they were the best.

It was for that reason that some time ago, privately with Oberleutnant

---

[1] Leutnant Hans Joachim Wolff of Jasta 11.

Bodenschatz, they had already touched upon whether it might be possible to bring the Rittmeister around. They had, for example, a very fine position for him: a supervisory position for all of the Jagdstaffeln where he could put his vast experience at their disposal. The Rittmeister laughed right in his adjutant's face when Bodenschatz, for his part, dutifully broached the subject with him in private.

'An ink-spilling spy? No! I'm staying at the Front!'

With that, the subject was closed. But, as for traveling to the Black Forest for a few days to see the father of his friend, Voss, he had nothing against that.

The east wind sweeps more strongly across the airfield and they all raise their heads and sniff the air. If it continues like this just a little longer, then the weather will soon clear and the 'lords' will come a dancing.

Around 10.30 a.m., the east wind has swept the clouds aside, and the weather clears up. The officers hurry to their machines. The commander, however, applies the brakes a bit and thinks they should still wait to take off, so the 'lords' would become really bold. It would then be so much easier to get them in front of their guns.

Just then, a telephonist comes running: there are a couple of Englishmen flying at the Front. In less than five minutes, the first triplanes were thundering across the field. Oberleutnant Bodenschatz saunters slowly over to the observation post and glues himself to the telescope. It was around 11.00 a.m. He sees the two flights of Jasta 11 flying towards the Front, the one led by Leutnant Weiss, the other led by the commander. They roar along the Somme towards the west. Then he also discovers the 'lords', and he can no longer distinguish friend from foe.

Around 12.00 noon, the Staffel comes flying back. One machine after another flattens out and lands. Suddenly, a realization goes through the adjutant like a bolt from above and he stares out at the field.

Richthofen is not with them!

Somewhat apprehensive, from his elevated seat he calls down to Leutnants Wenzl and Karjus, who have climbed out of their machines and now come running.

'Where is Richthofen?'

Leutnant Wenzl says hurriedly, 'I have a bad feeling. We were right near the Front, and over the lines came seven Sopwiths with red noses, the "Anti-Richthofen people".[1] The dogfight started; they had us outnumbered and we didn't really get a chance to shoot. The Rittmeister was

---

[1] A reference to an 'Anti-Richthofen' squadron, supposedly formed by the British for the express purpose of downing von Richthofen, which was given wide coverage in the German press. This, however, had no basis in fact.

flying within view and he now came flying over with his flight. But then seven or eight new 'lords' came wheeling down from overhead. There was a huge dogfight; everything was in confusion. We all gradually worked ourselves a little lower, and in the east wind, we all drifted further and further to the other side of the lines.[1] We broke off the fight and helped each other back across the lines. I have a bad feeling. As I flew back, I saw a small machine standing east of Corbie that hadn't been there before. I think it was a red machine!'

The men stare at him for a second, then Hauptmann Reinhard, the most senior officer of the Geschwader, immediately orders Leutnant Wenzl, Leutnant Karjus and Leutnant Wolfram von Richthofen (a cousin of the commander) to go up and reconnoiter the area around Corbie for the red machine.

The three machines race over the field and go aloft. They disappear overhead on their search. Leutnant Wenzl rushes stubbornly in the direction of Corbie, his teeth clenched. He goes down to 200 to 300 meters, and attempts to get close to the machine to establish its identity. Instead of one machine, he now sees two standing on that spot. From this distance, he cannot determine anything for sure; to do that, he would have to go over the lines. In a hail of machine-gun and anti-aircraft fire, he attempts it, but already English single-seaters are breathing down his neck. With all hell breaking loose, he gets through, nevertheless, and comes closer to the mysterious machines there on the ground. Then bullets chatter furiously into his machine. Three Sopwiths come sweeping in behind him. There is nothing else he can do; they are forcing him ever lower, as it is. There is now one hell of a chase. The English overtake him as he reaches his own lines, and now he risks it all: at an altitude of twenty meters, he sweeps over the German captive balloon standing there and then along the ground towards home.

So he brings back no new information.

In the meantime, the news that the Rittmeister has not returned has spread to the last man. The men stand around, somber. No one says anything. Leutnant Richard Wenzl had no sooner taken off than the adjutant dragged all of the air defense officers to the telephone. None of them can report anything. Now all of the sector's divisional headquarters are alerted. In frantic haste, over and over again, the same sentences are uttered: 'Jasta 11 has returned from a combat mission. The Rittmeister is missing. The men of Jasta 11 report that the Rittmeister went down. Has a

---

[1] The prevailing wind generally blew from west to east, which was greatly to the advantage of the German airmen. On this particular Sunday, however, the wind had shifted and blew from east to west, towards the Allied lines.

red triplane made an emergency landing in your sector? Have you observed a red triplane landing on this side or on the other side of the lines?'

And in the headquarters of the artillery and the infantry, all the phone clerks raise their voices and ask: 'Red triplane? . . . Red triplane? . . . Red triplane?' The couriers and the messengers stumble hurriedly through the communication trenches, passing it on with shouts and notes: 'Red triplane? . . . Red triplane? . . . Red triplane?' In the forwardmost trenches, all the telescopes, trench periscopes, and field glasses — all the eyes of the infantry — scour the terrain: Red triplane? . . . Red triplane? . . . Red triplane? God help us, every minute counts. If he has made an emergency landing somewhere, he must be helped immediately.

Finally, after what seems like an eternity, the General Staff officer of the First Division reports the following: 'The artillery observation post of Field Artillery Regiment No. 16, Oberleutnant Fabian, observed the fight perfectly from Hamel-East. Oberleutnant Fabian saw a red triplane land smoothly on Hill 102, north of Vaux-sur-Somme. Immediately after the landing, the English infantry came running up and pulled the machine behind the hill.'

At first, the dismay in Cappy is enormous, but then everyone breathes a sigh of relief. The commander made an emergency landing. That means he's alive.

Oberleutnant Fabian's report is immediately sent to the Commanding General of the Air Service. The Geschwader adjutant requests Hauptmann Reinhard's permission to go to the observation post of Field Artillery Regiment No. 16. Just maybe . . . with the trained eyes of an airman . . . the adjutant stares through the telescope for a long, long time. He searches the terrain thoroughly, practically centimeter by centimeter. He keeps the lens focused on Hill 102 for a long, long time, and puts some short, quick questions to Oberleutnant Fabian, in vain. At 2.00 p.m., the adjutant returns to the airfield, his eyes burning from the observation. Several infantry officers have passed on reports, but they contain nothing beyond what Oberleutnant Fabian has already reported.

With that, the time in which they could have aided the Rittmeister, somehow, some way, is just about gone. From now on, they can only hope he was forced to land on the other side of the lines, wounded at worst, unwounded at best. It wouldn't be the first time he'd made an emergency landing. He even managed to land smoothly when he was wounded.

In the telephone exchange of the Geschwader, inquiries are pouring in from all sides. At Army headquarters, an extraordinary step is suddenly decided upon. The General allows an inquiry to be radioed to the enemy, in clear language: 'Rittmeister von Richthofen landed your side of the lines. Request information as to his fate.'

There is no answer.

The airfield at Cappy carries on, silent, listening, depressed. In the afternoon, the east wind picks up and becomes cooler. This damned east wind! It drives anything that can longer resist it to the west, towards France. Anyone whose engine failed will be driven west. Maybe this damned east wind pushed the red triplane westward. Without it, perhaps it would have been possible for him . . . These are idle daydreams.

Towards evening, there is no other alternative but to notify Richthofen's father who is now the local commandant in Courtrai. Oberleutnant Bodenschatz climbs into an observation plane and takes the shortest route, over Douai and Lille. He calls Major Richthofen from the Courtrai airfield and asks if he might visit him immediately.

In the beautiful Courtrai town hall, the old gentleman, standing straight, comes through the dim room to meet the adjutant.

'I have the feeling that something has happened to Manfred,' he says quietly.

The Oberleutnant stands like a rock, seeking the Major's eyes. 'Herr Major, I must inform you that the Herr Rittmeister has not returned from a flight, as of yet. All of our inquiries, however, have given us hope that he is alive.'

The two men look at each other in silence. That he is alive? The old officer knows better. And as if lost in deep thought, he says slowly, 'Then he has fulfilled his highest duty.'

As they take their leave, the old gentleman walks back into the twilight of his room. To the adjutant it feels as if it were a walk into utter gloom.

The adjutant arrives back in Cappy that same evening. He hears the subdued conversation in the officers' mess. During the night, he sees the enlisted men standing on the landing field staring into the starry sky, as if someone they had been awaiting for so long would suddenly come gliding gently down and explain everything as a splendid joke.

There are still a couple of things for the adjutant to do. A telegram is sent to Schweidnitz, to his mother and brother: 'Manfred did not return from a flight and, according to reports received, probably landed uninjured on the other side of the lines.'

Hauptmann Reinhard wanders incessantly back and forth and winces when the adjutant throws himself into a chair, dog-tired, then suddenly stands up and fetches the iron box from the safe. He opens the box and from it he takes the grey, official envelope sealed with the official seal of the Geschwader. It has now come to this. One other time, he'd thought it had come to this, that time at Le Cateau. He opens the envelope.

A small piece of paper, no longer quite clean, lies inside. The adjutant skims it, hands it to the Hauptmann. There, in Richthofen's own hand, written in pencil, is one sentence:

10 March 1918

> Should I not return, Oberleutnant Reinhard (Jasta 6) is to assume command of the Geschwader.
>
> Freiherr von Richthofen,
Rittmeister

That is his entire will and bequest. It concerns only and solely his Geschwader. It is the will of a true soldier. There is nothing in it concerning his personal life. There is nothing in it about his personal concerns, nothing that might, perchance, need putting in order. No tender, backward glance to his mother, father, brothers. There is nothing in his private life that needs to be put in order. He had no private life. His life belonged to the Fatherland, without condition, reservation, or consideration. His life belonged to the Geschwader. Free and unburdened, he took off for each flight. He had seen to it that his Geschwader would be in the right hands, if he met his fate. For him, there was no need to worry further.

Oberleutnant Reinhard (who has since become a Hauptmann) and Oberleutnant Bodenschatz cannot imagine, however, that this modest piece of paper should now be valid. It is simply not possible that Manfred von Richthofen should have fallen to that same inexorable law of war to which all men who went to war eventually fell. There are exceptions, they think again and again. And he was, indeed, an exception. Anyone so pampered, so honored, so protected by the God of War simply cannot be forsaken by this same God of War from one hour to the next, to be betrayed and sold.

Somewhere, he must still be alive.

This hope, cherished by not only Jagdgeschwader I but the entire German Army, finds new sustenance in a strange enemy radio message that was picked up, but then suddenly interrupted. They could just make out:

> . . . famous German fighter pilot, Rittmeister von Richthofen, was shot down near Corbie and after landing, was . . . by Australian troops. . .

Here the radio message broke off.

They stood confronted by a mystery and they gradually became rather suspicious. Why did the enemy keep silent? Why did they not immediately announce to the whole world that they had succeeded in striking such a great blow, when in other cases they had been by no means shy?

Orders were given to thoroughly interrogate each and every captured Englishman. But the English airmen taken into German captivity knew only that the Rittmeister was dead. Others stated that a German pilot, whose name was being kept secret, had been taken to the field hospital at Amiens, severely wounded. Under such circumstances, any hope they may have had dwindled.

Rumors and speculations cropped up and these rumors were sometimes bitter. A few of them even said that Richthofen had been killed by Australian soldiers.

Finally, on the evening of 23 April, soldiers find an English message cylinder with streamers attached, in the vicinity of the airfield. It contains the announcement by the Royal Flying Corps that Rittmeister von Richthofen had been fatally wounded in air combat and had been buried with full military honors. On the same day, a Reuters news report containing the same information is released. Now, there was no longer any doubt. It was now certain that he was no longer among the living, but had entered that huge, silent kingdom of front-line soldiers who had given their lives for the Fatherland.

But how had it happened?

Oberleutnant Fabian's report did not prove to be totally correct. The Baron had already been fatally hit in the air, and his machine, therefore, heavily damaged upon landing. Later photographs have proven this conclusively.

It was not possible to clarify completely the circumstances of his death during the war. However, the last commander of Jagdgeschwader I, at that time Oberleutnant Hermann Göring, presently General of Aviation and Prussian Council President, did not give up until he had personally clarified every last remaining doubt, in discussion with numerous English fighter pilots after the war. General Göring gives the following absolutely clear and truthful account of Richthofen's last flight:[1]

On 21 April 1918, Richthofen took off with two flights of his good old Jasta 11 in the direction of Amiens. Moreover, he had also given take-off orders to one of his Geschwader's other Staffeln, and so this Staffel was in the air as well; without any connection to the Rittmeister, however, as it had a separate mission.

After he had reached the desired altitude, Richthofen flew over the enemy front and pushed forward into enemy air space because he had

---

[1] This is the account that appeared in the first, 1935 edition of the book. The second edition, published in 1938, contained an updated account which appears in the appendix.

observed enemy aircraft there. At first, it was a matter of an attack on a couple of enemy two-seaters, so-called 'artillery observation planes'. While in combat with these planes, he and his men were attacked by an enemy pursuit formation, vastly superior, numerically. As was his wont, he took up the fight against this manifold force.

The wind was unfavorable, and during their continuous turns the combatants were driven ever further behind the enemy lines. Richthofen fought splendidly as always, without being able to prevail against the enemy's superior numbers. He paid special attention to his comrades because they were so far inside enemy air space and there was a certain danger of their being cut off. For this reason, Richthofen was soon forced to fire on various opponents, in order to help his men. He couldn't, therefore, busy himself singlehandedly with a single opponent and bring him down, as was generally his rule.

His comrades watched as he suddenly went down in a dive, completely intact and under control. They were not in a position to cover him as every single one of them was busy with several enemy airplanes. The enemy's superior numbers took ever more effect and they completely routed the German Staffeln.

When Richthofen was not to be found in the predetermined rendezvous area, his now leaderless comrades sought their airfield in the hope that he had already landed. Sudden panic seized them, however, when they were forced to confirm the fact that this wasn't the case. Furthermore, shortly after their landing, from the Front there arrived an observation post's report that a red triplane had apparently landed smoothly behind the enemy lines following air combat. They still had a faint hope that Richthofen had only been taken prisoner.

The Jasta 11 flight which had just landed immediately took off again, under the command of Leutnant Wenzl, to undertake a search and once again thoroughly scour the area in which the airplane had been downed; and to ascertain, if possible, whether the airplane had, in fact, landed smoothly or had been destroyed. However, they did not succeed in reaching the air space where the fight had taken place, for a swarm of vastly superior English fighters was already keeping the weak flight of Jasta 11 from any approach to the Front.

A clear picture could not be obtained in this way, and so we continued to hover in the darkness between fear and hope until a few days later, when the enemy press reports left no further doubt that the greatest of all fighter pilots was no more.

The inquiries now began as to the manner of his death about which we had been in the dark for so long. I, myself, having had the great honor and the undeserved luck to be the last commander of this glorious Geschwader, naturally tried everything in order to finally get a clear description of what had happened.

This, however, I only succeeded in doing to my satisfaction during my visits to England. While there, I made inquiries of all the pilots, and I received the same explanation pretty much everywhere. This explanation, in particular, was further supported by an interesting conversation concerning this which I had here in Berlin with the successful fighter pilot, Major Bishop, the 'English Richthofen'. He gave me the following description of Richthofen's death, a description which coincides completely with those descriptions I had already obtained in England and which can today, in general, be considered as the official one.

After the above-described battle had been in progress for some time, for some reason or other Richthofen's engine must have suddenly quit, either as a result of a shot or some type of engine failure. This forced the Rittmeister into an immediate descent. However, since he found himself far behind enemy lines, it was impossible for him to still reach his own lines. He therefore made for enemy territory. In doing so, he encountered a young Canadian pilot who had been at the Front just a short time, and who had experienced just a few air battles. The Canadian, unaware of who was in front of him and apparently not knowing that his opponent was already defenseless, positioned himself behind him. Because Richthofen could no longer maneuver, his fate was quickly sealed, for the first shots fatally wounded him. This entire affair is said to have been played out to its conclusion at an altitude of just 300 meters.

This is the conclusion of General Göring's exacting inquiries. For their part, these inquiries once again find corroboration in the reports made to Oberleutnant Bodenschatz, Richthofen's adjutant, when he was ordered to a North American flying unit in 1927.

The young Canadian who shot down this eagle shot down a badly wounded eagle whose wings were crippled. As he made his last descent with a dead engine and heard the rattle of machine guns behind him, Rittmeister von Richthofen must have known that the end had come. With calm eyes, he will have looked for a moment at the novice noisily overtaking him. And before the bullet tore through that pure, brave heart, perhaps a small, grim smile will have flown across his face, the smile of the undefeated.

If the laws of war had decreed his death, his comrades would not have begrudged him falling in combat with someone of equal stature. But the laws of war are mysterious and unfathomable, for they are the laws of death.

On 24 April 1918, a radio message is sent to Courtrai:

> To Major Freiherr von Richthofen,
> Commandant of Courtrai
>
> The painful news of the heroic death of our good Rittmeister has
> shaken all of us deeply. With deepest sympathy, the entire Geschwader
> mourns with the father, mother, brothers and sister of our proud and
> chivalrous commander. With the solemn vow to continue the struggle
> in the way he demonstrated to us daily, he shall live on within us for all
> time as a shining example of the boldest spirit of a fighter pilot.
>
> Reinhard
Hauptmann and Geschwader Leader

Major von Richthofen's reply arrives the same day:

> To Jagdgeschwader I
>
> My proud son must live on as your model.
>
> Father Richthofen

The Commanding General of the Air Service telegraphs from Supreme
Headquarters:

> The hope which we all cherished, that Richthofen would be spared, has
> not been realized. He has fallen. Stronger than our words are his deeds.
> To him it was granted to live revered and recognized as a leader, and to
> be loved as a comrade. Let us turn our gaze not upon what he might
> have yet become, but rather, from what he was, let us derive our living
> strength, the strength to keep his memory ever alive in our deeds. I am
> thinking affectionately of his Geschwader and especially of his
> Jagdstaffel 11.

What the English were feeling is expressed in the report which came in from
Holland during these days of mourning. The English Reuters news report
read as follows:

> Reuters' special correspondent with the British Army reports that the
> German airman, Rittmeister von Richthofen, has met his death in an
> air battle at the Front. His body will be buried with military honors. It
> is anticipated that this ceremony will be very impressive and worthy of
> this airman's remarkable record.

The war correspondent for the English newspaper, *The Times*, writes: 'All British pilots concede that Richthofen was a great pilot and an honorable opponent.'

The obituary sent out by Jagdgeschwader I read:

> His love for his Fatherland, his heroic, modest way of thinking, his exemplary life as a German soldier were sealed with a hero's death upon the battlefield by our admired and beloved commander, Royal Prussian Rittmeister
>
> Manfred Freiherr von Richthofen
> Knight of the Highest Order.
>
> On 21 April, he departed from us. Bereft and robbed of its leader, the Geschwader mourns the irreparable loss of its proud commander.
>
> Loved and admired by Germany's people, respected by his enemies, he who was so accustomed to victory died undefeated, as a victor.
>
> To all of us, he was the model, the adviser, the friend whom we can never replace.
>
> With the solemn vow, 'What you began — your life's work — we will finish, and we must finish', Richthofen's brave fighting spirit shall live on in us for all time.

Great was the mourning in Germany. Condolences arrived in endless numbers. Much was written about him, and much had been told of him. Countless legends had sprung up around him. But what he really was, in air combat where the enemy aircraft saw him, and at home with his Geschwader where only his fellow soldiers, his comrades saw him, emerges from the following description.

First and foremost, he was a soldier. And, as a soldier, the fighter pilot was the ultimate to him. He subordinated everything else to this concept. Nothing was too difficult for him, nothing was impossible for him, if it meant achieving something for his combat flying and his Geschwader. As a 25-year-old Rittmeister, at the same time he held the position of a Jagdgeschwader commander, an assignment for which there were as yet no criteria, and no model. Accomplishing this was really Richthofen's responsibility. Indeed, he had established the standards himself. The concept of a 'Jagdgeschwader' originated with him.

Very few people know all he accomplished, aside from his flying activity. His work on the ground was no less important than his work in the air. No sooner had he returned from a flight than you would find him already at work in his hut. Nothing went on in the Geschwader that he did not know about. He dealt with the 'paperwork war' in next to no time, and just as dependably as he dealt with the war in the air. For example, if he had some paperwork to plough through, important matters to deal with which could be best gotten out of the way directly and immediately at the highest levels, he got into his triplane and took off. He flew to headquarters, laid the stuff on the table, and took care of everything on the spot. On one occasion, during weather so unbelievable that any mouse would have stayed in its hole, he flew to army headquarters, unconcerned, in order to settle some important matter.

Only a healthy physical constitution like his could be equal to these kinds of demands. No matter how much work he might already have behind him, he always looked fresh and rested. He made demands for comfort only when they were inexpensive and to be had without detriment to flight operations. His clothing was as simple as possible. Around us, most of the time he ran around in just a knitted sweater and his deerskin trousers, the *Pour le Mérite* at his throat. If it was cold, then over these he'd have a leather jacket. You saw him in uniform only on festive occasions, or when guests were there. During the early days, he suddenly came rushing in to the adjutant to borrow gloves and a belt, because he had to quickly report to 'the gentleman from Brunswick'. He then came back grinning. He had gotten the inevitable house order, for the second time.[1] 'But I can't very well tell the man that!'

He took real pleasure in good food, especially when the requisite mustard (which he used on anything and everything) was at hand. But if there was no other way around it, he was highly satisfied with everything. He didn't have 'prima donna' type moods, although he could have indulged in them. He never turned down a good wine either, but you always saw him sober, even if a drunken atmosphere prevailed all around him.

He held comradeship above everything else; he openly cultivated it. He held to the sensible principle that his men could do and should do whatever they liked after a flight. He took part in many a joke and he put up with a lot. I can still see his exuberant face that time when Supreme Headquarters sent some members of the Reichstag to visit. That evening, the visitors went to bed in a corrugated-iron hut and, in the still of the night, Reinhard and a couple of helpers staged a bombing raid. As the signal flares, which were ideally suited for the purpose, traveled through the stove pipe and into the metal hut, explosions flashed from the flares' cardboard coverings with a terrifying crash and stench, and the guests came rushing out of the hut, more than a little terrified, their faces white as death. And right in front of the door, they came within a hair's breadth of running over the commander. However, he quickly slipped away into the darkness . . .

---

[1] The Brunswick War Merit Cross, 2nd Class.

If, however, Richthofen believed there to be some kind of disagreement between two comrades, he intervened immediately. Thus, one fine day, one man was ordered in to see him because Richthofen had taken a loud and somewhat excited exchange of words seriously. The man received a fatherly admonition, and promptly got into a huff. At that time, we still didn't know that side of him. Only later did it dawn on us that he had meant it for our own good. Almost every one of us had to put up with these 'fatherly admonitions'. There were even those among us who received these admonitions in a very heavy manner, because it seemed necessary to him.

'The Staffel will conduct itself in the air just as it conducts itself on the ground.' That was his ironclad training principle and he applied it not only to his own Jasta 11, but extended it to the entire Geschwader as well. He visited the other Staffeln on a day by day basis, and he knew each and every one of us on the ground and in the air.

He shared a close friendship with his adjutant, Oberleutnant Bodenschatz, and with Hauptmann Reinhard, at that time leader of Jasta 6. But his acknowledged favorite was 'Wölfchen', Joachim.[1] 'Wölfchen' had been with the Geschwader a long time, had been wounded three times, and had the surefire bad luck to get his crate completely shot up at each and every opportunity. As a result, his activity as a fighter pilot was at first merely passive. Nevertheless, Richthofen kept him in the Geschwader, whereas otherwise he immediately and ruthlessly got rid of anyone not meeting his harsh requirements. 'Wölfchen', however, had pulled the Rittmeister out of a bad situation once, and Richthofen 'smelled' the good fighter pilot in him, despite his initial failures. And under Richthofen's guidance, 'Wölfchen' suddenly got it right. He took off, tore into the enemy squadrons like a devil, and within a short time, he shot down ten opponents.[2]

To speak of Richthofen as a fighter pilot is really superfluous. He was probably the best fighter pilot who ever lived. Even though he writes in his book that he shot down his first twenty opponents without being able to fly correctly, later that was no longer true. He combined excellent eyesight and a certain 'nose' for the hunt with great flying ability. Wherever he flew, there was always something afoot. He then shot quite splendidly. Most of the time, his opponent was lost after his first rounds, and burned immediately. That is the whole secret of his great successes. He had no other secrets. He knew no special, carefully guarded trick. At most, he had one

---

[1] A nickname meaning 'Wolfie' or 'little Wolff' given to Lt Hans Joachim Wolff.
[2] Lt Wolff joined Jasta 11 on 6 July 1917, but did not score his first victory until 18 March 1918.

single trick and no doubt it was one that all experienced fighter pilots had: during the flight, he kept a close eye on his 'young hares', meaning he paid close attention to the novices of his Geschwader. Now, as the enemy squadrons came nearer, naturally they too recognized the novice pilots. As soon as a 'young hare' was set upon by an opponent, Richthofen took the attacker on, for the enemy pilot was occupied with the 'young hare' and was taking nothing else into consideration. Any attacker who took the bait was usually lost, for Richthofen would come roaring up to within ramming distance behind him. And Richthofen shot splendidly.

'Anyone who flies a lot, experiences a lot' was also a maxim of his. 'On good days, an average of three take-offs can be made in the morning.' Then, of course, he still flew steadily in the afternoons and evenings. The rest of the time he stood with his men on the landing field, pretty much suited-up, his knobbed walking stick in his hand and Moritz, his big Great Dane, next to him. Here he impatiently awaited the enemy and ordered the deployment of his Staffeln. He had not the slightest sympathy for those with sickly and frail constitutions. For many people that was very hard.

VI OUTSIDE AMIENS

The Cappy airfield lies in a foggy dampness. The spring wind wafts mildly over the dull landscape and pushes a few, isolated grey clouds along low in the sky.

The days of feverish combat have suddenly ceased, as if with a thunder-clap. Occasionally now and then, an anti-aircraft gun growls somewhere and the pilots lift their heads and listen. But there is nothing. The air space over this sector remains strangely empty. Not one Englishman is to be seen, not one captive balloon is sighted. No bombers attempt to come over the Front.

Nothing.

On 27 April, Hauptmann Reinhard's official appointment as commander of Jagdgeschwader I arrives and with that, Richthofen's last wish is fulfilled. And as if the thunderclap of Richthofen's death has faded away over the fronts once this void is filled, English airmen again come sporadi-cally at first light. On the other side of the Front, they roar up and down at low altitude, then climb aloft, disappearing into the clouds, and do not return.

On the next day, 28 April, however, the sky is again empty. On the Cappy airfield, hour after hour, they turn their telescopes back and forth. Nothing. The air defense officers crouch in their forwardmost observation posts and search every cloud. Nothing.

On 29 April, it is exactly the same.

On 30 April, it appears no different.

On the first day of May, this same, strange stillness prevails in the air overhead. During these few days, the weather was bad and the air was hazy, but they had certainly flown in worse weather. The English preferred to give themselves a rest.

On 2 May, however, all of the air defense officers' telescopes finally clamped on to something: brisk enemy air activity at the Front. The men of the Cappy airfield went aloft. Once again, the time had come. The English were coming once again! But coming was all they were to do. They encountered a Jagdgeschwader carrying not only the designation 'No. I', but a great name as well. They encountered the 'Jagdgeschwader Freiherr von Richthofen', so designated from this time forth, by decree of His Majesty, the Kaiser. At 12.30 p.m. on this particular day, Leutnant Löwenhardt brings down a single-seater. It smashes into the shell holes north of Montauban.

Already in these first, new air battles, they noticed that the pilots on the other side had received a new type of airplane, built from the unlimited materials of ever-better quality which were ever at their disposal. These airplanes easily surpassed the German triplanes; they were tremendously maneuverable. They were the first models of the brand-new, modified Sopwith Camel brought out with a 150 hp Vickers engine and made almost totally out of aluminum. What did the Cappy airfield have to put up against these new airplanes? They were flying their old triplanes. In these old triplanes, however, sat Richthofen's resolute heirs. They had nothing else with which to oppose the English.

So what!

On 3 May, at 11.00 a.m., under the machine guns of Leutnant Hübner, a two-seater catches fire and blazes slowly to earth. At 12.15 p.m., a Bristol Fighter disintegrates under Offizier Stellvertreter Aue's shots to its fuselage and wings, and flutters into nothingness. At 12.20 p.m., at ramming distance in front of Leutnant Bretschneider's propeller, a Spad goes over on its nose and, with its engine shot to pieces, races straight down, shattering into a thousand pieces on the ground. At 12.50 p.m., an English pilot in his Spad collapses under the first shots of Leutnant Kirschstein, and goes down in a spin until his machine breaks apart.[1] At 5.50 p.m., in front of Leutnant von Rautter's gunsights, a Bréguet starts to smoke, sends a spurt of flame from out of its fuselage, and shoots downwards like a piece of wood. At 6.50 p.m., Leutnant Friedrichs pumps a machine-gun burst into a de Havilland near Fontaine lès Cappy, and its wings break apart. At 8.05 p.m., before the eyes of Leutnant von Winterfeld, an Armstrong lifts its left wing to bank and does not level off again. Under his first dozen rounds, it goes roaring downward and disintegrates. On this day, seven Englishmen have been taken out of the air by Richthofen's heirs.

These have been hard, particularly bitter battles. It seems as if, beneath their helmets and goggles, the faces of the Germans have become somewhat more impassive and somewhat stonier, and it seems as if their machine guns made a noise more brutal than before.

The Jagdgeschwader knows how things stand. Day after day, they are growing more numerous over there on the other side. It is nothing unusual, no longer even an act of bravado, but almost a habit for four of them to shoot it out with eighteen to twenty Englishmen. When they again land in Cappy, their machines look quite moderately . . . bullet-riddled, to be precise. These are bitter battles and the God of Battle no longer seems to allow himself any particular favorites. He grasps blindly and by no means spares the Jagdgeschwader Richthofen.

Leutnant Weiss, splendid, calm, and daring, encounters six to eight of those brand-new Sopwith Camels with his Staffel. In no time flat, these

---

[1] If this was indeed a Spad, it was not English, as the British were no longer flying them.

machines had climbed above the Staffel, which was forced to remain below. Only Leutnant Weiss was able to maintain his altitude with his airplane, and his comrades saw how he fought it out up there in his triplane, completely alone. He'd had his airplane painted completely white, and there overhead, he flashed in the midst of the Englishmen. He got behind one of them and stuck with him. Then from overhead, another Englishman raked him with a machine-gun burst sideways into the cockpit. Leutnant Weiss put his machine on its back and the plane shot downwards. He could no longer break the dive. He had taken a shot right through the middle of his forehead.

On this same day, 2 May, Vizefeldwebel Scholtz, whose name was highly respected in the Geschwader, crashed over the Cappy airfield shortly after take-off. He was already dead when they pulled him from under the wreckage. An hour later, a short telegram came in to the Geschwader's adjutant. Oberleutnant Bodenschatz read it and laid it aside in silence. It contained Vizefeldwebel Scholtz's promotion to the rank of officer.

During these days, glorious Jasta 11 had at its disposal just one solitary pilot who was fit to fly. That was Leutnant Richard Wenzl. Weiss and Scholtz were dead; Just was wounded; Karjus, who had only one hand (but had flown with just the one hand) had been transferred;[1] Steinhäuser couldn't fly;[2] and Wolff and Richthofen's cousin had traveled to Berlin for the Rittmeister's funeral service.[3]

The month of May had truly begun with a dirge, but in the midst of this dirge, strewn somewhere in the shell holes, blazed the remains of many an English machine. And that is all that mattered. In the name of their fallen leader, that was all that mattered. That and nothing else.

The thunderclap of 21 April had died away.

With every engine, and with every machine gun, they struck up the new chorus of the Jagdgeschwader Richthofen. This new chorus was already dreaming of a new airfield in Amiens. But Amiens was to remain a dream for ever.

From both near and far, the English and French army commanders hurriedly pull together what they have in the way of troops. In frantic haste and with the last of their energy, they mend the breach. Indiscriminately, with almost no plan, they hurl themselves blindly against their German opponents in frantic counterattacks, wherever the Germans have

---

[1] Walther Karjus, who had his airplane's controls modified to allow the control column and the firing lever to be operated with one hand, was transferred to Armee Flug Park II on 29 May 1918. He was later given command of Jasta 75.
[2] He had been wounded in the foot on 13 March 1918.
[3] The service took place on 2 May 1918, on what would have been Richthofen's 26th birthday, in the old garrison church on Neue Friedrichstrasse in Berlin.

penetrated. They have in mind only the next few hours and stopping the Germans at any price.

They hurriedly assemble what they can in the air as well, throwing countless fighter pilots, bombing squadrons, infantry- and ground-support planes at the Front. These always come only during the evening hours, for the visibility is poor during the day. The evenings are thus filled with bitter air battles.

Come they might, when they wanted and as far as they wanted, but time and time again, the vastly superior numbers of the enemy air service encountered this same small, wonderful élite group of German airmen.

From 9 to 16 May, thus in just eight days, this élite group dispatched thirty-two enemy aircraft, and lost for their part neither a single man nor machine. On 9 May, at 1.15 p.m., Leutnant von Rautter knocks a DH 9 out of the air near Wiencourt. In flames, it flutters downward, his sixth air victory. At 7.50 p.m., Leutnant Löwenhardt gets his nineteenth opponent near Hamel. At precisely 8.00 p.m., the commander, Hauptmann Reinhard, drives a Sopwith into the shell holes west of Morlancourt. Vizefeldwebel Hemer can report that he dispatched his eighth opponent, an RE, east of Cachy at 12.30 p.m.

On the following day, 10 May, there is a great harvest: Leutnant von Rautter, a Bristol near Chuignes, his seventh air victory; Leutnant Paul Wenzel, a Sopwith south-west of Caix, his second air victory; Leutnant von Winterfeld, a Sopwith north of Hamel, his second air victory; Vizefeldwebel Hemer, a Sopwith this side of Chérisy, his ninth air victory; Leutnant Kirschstein, a Sopwith this side of Chipilly, his eighth air victory; Oberleutnant von Wedel, a Sopwith in the area of Chérisy, the first air victory of his life; Leutnant Steinhäuser, a Sopwith north of Chérisy, his fifth air victory; Leutnant Wolff, a Sopwith south of Sailly Laurette, his ninth air victory. Leutnant von Rautter gets hold of his second airplane of the day this side of Rosières. The DH 9 is his eighth air victory. Leutnant Paul Wenzel gets yet another DH 9 in front of his machine guns on this day, and brings it down, his third air victory. Leutnant Löwenhardt gets his twentieth opponent this side of Chaulnes.

This fierce day seems to have driven the English to their knees somewhat, for on the following day, 11 May, no engagements take place. From 12 May to 14 May, the weather is bad. Rain and clouds drift along in thick curtains low in the sky.

On 15 May, however, the music of the machine guns again begins to roar in Flanders' skies. Once again, a day of rich harvest for the Geschwader and an awful spring day for the English. Leutnant Friedrichs starts the dance off at 8.15 a.m. with the downing of a Sopwith, his fourth air victory. Leutnant Paul Wenzel gets a de Havilland at 11.15 a.m., as his fourth air victory;

Leutnant von Gluszewski, a Bréguet, as the first victory of his life; Leutnant Kirschstein, a Sopwith at 12.05 p.m., as his ninth opponent; Sergeant Schmutzler, a Sopwith at 12.10 p.m., as the first victory of his life; Leutnant von Rautter, 12.15 p.m., a Sopwith as his ninth opponent; Leutnant Janzen, 12.50 p.m., a Bristol Fighter as his sixth opponent; Leutnant Löwenhardt, 1.25 p.m., a Bristol as his twenty-first air victory. Leutnant Kirschstein gets his second opponent of the day, a Bristol at 3.15 p.m., as his tenth air victory; Leutnant Wolff, a Bristol at 3.10 p.m., as his tenth air victory; Oberleutnant von Wedel, a Bristol at 3.15 p.m., as his second air victory. Leutnant von Rautter also gets his second opponent of the day, a Bréguet at 6.05 p.m., as his tenth air victory. At 6.20 p.m. on this late afternoon, one of the boldest of the bold, Leutnant Kirschstein, finishes off the list for 15 May by shooting down his third opponent, a Bristol. With it, he has increased his victory list by three within just a few hours; it was his eleventh victory.

On the next day, the dance continues. Leutnant Kirschstein does not slacken off. At 2.40 p.m., he brings down his twelfth opponent, and his thirteenth at 8.10 p.m. Leutnant Löwenhardt shoots down his twenty-second opponent, and Leutnant Richard Wenzl, his third. That makes thirty-two airplanes in eight days without a single casualty, in the face of a staggering, numerical superiority on the opposing side.

At 8.20 a.m. on 16 May, however, Leutnant Wolff is shot down in air combat north of Lamotte. He caught two lethal shots right below the heart. In silence, the Geschwader mourned for this bold, tenacious, and bullet-riddled heart.

As 20 May dawned, the four Staffeln had shot down fifty Englishmen in ten days. A telegram from the Commanding General is able to congratulate the Geschwader on its 300th air victory.

Around this time, the English and French army commanders have finally accomplished their aims with the superior strength of their men and machines: the German assault sinks slowly once again into the trenches and shell holes, and the Front solidifies into a war of position.

VII ABOVE THE CHEMIN DES DAMES ON THE MARNE

In the meantime, the Army High Command finished its preparations for a breakthrough on the Chemin des Dames.[1] As part of these preparations, they again employed the ace card of their Air Service. The Jagdgeschwader Richthofen takes its leave of the Second Army and moves to Guise, where it is placed at the disposal of the Seventh Army for the breakthrough.

For five whole days there in Guise, the Geschwader can rest in peace. During this time, the new airfield at Puisieux Farm, five kilometers northeast of Laon, is being prepared. The machines are looked after. During these days off, some of the men familiarize themselves thoroughly with the new Fokker DVII, a biplane with a 160 hp Mercedes engine. Less maneuverable than the triplane, it is all the faster for it. If it climbs a little slow down below, it climbs surprisingly well higher up because its high-compression engine is designed for high altitudes. In the area of the attack, the same game of hide-and-seek is being repeated as before the great offensive in March. At night, the whole hinterland swarms with marching columns as the artillery and the infantry assume their assault positions. During the day, the hinterland lies still and motionless.

On the eve of the attack, on 26 May, as the deepening dusk falls, tents sprout up suddenly on the airfield at Puisieux Farm and one airplane after another lands in the darkness. One last friendly and grateful radio message follows the Geschwader from the Second Army:

> Upon its departure from the Second Army, I express my deepest appreciation to the Jagdgeschwader Richthofen for its successful action during the time period of 17 November to 18 May. Its 184 victories attest to the bravery of its pilots and show to what extent the Geschwader contributed to the successes of the Second Army by fighting in true, devoted cooperation with all of the other branches of the service.
>
> Its commander, whose name the Geschwader has been granted by order of His Majesty, found a hero's death on our Front. May the spirit that radiated from this loyal, brave, and beloved leader accompany the Geschwader in further battles and successes.
>
> The Commander in Chief,
> von der Marwitz

---

[1] A ridge running from east to west midway between Soissons and Laon along which a road had been constructed for the daughters of King Louis XV.

On 27 May, at 2.00 a.m., the German heavy barrage leaps from its hidden gun emplacements. The members of the Jagdgeschwader Richthofen, who have gradually grown accustomed to being deployed during the great offensives and to listening to the preparatory barrages, stand around on the airfield and listen raptly. In all their years of war, they have never yet heard such a hurricane.[1] The whole earth and everything on it — ground and trees, houses and huts, man and beast — seem to tremble and shake incessantly, and the air layers seem to whirl. High in the air and deep within the earth, millions of sounds pound and thunder, howl and roar; noises that soon collapse within their ears into a single, unbroken, deep, and powerful organ note of immeasurable strength. The organ of the German artillery is playing the overture for the breakthrough of the Chemin des Dames.

At the very minute when its brutal melodies are traveling on to resound further in the distance, at 4.20 a.m. in the early morning, the officers of the assault troops lift their bleary eyes from their wristwatches. Fists are raised in the air, brief shouts go from man to man, and beneath hundreds of thousands of steel helmets, eyes begin to shine. The German infantry climbs out of its trenches. Marshal Foch describes in his memoirs how they surged forward:

> . . . Preceded by a dense, creeping barrage and supported at various points by tanks, it penetrated with a single rush far into the French positions. The surprise had been practically complete and the results were most important . . . In the center, the French 22nd Division and the British 50th Division were literally submerged under the German flood. Rapidly gaining possession of the plateau along which runs the Chemin des Dames, the enemy pushed right up to the Aisne. At 10.00 a.m. he was in possession of the river from Vailly to Oeuilly . . . At 11.00 a.m. no further illusion was possible.[2]

At Puisieux Farm, they hear right away of the enormous leap which the infantry has made in almost a single breath. The Staffeln that dance across the field shaking with impatience and lift off for their first flight against the enemy, find the sky empty over a wide radius. They are disappointed, although they were prepared for this. The hammers of the artillery and the fists of the infantry have smashed the French–English front. The wreckage of the two armies flees to the rear in disarray. Anything not yet pulverized by the batteries, anything still capable of moving to any extent, gets out of

---

[1] The Germans employed 4,600 guns for their opening barrage of the Third Battle of the Aisne River.
[2] *The Memoirs of Marshal Foch*, William Heinemann Ltd, London, 1931.

there. The landscape is strewn with 'Frenchies' and 'Tommies' running for the rear.

On the airfields as well, they had no alternative but to roar off at once. The huts are vacated in a mad rush. If there is still time, they torch anything that will burn, demolish those aircraft they are unable to take with them, and destroy their provisions. The airfields soon lie deserted, smoking and desolate. And the sky is empty as a result.

Hauptmann Reinhard, commander of the Jagdgeschwader Richthofen, grows extremely impatient. That small, harsh word burns just as fiercely within him as it burned within his fallen predecessor. *Onward!*

The airfield is situated much too far to the rear for his liking. Reinhard puts up with the situation for two days, then the adjutant, Oberleutnant Bodenschatz, squeezes himself into an observation plane and flies up ahead to look for a new airfield. He has already figured out where he is going to look. If he is not mistaken, the French airfield at Beugneux is already in the hands of the infantry and he won't need to look any further. It doesn't take long before he is circling over the field. There below, however, there is still heavy firing. The infantry is still fighting on the south edge of the airfield. He sees the rounded dots of German steel helmets leaping back and forth, sees the flat helmets of the French swarming, and hears rifle fire bubbling up. In short, the time for them to occupy this airfield doesn't seem to have arrived yet. That is not to say that the adjutant deems the moment premature for a preliminary landing, as far as he's concerned, however. So he cuts the engine and, with faith in God, he glides down to the churned-up terrain and lands smoothly amid the shell holes.

For the moment, he can't concern himself with the infantry action in the area. The airfield must be inspected. This inspection yields a fairly gratifying picture. The French, justifiably angry, have, of course, burned all but three of the hangars and completely demolished all of the airplanes they had been unable to take with them: ten Voisins, one Bréguet, and twelve Spad single-seaters. That cannot be undone. Except for that, however, the field was quite good, not overly shot up, and it needed only slight improvements. Above all, they could observe the enemy's air operations splendidly from here.

When the adjutant has stumbled around the smoldering, stinking ruins long enough and gets out of the smoke somewhat, with pleasure and a well-satisfied eye, he spies a flock of more than three hundred sheep grazing in biblical harmony there on the grassy turf, without a shepherd. In a flash, these future soup and meat dishes for the Jagdgeschwader Richthofen are secured in a pen.

On 31 May, the enemy with his weakened forces ventures to make contact for the first time. The enemy is turned back. That evening, the

Geschwader can report five air victories. The loss of one of their best is irreparable, however: the loss of Leutnant von Rautter who had just achieved his fifteenth victory during the noon hour. He failed to return from a patrol.[1]

On 1 June, they occupy the Beugneux airfield. At the same time, there occurred a slight mishap, over which Hauptmann Reinhard did nothing more than raise his eyebrow slightly. A pilot from Jasta 10 had made an emergency landing somewhere towards the Front, and a newcomer to the Staffel was to collect his comrade with the two-seater. They described the field to him precisely and vividly, clearly and painstakingly indicated the route which he could not miss, and impressed upon him that it was the first airfield on the other side of the Chemin des Dames. There would be seven or eight abandoned French airplanes standing there. The newcomer just flew off and landed, as ordered, at the first airfield where he saw French machines. Something was not quite right, however. The machines standing there had not been abandoned, and the airfield was swarming with French uniforms. Unfortunately, it was a different French airdrome, and completely intact. The newcomer had gotten himself lost, 'verfranzt' so to speak,[2] and in this way wound up in French captivity.[3]

Otherwise, the move to the new airfield proceeded quickly and without incident. They had to be prepared for the fact that the French had gotten their nerve back, and that the resistance would be resumed in the air, as well. And so it was. On 2 June, the first enemy aircraft were spotted on the other side of the lines. Jagdgeschwader Richthofen, long since impatient, went roaring up against the squadrons, and it was a bad day for the French. For the first time, the German fighter planes were not up against the English, but the French instead. And both sides felt the difference: if the Englishman was a perfect daredevil, then the Frenchman was very cautious.

Jagdgeschwader Richthofen's breaching of the enemy squadrons' defenses had bitter consequences for their adversaries. The commander, Hauptmann Reinhard, shot down three: a Spad at 5.45 p.m., another Spad at 8.30 p.m., and his third Spad at 9.00 p.m. Leutnant Kirschstein got two, a Spad at 5.35 p.m. and a second Spad at 9.00 p.m. Leutnant Udet got his twenty-fifth victory at 11.25 a.m.; Leutnant Janzen, 5.20 p.m., his tenth victory; Leutnant Steinhäuser, 5.45 p.m., his eighth opponent; Leutnant Löwenhardt, 5.45 p.m., his twenty-fifth opponent; Leutnant Maushake,

---

[1] Killed in action near Soissons.

[2] This verb derived from the German nickname 'Franz', given to observers. Pilots were traditionally known by the nickname 'Emil'.

[3] The pilot was Lt Rademacher who joined Jasta 10 on 14 May 1918 and was listed as missing on 31 May 1918.

6.20 p.m., a Bréguet which he forced to land on its own side of the lines.[1] That evening, one select man found his reward. The *Pour le Mérite* arrived for Leutnant Löwenhardt.

The French, however, felt nonstop the full force of whom they were up against. On 3 June, at 12.50 p.m., the French lose a Spad, due to the second victory of Leutnant Skowronski. At 6.30 p.m., a Spad falls as the twenty-sixth victory of Leutnant Löwenhardt. Between 7.30 and 7.35 p.m., within five minutes, they lose two Bréguets due to the nineteenth and twentieth victories of the incomparable Leutnant Kirschstein, and another Bréguet as the fourth victory of Leutnant Bretschneider.

On 4 June, at 5.25 p.m., Leutnant Wolfram von Richthofen, cousin of the late commander, puts the first opponent of his life into the shell holes. In the same minute, Hauptmann Reinhard gets his eighteenth victory. At 6.45 p.m., Leutnant Drekmann shoots down his third opponent. At 8.40 p.m., Oberleutnant von Wedel downs his fifth opponent.

On 5 June, upon returning home, the Geschwader draws up a victory list of thirteen opponents: 7.45 a.m., a captive balloon by Leutnant Grassmann, first victory; 11.20 a.m., a captive balloon by Leutnant Friedrichs, seventh victory; 11.35 a.m., a Spad by Leutnant Kirschstein, twenty-first victory; 11.37 a.m., a Spad by Leutnant Janzen, eleventh victory; 12.00 noon, a Spad by Leutnant Udet, twenty-sixth victory; 5.35 p.m., a Bréguet by Leutnant Kirschstein, twenty-second victory; 5.35 p.m., a Bréguet by Leutnant Skowronski, third victory; 5.40 p.m., a Bréguet by Leutnant Richard Wenzl, fourth victory; 6.45 p.m., a Spad by Leutnant Löwenhardt, twenty-seventh victory; 6.45 p.m., a Spad by Leutnant Heldmann, sixth victory; 8.10 p.m., a captive balloon by Leutnant Friedrichs, eighth victory; 8.25 p.m., a Spad by Leutnant Kirschstein, twenty-third victory; 8.25 p.m., a Spad by Leutnant Janzen, twelfth victory.

On 6 June: 7.25 a.m., a captive balloon by Leutnant Friedrichs, his ninth victory; 7.50 a.m., another captive balloon by Leutnant Otto, his first victory; 11.40 a.m., a Spad by Leutnant Udet, his twenty-seventh victory.

On 7 June, the enemy is more than cautious. But if the enemy won't come, then the Jagdgeschwader Richthofen will try to keep busy with a couple of flights over the lines. 7.00 a.m., a Spad falls to Leutnant Udet, his twenty-eighth victory. Five minutes later, another Spad crashes due to Leutnant Janzen, his thirteenth victory. Five minutes after that, at 7.10 a.m., Leutnant Kirschstein shoots down his twenty-fourth opponent.

On the next day, 8 June, not one enemy airplane comes over the German

---

[1] This victory is listed in the squadron log as confirmed despite landing behind enemy lines.

Top: Karl Bodenschatz, second from right, poses with his fellow cadets from the War Academy at Metz, 18 August 1910 (*Bodenschatz family via George Williams*).

Middle left: 'In The Field' by Professor Arnold Busch, July 1917 (*WWI Postcard – Public Domain*).

Bottom left: Fähnrich (Officer Candidate) Manfred von Richthofen, 1912 (*Author via Sue Hayes Fisher*).

Bottom right: Oswald Boelcke, reportedly just before his last flight (*Author*).

Top left: Château Marckebeke. The front steps of the château were a favorite photo location for Jagdgeschwader I (*Author*).

Top centre: Oblt Eduard Dostler, leader of Jasta 6. Killed in action 21 Aug 1917 (*George Williams Collection*).

Top right: Lt Kurt Wolff, leader of Jasta 11. Killed in action 15 Sept 1917 (*Original book: Sanke card*).

Bottom left: The men of Jasta 11, as sketched by Professor Arnold Busch in July, 1917. A framed copy of this drawing hung in the Bodenschatz

home in Erlangen for many years. Clockwise from top: Lt v. Schönebeck, Lt Niederhoff, Lt Busch, Lt Groos, Lt Brauneck, Lt Stapenhorst, Lt Krefft, Lt Meyer, Lt Lothar von Richthofen, Lt Kurt Wolff, Oblt Reinhard, Lt Joachim Wolff, Lt Müller, Lt Mohnicke, Manfred von Richthofen in middle, Lt Bockelmann, Oblt Bodenschatz, and Oblt Scheffer. (*Bodenschatz Family via George Williams*).

Bottom right: Oblt Ernst Frhr von Althaus, leader of Jasta 10 (*Sanke Card – Public Domain*).

Top left: A jovial Kurt Wolff and Manfred von Richthofen grin for the camera from the rear cockpit of a Rumpler CI piloted by Lt Krefft (*Public Domain*).

Top right : Manfred von Richthofen in hospital, several days after being wounded (*University of Maine – Floyd Gibbons Collection*).

Middle left: Karl Bodenschatz with Jasta 11 (*Original book*).

Middle right: This photo of the helmet worn by von Richthofen on 6 July shows clearly just how close he came to being JG I's first casualty (*University of Maine – Floyd Gibbons Collection*).

Bottom: Jasta 11 Albatros Scout practising against a ground target (*Original book*).

Top left: Feldlazarett No. 76 (St Nicolas Hospital) Courtrai. It was torn down in the 1960's to make way for a new, much larger facility (*Courtrai Historical Society*).

Top right: Manfred von Richthofen and Kurt Wolff visit Château Marckebeke from hospital on Friday, 20 July 1917. Top row, standing from left to right: Mohnicke, Reinhard, Nurse Käte Wienstroth, Major Albrecht von Richthofen, and Scheffer. Middle row from left to right: Müller, Bodenschatz, MvR, Joachim Wolff, and Niederhoff. Front row left to right: Krefft, Brauneck, Bockelmann, Kurt Wolff, Professor Arnold Busch (visiting artist), Meyer, and von Schönebeck (*Bodenschatz family via George Williams*).

Bottom left: Another photo of von Richthofen

taken on the front porch of Château Marckebeke, quite possibly on the same afternoon (*University of Maine – Floyd Gibbons Collection*).

Middle right: Major General von Lossberg, Chief of Staff Fourth Army, talking to aircraft designer Tony Fokker, who is seated in the cockpit of Fokker FI 102/17, while MvR and Lt Adam look on. Less than a month later, Lt Kurt Wolff would lose his life in this same machine (*University of Maine – Floyd Gibbons Collection*).

Bottom right: Manfred von Richthofen in conversation with Lt F. A. Bird of 46 Squadron RFC, who was forced down behind German lines near Bousbecque on 3 Sept 1917 (*Original book*).

Top: St Joseph's Church, Courtrai. It was destroyed in a bombing raid during WWII (*Courtrai Historical Society*).

Middle left: Lt Werner Voss, leader of Jasta 10. Killed in action 23 Sept 1917 (*Original book*).

Above: Kurt Wolff's funeral procession (*Joe Nieto Collection via George Williams*).

Bottom left: Lt Lothar von Richthofen, Manfred's handsome, but no less deadly, younger brother (*Original book*).

Lt. Wüsthoff

Oblt. Frhr.v. Boenigk

Lt. Adam

Oblt. v. Döring

Lt. Klein

Lt. Niederhoff

Lt. Brauneck

Lt. Mohnicke

Lt. v. Schöenebeck

Lt. Bockelmann

Lt. Küppers

Oblt. Weigand

Top left: A popular postcard showing Rittmeister von Richthofen 'in his finest uniform with all of his medals, and his most winsome face' (*Sanke card*).

Top right: The two famous von Richthofen brothers pictured here in the garden behind Château Marckebeke (*Sanke card*).

Lt Meyer

Vzfw. Clausnitzer

Lt. Tüxen

Lt. Krefft

Lt. Bohlein

Lt. Gerstenberg

Top right: Rittmeister von Richthofen in conversation with two unidentified officers (*University of Maine – Floyd Gibbons Collection*).

Middle right: Jasta 11's best pilots, pictured here at Roucourt near Douai in April, 1917. From left: Sebastian Festner, Karl Emil Schäfer, Manfred von Richthofen, Lothar von Richthofen, and Kurt Wolff. Just one year later, Lothar von

Richthofen alone survived (*Sanke card & George Williams Collection*).

Bottom right: Manfred von Richthofen with Major Thomsen (left) and Gen Lt Ernst von Hoeppner, May 1917 (*Sanke card*).

Bottom left: Manfred and Lothar von Richthofen at Roucourt in April, 1917 (*Public Domain*).

Top left: A mechanic helps Lothar von Richthofen down from his Albatros DIII. Lothar's airplanes always carried his chosen color of yellow, the regimental color of his former unit, Dragoon Regiment 'von Bredow' No. 4. The regimental color of Manfred's original unit, Uhlan Regiment 'Kaiser Alexander III of Russia' No. 1 was red. (*University of Maine – Floyd Gibbons Collection*).

Top right: Lothar von Richthofen, in the same flying attire as above, greets his father after a flight. One can only wonder if his first words were "Hello, Papa, I have just shot down an Englishman" (*University of Maine – Floyd Gibbons Collection*).

Bottom left: Major Albrecht Freiherr von Richthofen (*Original book*).

Middle right: Fokker Dr1 F.102/17 in which Wolff was later killed (*via Norman Franks*).

Bottom right: Richthofen visits Jasta 10, Awoignt, March 1918. From left to right: Löwenhardt, Bodenschatz, Kühn, von Richthofen, Heldmann, Schäfer, Aue, and Grassmann (*Original book*).

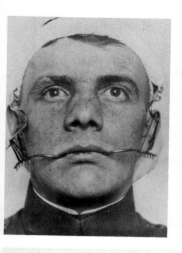

Top left: Lothar following his crash of 13 March 1918. The injuries to his nose and right eye are clearly visible (*University of Maine – Floyd Gibbons Collection*).

Top right: Taken at Lechelle, von Richthofen and pilots March 1918, left to right: Wolfram von Richthofen, Scholz, Karjus, Joachim Wolff, Lischke, MvR, Löwenhardt, Steinhauser and Weiss. Note parachute harness (*via Norman Franks*).

Middle: Richthofen's quarters at Lechelle airfield. If you look closely, you can see Moritz lying on the stacked material in front of the windows. (*Original book*).

Bottom left: Richthofen with his dog, Moritz (*Public Domain*).

Bottom right: Udet's quarters at Lechelle (*Public Domain*).

Top left: Richthofen's simple will naming Reinhard as his successor (*Original book*).

Top right: Jagdgeschwader I's tent encampment at Cappy, April 1918 (*Original book*).

Middle left: Willi Reinhard's lucky escape in a Fokker Triplane.

Middle right: The note and photo confirming Richthofen's death which were dropped on the Cappy airfield by the Royal Air Force on Tuesday evening, 23 April 1918 (*Original book*).

Bottom left: A newspaper photo of Richthofen's memorial service on Thursday, 2 May 1918 in the old Garrison Church in Berlin. Four machine guns and an airplane propellor adorned the catafalque on which rested a black pillow (*ordenskissen*) displaying von Richthofen's man medals. An honor guard of airmen stood to either side, between four towering columns, each one topped by a bronze urn in which a flame burned. A fitting farewell to Germany's greatest airman (*University of Maine – Floyd Gibbons Collection*)

Bottom right: Wilhelm Reinhard, second commander of Jagdgeschwader I. Killed during test flight at Berlin-Adlershof on 3 July 1918 (*Original book*).

Lt. Kirschstein

Lt. Weiss

Lt. v. Rautter

Lt. Wenzel

Lt. Joachim Wolff

Offz. Stellv. Aue

Lt. Janzen

Lt. Groos

Vzfw. Scholtz

Lt. Steinhäuser

Lt. v. d. Osten

Lt. Just

Lt. Grussmann

Lt. Stapenhorst

Feldw.Lt. Schubert

Lt. Lübbert

Lt. v. Raffay

Above: The graves of Eiserbeck, Weiss, Scholtz, and Wolff at Cappy. The cross inscription is dedicated to 'their unforgotten comrades' from Jasta 11. The markers read that each man 'died a hero's death for his Fatherland'. Below the man's name is his date and place of birth, and date and place of death.

Lt. Laumann

Lt. Neckel

Lt. Grassmann

Lt. Maushake

Lt. Heldmann

Lt. Hemer

Lt. Koepsch

Lt. Schulte-Frohlinde

Lt. Noltenius

Lt. Wedel

Vzfw. Gabriel

Lt. Wolfr. v. Richthofen

Lt. Richard Wenzl

Lt. Friedrichs

Lt. v. Gluszewski

Vzfw. Niemz

Right: Löwenhardt,
Hugo Schäfer, Udet
(behind the wheel),
Meyer and
Bodenschatz
(*Original book*).

Top left: Ernst Udet after his parachute jump on 29 June 1918. Drekmann stands on the right (*George Williams Collection*).

Top right: Oblt Hermann Göring, last commander of the Jagdgeschwader Richthofen (*Original book*).

Middle left: Oblt Löwenhardt, leader of Jasta 10.

Killed in action 10 August 1918 (*Original book*).

Middle right: Lothar von Richthofen and Otto Förster, summer 1918 (*George Williams Collection*).

Bottom: Jasta 10, ready for take-off. From left: Hennig, Schibilsky, Grassmann, Heldmann, Aue, Kohlbach, Klamt and Baehren (*Original book*).

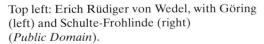

Top left: Erich Rüdiger von Wedel, with Göring (left) and Schulte-Frohlinde (right) (*Public Domain*).

Top right and bottom left: Lothar von Richthofen after the war (*University of Maine – Floyd Gibbons Collection*).

Middle right: Richthofen's former gravesite in the Invaliden Cemetery in Berlin following the dedication of the huge granite marker in November, 1937. The large wreath in front is from the new Jagdgeschwader Richthofen.

Bottom right: The Richthofen home in Schweidnitz as a musuem in the mid 1930s (*Old Postcard via Sue Hayes Fisher*).

Four views of the Richthofen museum (*Sue Hayes Fisher*).

GEDÆCHTNISSTÆTTE FÜR

MANFRED FREIHERR VON RICHTHOFEN

GEBOREN AM 2. MAI 1892   GEFALLEN AM 21. APRIL 1918

DEM
ERFOLGREICHSTEN
KAMPFFLIEGER
DES
WELTKRIEGES

DEM
UNUEBERTROFFENEN
SIEGER
IN
80 LUFTKÆMPFEN

IM JAHRE 1928 ERRICHTET
AUS SPENDEN DER DANKBAREN HEIMAT

Top left: The Richthofen memorial erected in the park across the street from his parent's home in Schweidnitz (*Old Postcard via Sue Hayes Fisher*).

Top right: Today the Richthofen memorial is crumbling away, and the bronze plaque has long since disappeared (*Author*).

Middle: Close-up view of the plaque. The inscription reads: 'Memorial for Manfred Freiherr von Richthofen. Born 2 May 1892. Fell on 21 April 1918. (Left) To the most successful combat pilot of the World War. (Right) To the undefeated victor of 80 aerial combats. (Below) Erected in the year 1928 from contrib-utions of his grateful homeland' (*Old Postcard*).

Bottom left: The Richthofen home today. The former No. 10 Striegauerstrasse stands in a sad state of disrepair. It is now an apartment house (*Author*).

lines. Instead, very early in the morning, at 7.10 a.m., Leutnant Friedrichs roars over an English balloon and brings it down, his tenth victory. With that victory, Jagdgeschwader Richthofen, called 'JG I' in the succinct jargon of the Air Service, has shot down approximately forty French airplanes in eight days. On their airdromes on the other side of the lines, the French can no longer delude themselves with talk of bad luck or chance. They now know that the Richthofen people are at work in their midst, and from now on, the blue, white, and red cockades become extremely cautious. There is scarcely a time when a French plane approaches the German lines. They give up their bombing almost entirely. Their single-seater fighters are seen flying around, very cautiously, in the sky far behind their own lines.

On the ground, however, the German attack suffocates and sinks again into the trenches and shell holes. Its tiger-like leap across the Chemin des Dames has succeeded, but the claws of the attacker are paralysed by the enemy's superior strength.

The Jagdgeschwader Richthofen feels the force of this superiority in the air as well and, now and then, a sure quarry will escape it. Despite this superiority, they always have a sure quarry on the run somewhere, whether it be bombing squadrons, ground-support or infantry-support planes, or captive balloons. It is just a matter of their getting the information in time. On this day, a relevant report is sent to headquarters:

> This morning, between 10.00 and 11.00 a.m., three enemy bombing squadrons coming from the Marne broke through and systematically bombed the Fère-en-Tardenois region.
>
> These squadrons were reported much too late. It is absolutely essential that balloon observers report the assembly of such bombing squadrons on the other side of the lines. Only in this way is successful opposition possible.

On 9 June, the Jastas take off to protect the flanks of the Eighteenth Army in conjunction with Jagdgeschwader III. The day's monotonous report: 9.00 a.m., a Spad by Leutnant Steinhäuser, his ninth victory; at almost the same minute, a Spad by Oberleutnant von Wedel, his sixth victory; and again at almost this exact, same minute, 9.00 a.m., a Spad by Hauptmann Reinhard, his nineteenth victory; 12.20 p.m., a Spad by Leutnant Steinhäuser, his tenth victory; 12.20 p.m., in the same minute, a Spad by Leutnant Wolfram von Richthofen, his second victory; 4.30 p.m., a Bréguet by Leutnant Friedrichs, his eleventh victory.

That evening, the Geschwader looks back on an incredibly proud list of victories. Since its inception, the Geschwader has shot down four hundred enemy airplanes — an almost unparalleled figure! The joy over this is not without sorrow. Leutnant Janzen, an excellent fighter pilot, did not return from a patrol. Unfortunately, he was taken prisoner.[1]

At this time, the German Army High Command tries once again to take the bull by the horns. With a savage energy, they attack with their Eighteenth and Eighth Armies, as Compiègne is decided upon as their strategic objective. Jagdgeschwader Richthofen undertakes the protection of the Eighteenth Army's flanks in the area of Noyon–Compiègne–Vic-sur-Aisne.

On 12 June, Hauptmann Reinhard shoots his twentieth opponent to pieces.

With an iron energy and constant attentiveness, the commander keeps his eye on the activity of the enemy pilots, and on the deployment of his own. His official report from this time period is of painstaking precision:[2]

> . . . If the breakthrough offensive turns into a war of movement, then deployment according to a timetable is to be unconditionally discarded. If a change of airfield is undertaken, from that moment on, each Jagdgruppe or Geschwader must work independently, for any telephone communication is as good as impossible . . .
>
> In the army, the only things which would have to be ordered each day in advance, for the following day, are:
>
> 1. The first take-off at dawn. Reason: The other Jastas are thereby given the chance to sleep in.
>
> 2. The afternoon take-off between 1.00 and 2.00 o'clock. Reason: If I require continuous take-offs against the enemy from my Jastas, then they need an hour during the day to rest.
>
> 3. The third take-off ordered is the last take-off before dark. This take-off is necessary since it is more practical not to fly late in the evenings, but to get the machines ready for the next day instead. In the meantime, freelance pursuit is the only possible way to provide relief to the infantry. It is to be understood that 'freelance pursuit' does not mean hunting with the adjacent armies, or in the support area behind the lines, but destroying the enemy upon the battlefield of the infantry from the lowest altitude as well, and flying as often as one can accomplish anything at all with his Staffeln.

---

[1] Lt Janzen had taken command of Jasta 6 when Hptm Reinhard was appointed commander of JG I.

[2] The first part of this report comes straight from the operations manual which Rittmeister von Richthofen completed just before his death.

Practical experiences in combat with the French pilots: In the first few days following the breakthrough, hardly any enemy airmen showed themselves. During the advance, there was a deployment of powerful bombing squadrons, apparently as a substitute for artillery. Since the beginning of the planned assault, the Frenchman has been very cautious. He is completely on the defensive, and only rarely pushes forward over the lines. The individual French pilot is technically very skilled, but avoids serious combat. The enemy captive balloons are situated on the average of ten kilometers on the other side of the lines, at a relatively low altitude, and are protected by enemy single-seater fighters. Attacks are very difficult and are successful only with the element of surprise . . .

Attached to this report is quite a modest request. This request has been expressed more than once, and one would think that it would have been approved long ago as a matter of course. The Jagdgeschwader, in bitter combat day after day, and practically hour after hour, has never had a doctor. The commander's request is almost timid:

The lack of a permanent medical officer has made itself felt very unpleasantly. The Geschwader has an effective strength of around 700 men, counting detached personnel, and is always wholly situated on an airfield. The distance to the nearest local doctor or field hospital is often very far. With wounded pilots returning to their own landing field, the frequent enemy air raids, and in the interest of preventive health measures, the Geschwader must have its own doctor at its disposal.

They were to wait a very long time yet for their own doctor. They waited patiently and occasionally, when someone came back wounded from a flight, the medical orderly patched him up to the best of his ability. In severe cases, the car just rumbled along for hours to the nearest field hospital, and the wounded man simply accepted the risk that entailed. They weren't very sentimental about themselves.

On 18 June, Hauptmann Reinhard travels to Adlershof near Berlin with Leutnant Kirschstein.[1] There they are to test new aircraft types as to their suitability for utilization at the Front. Richthofen himself had pushed for such tests to be carried out only and exclusively by field pilots. They alone

---

[1] This seems unlikely in view of the victory scored by Lt Kirschstein just six days later. Kirschstein most likely joined Hptm Reinhard at Adlershof sometime after 24 June 1918.

were in the position to determine which airplane types were suitable for the Front and which were not. All of the Jagdstaffeln of the Field Army sent representatives to these trials. They put the individual machines through their paces and then they submitted their opinions. As Hauptmann Reinhard bid his Geschwader goodbye, no one could possibly know that it was goodbye for ever.

In the meantime, the Geschwader is operating in the midst of the French units with an eerie regularity. In the time period from 20 to 28 June, the Geschwader shoots down 26 airplanes.

On 20 June, Leutnant Paul Wenzel, a Bréguet, fifth victory.

On 22 June, Leutnant Löwenhardt shoots down his twenty-eighth opponent.

On 23 June, 9.45 a.m., a Spad by Leutnant Heldmann, seventh victory; at this same time, a Spad by Sergeant Schumacher, first victory; at the same minute, a Spad by Leutnant Friedrichs, thirteenth victory; 12.10 p.m., a Bréguet by Leutnant Udet, thirty-first victory; 8.15 p.m., that truly splendid fighter pilot, Leutnant Udet, gets his thirty-second opponent.

On 24 June, 9.45 a.m., a Bréguet by Leutnant Kirschstein, as his twenty-seventh victory; 10.00 a.m., a Bréguet by Leutnant Udet, as his thirty-third victory.

On 25 June, 6.45 p.m., two Spads by Leutnant Udet, his thirty-fourth and thirty-fifth victories; 8.40 p.m., a balloon by Leutnant Friedrichs, number fourteen on his victory list.

On 26 June, at 8.25 p.m., Sergeant Schumacher shoots down a balloon, his second victory. Leutnant Steinhäuser, one of the Geschwader's first-rate pilots, crashes to his death following air combat.

On 27 June, 9.00 a.m., a Spad by Leutnant Friedrichs, his fifteenth victory; 9.15 a.m., another Spad by Leutnant Löwenhardt, his twenty-ninth victory; 1.00 p.m., Leutnant Friedrichs brings down yet another Spad, his sixteenth victory; 8.00 p.m., Leutnant Drekmann sets a balloon on fire with his machine guns, his fifth victory.

On 28 June, 8.20 a.m., a Spad by Leutnant Löwenhardt, thirtieth victory; 8.30 a.m., a Spad by Leutnant Friedrichs, seventeenth victory; 9.05 a.m., a Spad by Leutnant Mohnicke, eighth victory; 9.00 a.m., a Spad by Leutnant Mohnicke, ninth victory; 9.45 a.m., a Spad by Leutnant Maushake, second victory; 9.50 a.m., a Spad by Leutnant Meyer, second victory; 9.50 a.m., a Spad by Leutnant Drekmann, sixth victory; 12.30 p.m., a Spad by Vizefeldwebel Hemer, eleventh victory; 12.30 p.m., a Spad by Leutnant Löwenhardt, thirty-first victory.

On 28 June, a dispatch arrives for Leutnant Kirschstein, and is immediately forwarded to him in Adlershof with hearty congratulations. And on the next morning when Leutnant Kirschstein shows up on the airfield there, he is wearing the order *Pour le Mérite*.

On 29 June, another 'ace' has an experience that only a man as bold, fearless, and cold-blooded as the devil can live to tell about. Leutnant Udet's report concerning his jump from a Fokker DVII using a parachute:

> On 29 June 1918, I took off at 7.15 a.m. with my Staffel on a patrol. At 7.40 a.m., over Cutry, I attacked an infantry-support plane flying at an altitude of 800 meters over the area which was under heavy French shell fire. Upon my first attack, the Bréguet turned towards me and flew under me. As he did so, I observed that the observer was no longer standing at the machine gun. I therefore assumed that I had already hit the observer and, contrary to my usual habit, I attacked the enemy pilot from the flank. I suddenly noticed, however, that the French observer had reappeared from the body of the plane and, at that same moment, I took several hits, including one in the machine gun and another in the fuel tank. At the same time, the elevator and aileron cable must have been shot through, because my Fokker DVII plunged out of control. I tried everything possible to bring the plane back under control, but in vain. At an altitude of about 500 meters, the machine went over on its nose, and I could no longer bring it out of this position.
>
> It was high time to get out. I unbuckled myself, positioned myself up on the seat, and in the next moment, I was flung backwards by a tremendous draught of air. At the same time, I felt a violent jerk and realized that I had gotten hung up by my parachute harness on the front tip of the rudder. Summoning up the last of my strength, I broke the tip off and I fell free behind the airplane, tumbling repeatedly head over heels. I had already assumed that the parachute had failed when I suddenly felt a slight slowing and shortly afterwards, I hit the ground. The 'chute had opened after all, at about 80 meters. The ensuing landing was pretty hard and I sprained my left leg. I had come down west of Cutry in the middle of a heavy barrage. The enemy fired on me with machine guns shortly before and after landing. I unbuckled myself from the parachute and ran in an easterly direction. Just then I received a hard blow to the back of the head, and was knocked to the ground by a blast of air. Apparently, a dirt clod thrown up by the impact of a large-caliber shell had hit me. Shortly after that, my left cheek was hit by a small stone thrown up as well by the impact of the numerous shells around me. I ran with all my might and luckily came to the edge of the ravine north of Missy where I was met by the 16th Infantry Regiment. I was aware that I was nauseous and coughing heavily, as I had covered the distance of roughly three kilometers without a gas mask. After about three hours, the gas attack let up. I was able to reach the Paris

road and from there, Courmelles, where I was able to contact the Geschwader by telephone. I was picked up by car, and by that afternoon, I was able to carry out a more auspicious patrol.

Leutnant Udet didn't need to let the shock to his nerves subside. He hadn't even had a shock. On 30 June, he shoots down his thirty-sixth opponent; on 1 July, his thirty-seventh and thirty-eighth; on 2 July, his thirty-ninth; and on 3 July, his fortieth.

Jasta 11 and the leaders of the Geschwader's other Jastas received new machines: a Fokker with a 220 hp BMW engine. The performance of these new machines was extraordinary for the time, reaching 6,000 meters in twenty-four minutes.

On 3 July, a short radio message arrives from the Commanding General of the Air Service. Radio messages of such brevity from him are either congratulations or . . . . 'The commander of Jagdgeschwader Richthofen, Hauptmann Reinhard, crashed fatally on 3 July 1918 during a test flight at Berlin-Adlershof.'

Richthofen's successor is dead. Fate goes its strange ways. The new machine which was to be tested had been flown first there at Adlershof by the leader of Jasta 27, Oberleutnant Hermann Göring. After Göring landed, Hauptmann Reinhard climbed into the seat and took off. At an altitude of 1,000 meters, the struts broke. Miraculously, Providence watched over Oberleutnant Göring, as if ordered to preserve him for a different path, one which was some day to be prepared for the German people, on the other side of all the darkness.

Thus, five weeks after Richthofen's death, his successor dies. Richthofen's father sends a telegram: 'Heartfelt sympathy on the loss of your proud leader. May Richthofen's spirit live on in the Jagdgeschwader.' Everyone knows what this loss means, even the officials of the High Command. The Commanding General of the Air Service telegraphs:

I am deeply sympathetic over this new, grievous loss suffered by the Jagdgeschwader. Hauptmann Reinhard proved himself worthy of the weighty task of being Richthofen's successor. Under him, the Geschwader scored victories that honored the proud name which it bears. To me, that is proof that the spirit of Richthofen's victories is firmly ingrained in the Geschwader. We will all gratefully remember Hauptmann Reinhard, who was taken from us so early and so unexpectedly.

VIII UP AGAINST A SUPERIOR FORCE

On the evening of 3 July, the Geschwader adjutant went pensively into the commander's room and took into his safekeeping the *Geschwaderstock*, the stick with the thick knob that Richthofen and Reinhard had both carried. Who was to carry it now? What would be the name of the new commander? Into whose hands was the ace card of the German Air Service, the Jagdgeschwader Richthofen, to be given? That was not an easy question to answer. The adjutant was not the only one pondering the answer. The personnel advisor to the Commanding General of the Air Service was racking his brains over it, as well. The selection of candidates was not very large. Jagdgeschwader Richthofen had to get a first-rate man. The new Jagdgeschwadern II and III were led by Hauptmann Rudolf Berthold and Oberleutnant Bruno Loerzer. These two mustn't be recalled, but who should get Jagdgeschwader I? Who should be Richthofen's heir?

In five days, the decision is made. In accordance with Order No. 178654 of the Commanding General of the Air Service, under the date of 8 July 1918, Oberleutnant Hermann Göring is appointed commander of the glorious Jagdgeschwader Richthofen.

The Geschwader breathes a sigh of relief. This man is not unknown to them. He is the splendid leader of Jasta 27, victor of twenty-one aerial combats, and wears the order *Pour le Mérite*. He is the man who fulfills all of the requirements that will be tacitly placed on the commander of the first and most famous Jagdgeschwader of the Army, by both his superiors and his subordinates: he is himself a first-rate fighter pilot; in a position to command the most daring fighter pilots of the Air Service; capable of keeping the historic, heroic spirit of the Geschwader ever alive; and capable of putting these élite men into action together as a large unit against a numerical superiority of men and machines which was rapidly growing in every tactical aspect of the air war. The new commander was 'right'; he was a 'personality'.

There were still a few days to go before his arrival. These days were filled with preparations for support of the new push being planned by the Army High Command. Theirs was a bold plan: the capture of the old coronation city of Reims,[1] a breakthrough across that old, fateful river, the Marne, and the conquest of Epernay and Châlons.

On 14 July, the new commander arrived at the Geschwader in Beugneux.

---

[1] The coronations of most of the French kings took place in the cathedral here, the most famous coronation being that of Charles VII who was crowned there in 1429 in the presence of Joan of Arc.

The impression he made met their high expectations in every respect. He was the finest type of young, active officer.[1] In the quiet, well-proportioned features of his face there dwelt cold-bloodedness and energy. His eyes were clear, arresting, and calm, and when his face and eyes relaxed, one discovered the unerring common sense sparkling behind them. The man was tough. They saw that in the way he moved; they heard it in his words. It breathed from his very being. He had the Geschwader well in hand in no time.

Oberleutnant von Wedel reports that the Geschwader, Jasta leaders, and pilots have fallen in. The commander makes a short speech. He speaks of the special honor of being the commander of this unit; of the spirit in which he intends to lead the formation; of the great, fallen fighters who founded this spirit and gave it their lifeblood; and he speaks of the difficult days now in store for all of them.

Oberleutnant Göring's speech, short as it is, has an intense, illuminating power. It is not a prepared speech, but rather words formulated from the moment itself and spoken in a strangely penetrating voice. After the speech, the adjutant, Oberleutnant Bodenschatz, presents the *Geschwaderstock* to the new commander. The wooden stick, which both Richthofen and Hauptmann Reinhard had carried, is now handed over to Göring with a few respectful and heartfelt words. It had been made by the shop foreman, Holzapfel, for Richthofen in his day, and he had presented it to the Baron who had taken real pleasure in this sturdy walking stick. As the officers disperse, they are in agreement with each other and their new commander down to the last fiber of their beings. Here stands the right man in the right place at just the right time, twenty-four hours before the great offensive.

On 15 July, the artillery's well-orchestrated and terrible clockwork engine thunders forth and the infantry scrambles through the crater field in one of their wonderful advances. Over the valley of the Marne, the sky is swarming with enemy airmen. In the afternoon, the sky is filled with powerful squadrons of English single-seaters at all altitudes. The English have reappeared! That means things are coming down to the final act.

From out of these scattered squadrons, Leutnant Löwenhardt brings down his thirty-sixth opponent. With a bold dash, Leutnant Paul Wenzel shoots down a captive balloon despite vigorous defense from a veritable hurricane of machine guns, anti-aircraft guns, along with single-seater fighters. Leutnant Meyer sends a Spad smashing to the ground.

Despite these three victories in the midst of a tremendously superior

---

[1] A regular or career officer, as opposed to a reserve officer having only a wartime commission.

force, it is a bitter day for the Geschwader. Leutnant Friedrichs, one of the most cold-blooded and most daring 'balloon killers', falls. He falls, not to a skillful and lucky opponent, but to a twist of fate, one to which Leutnant Bender almost falls victim the next day as well. Geschwader Commander Göring's report concerning these two unfortunate events reads:

> On 15 July 1918, at 9.00 p.m., Leutnant Friedrichs, Jasta 10, took off on a front-line patrol, flying airplane Fokker DVII 309/18. At an altitude of 1,700 meters, the pilot flying next to Leutnant Friedrichs suddenly noticed a white trail of smoke to either side of the latter's gas tank. Leutnant Friedrichs then pointed his airplane downwards very sharply and, in the next moment, the airplane began to burn. Leutnant Friedrichs immediately jumped from the aircraft but got caught with his back to the stabilizer fin. The parachute opened properly, but in any case, it tore away as a result of the excessive weight due to the dangling body. The cords tore away roughly ten centimeters below where they were spliced to the parachute. Even during Leutnant Friedrichs' leap, several rounds were suddenly heard to go off. The airplane crashed, burning brightly, and burned to ashes on the ground. The course of events was established by several ground witnesses in the same manner. Leutnant Friedrichs' crash was fatal.
>
> According to the indisputable statements of witnesses on the ground and in the air, it must be accepted that the airplane fire was caused by the development of a leak in the gas tank. As a result of the prodigious heat in the Fokker DVII which is not drawn off adequately, the gasoline expands considerably under pressure. Development of a gas-tank leak is easily possible, since all of the gas tanks in the Fokker DVII have already given cause for complaint due to poor workmanship.
>
> Moreover, the possibility exists that, following development of the gas-tank leak, the gasoline spurting around was ignited by the phosphorus ammunition in the feed belts. A third possibility as to the originating cause of the fire can arise from sparks coming from the short muffler. Also, after the exhaust gaskets burn through, the sparks fly backwards right over the gas tank. Ignition of any gasoline squirting around is also possible here . . .
>
> A similar airplane fire occurred on 16 July, at 7.30 p.m., shortly after take-off with Fokker DVII 2063. Pilot: Leutnant Bender, Jasta 4. The airplane started to burn at an altitude of 200 meters. The pilot, Leutnant Bender, who landed smoothly by parachuting out, made the following statement concerning the incident:
>
> 'Immediately after take-off, I noticed a great heat in the airplane.

After I was about 200 meters up, I suddenly heard a couple of rounds go off. At the same moment, gasoline started spurting around inside the airplane, and the airplane began to burn. The only way to protect myself from burning was to jump immediately. I had switched off the gas and the ignition. The airplane was in a turn. I unbuckled myself, propped myself up, and was immediately hurled out of the airplane. After a short time, I felt a violent jerk on my body. The parachute harness had pulled tight around my arms and legs and I noticed that I was nearing the ground at a slow speed. I landed on my back and in doing so, I sprained my left foot.

This incident was also observed by witnesses on the ground. They saw a white trail of smoke by the airplane and heard some rounds go off at the same moment. Shortly after that, the airplane began to burn. The airplane burned almost completely in the air, and burned to nothing on the ground after impact. Since what was left of the airplane was almost totally destroyed, no other details could be determined from the remains of the gas tank.'

About an hour later, a similar incident occurred with one of Jasta 45's Fokker DVIIs. The airplane came to earth in the vicinity of Jagdge-schwader Richthofen's airfield. Consequently, the incident could be observed clearly. In the opinion of the pilot, who was still able to escape the burning airplane after impact, the gas tank first developed a leak, the gasoline spurting out in a white trail of smoke. Only later did the shots go off and the airplane begin to burn. The course of events was observed in the same way from the ground. The airplane's gas tank had taken no hits . . .

The Geschwader commander immediately orders a couple of modifications to be made on the Fokker DVII and he also suggests similar modifications of this aircraft type to headquarters.

The loss of Leutnant Friedrichs hits the Geschwader hard. Every one of these men knew that Death was playing no lottery game with them. Death had dispensed with that. He took the boldest ones. And Leutnant Friedrichs had been more than bold. He was what they called a 'crazy man'; a robust body and soul, a man with strong nerves, no matter what came at him, a soldier without faults or shortcomings, a daredevil . . . no, that word was much too soft for him. He had chosen the most daring of all attacks: the attack on captive balloons. That suited his daredevil disposition. He died in an accident. He died undefeated.

On 16 July, five airplanes are shot down from out of the enemy squadrons and destroyed. On the same day, an almost stupid accident strikes and again kills one of the best: Leutnant Kirschstein. He wanted to fly his airplane to the aviation park at Fismes. Since the plane was to remain there,[1] and he wanted to return immediately and as quickly as possible, he took along with him a rookie pilot from the Staffel,[2] who flew alongside him in another airplane, a Hannover. In Fismes, Kirschstein climbed in behind the new pilot for the return flight. This new pilot was not sufficiently familiar with the machine, he overcontrolled it, and they crashed from a height of fifty meters. They both died within just a few hours.

The Geschwader was dwindling away.

Time and again, there came promising new replacements and from the old stock emerged new names that achieved fame and honor in the Richthofen Geschwader: Leutnant Richard Wenzl, Leutnant Heldmann, Leutnant Paul Wenzel, Leutnant Bretschneider, Vizefeldwebels Hemer and Gabriel, Oberleutnant von Wedel, Leutnants Drekmann, Maushake, Wolfram von Richthofen, Meyer, Koepsch, Groos, Grassmann, Mohnicke, Just, Offizier Stellvertreter Aue, and Sergeant Schumacher.

The numerical superiority on the other side grew greater and greater, however. With a daring beyond compare, these few fighter pilots threw themselves up against those innumerable squadrons which often darkened the skies in the truest sense of the word. It had long since ceased to be an equal fight.

On 17 July, five airplanes were plucked from that wall of English squadrons.

On the ground, as well, it had not been an equal contest for a long time. The attack with the bold objectives which had begun so splendidly and which had advanced so splendidly all the way to the Marne, had at first penetrated into a void. This time, however, the void did not have its origin in a retreat by the enemy. This void was a trap. The enemy had been well-informed as to the attack. The enemy allowed the German infantry to easily overrun their weak, and almost empty front lines, lured it into their pincers . . . and then snapped them shut.

On 18 July, the enemy struck a murderous blow. After an insane barrage, the French attacked fiercely between the Aisne and the Marne with their enormously superior numbers.[3] They smashed the German front, and there were heavy casualties.[4] The retreat from the Marne became inevitable.

---

[1] For overhaul and maintenance work.

[2] Lt Johannes Markgraf who had joined Jasta 6 just five days earlier, on 11 July 1918.

[3] The Allied counteroffensive in the Marne salient by the Tenth and Sixth French Armies, and supported by 14 Allied divisions and 350 tanks.

[4] By the end of the Second Battle of the Marne, the Germans had lost approximately 168,000 men, compared to French losses of approximately 95,000.

The French and English came at them in the air as well, with a massive deployment of squadrons. Here, however, they stuck their heads in a bit too far.

Here in the French heavens, the Jagdgeschwader Richthofen wrote its deadly victory list: 6.20 a.m., a Spad by Leutnant Löwenhardt, his thirty-eighth victory; 6.20 a.m., a Spad by Vizefeldwebel Schumacher, fifth victory; 7.35 a.m., a Spad by Leutnant Heldmann, eighth victory; 8.15 a.m., a Spad by the commander, Oberleutnant Göring, his twenty-second victory.[1] ('On 18 July 1918,' read his brief, official report, 'at 8.15 a.m. I attacked a couple of Spads. I forced one Spad down and, after a dogfight, shot it down. It fell in the forested ravine near Bandry. Shortly thereafter, I observed the downing of a second Spad by Oberleutnant von Wedel. A third Spad was shot down by Oberleutnant Mohnicke.'[2]); 8.30 a.m., the Spad referred to in this report by Oberleutnant von Wedel, seventh victory; 9.15 a.m., a Bréguet by Vizefeldwebel Hemer, fifteenth victory; 9.25 a.m., a DH 9 by Leutnant Maushake, third victory; 9.30 a.m., a Sopwith by Leutnant Meyer, fourth victory; 9.50 a.m., a Spad by Vizefeldwebel Gabriel, eighth victory; 10.00 a.m., a Spad by Vizefeldwebel Gabriel, ninth victory; 10.22 a.m., a Bréguet by Vizefeldwebel Gabriel, tenth victory; 2.30 p.m., a Spad by Leutnant Löwenhardt, thirty-ninth victory; 3.30 p.m., a Spad by Vizefeldwebel Gabriel, eleventh victory. That is Jagdgeschwader Richthofen's list of victories for 18 July, a day of glory for everyone in Beugneux, from the commander down to Vizefeldwebel Gabriel, who brought down four enemy airplanes on this one day.[3]

One day earlier, the Geschwader commander sent his first official report concerning the combat situation in the air to the Commander of Aviation for the Seventh Army:

> Up till now, only French air units appeared on the Front of the Seventh Army. Since the beginning of the attack, powerful English reinforcements have arrived, numerous single-seater echelons in particular. In the area of the attack, especially in the Marne valley between Méry and Dormans–Verneuil, enemy air activity, which is numerically far superior, prevails in the afternoon and evening hours.

---

[1] This was Göring's only victory while commander of JG I.
[2] The Spad downed by Lt Mohnicke (whose rank is erroneously given as Oberleutnant here) does not appear in the squadron log as an accredited victory.
[3] Vfw Gabriel's first three victories were scored in direct defiance of Oblt Göring, who had signalled for the Geschwader to return to the airfield. He then took off again and scored his fourth victory after Göring had forbidden him to fly. The same day that Göring returned from leave, 22 August 1918, Vfw Gabriel was transferred to Armee Flug Park II and saw no further combat.

The English single-seaters, generally in several strong flights staggered in altitude, give a good account of themselves in the good, old way. The French fighter pilots, on the other hand, only rarely venture over the Front, and avoid any serious combat. In contrast to this, the French two-seaters always appear in strong squadrons flying together. They carry out their bombing raids ruthlessly, partly at low altitudes. The twin-engine Caudrons are similar in this predilection. Experience has shown that their armor plating is not penetrated by our armor-piercing ammunition even after repeated attempts. Armament consists of six machine guns (two sets of double machine guns in the back, two machine guns in front).[1] The enemy Caudron squadrons carry out their orders without regard to German fighter pilots. On 15 July 1918, during an attack on a Caudron from close range, I myself fired almost all of my ammunition. The Caudron calmly flew on without worrying about me. A serious engagement with these armored and well-armed aircraft would demand heavy sacrifices. The flak batteries must be called upon primarily for combating the Caudrons. They always fly close together and thus present a favorable target for the anti-aircraft guns.

The Geschwader was first put into action on the right flank of the Army for defense against the enemy air units advancing from the south-west. The superior enemy air operations on the battlefield south of the Marne automatically drew the Geschwader into this attack area where our troops were fighting. The individual Staffeln were taking off, in part, five times during the day. The pilots and machines cannot provide this kind of effort indefinitely.

Combining the Staffeln into a half-Geschwader and putting the whole Geschwader into action were very soon necessary. While the Geschwader was flying at the Front in these stronger, closed formations, air mastery was assured. The enemy, who is numerically far superior, can always send in fresh forces. The enemy quite cleverly takes advantage of those moments when our fighter pilots are less numerous to venture across our lines unexpectedly. Despite immediate take-offs upon relatively quick incoming reports, only in rare cases have we been able to reach and combat these squadrons which have broken through in time. The lack of direct telephone connections between Geschwader and Jagdgruppe makes uniform deployment very difficult. The laying of urgently needed lines must, at all costs, be already completed by the army prior to the attack.

The Geschwader is well-equipped with airplanes. The Fokker DVII

---

[1] The Caudron R11 was actually equipped with five Lewis machine guns, two in each cockpit, and another that fired downward.

with the BMW engine is comparable, and in part superior, to the enemy airplanes; the Fokker DVII with the high-compression Mercedes engine is a thoroughly comparable machine as well.

In the last few days, different airplanes have crashed in flames as a result of the easy ignition of the phosphorus ammunition. I have banned this ammunition. Remedy is urgently needed since attacks on captive balloons are impossible until further notice.

Göring, Oberleutnant and
Geschwader Commander

The German front was forcibly pushed back. The reports of the infantry-support pilots said that the French had broken through, nothing more and nothing less. In the early afternoon of 18 July, the members of Jagdgeschwader Richthofen saw the enemy captive balloons already standing close to their airfield at Beugneux. Towards evening, when the first enemy artillery shells struck the airfield, Oberleutnant Göring was forced to yield. They scouted out a new airfield back near the Monthussart Farm, northeast of Braine on the Vesle River. The Geschwader moved during the night.

On 17 July, Leutnant Friedrichs had been buried from the Beugneux field hospital. They were forced to leave a fine man behind in the French earth.

Mass attacks by the French followed incessantly, one after another. South of Neuilly, the first Americans appeared and, step by step, almost centimeter by centimeter, the German infantry gave way. They slowly evacuated the bridgehead at Dormans, they slowly evacuated the Marne line, and then tenaciously held the Coulonges–Fère–Oulchy front.

Flying out of the new airfield, Leutnant Löwenhardt gets his fortieth and forty-first victories on 19 July. On the same day, the brother of the late Rittmeister, Lothar Freiherr von Richthofen, having recovered from his wounds, returns and takes command of the old, glorious Jasta 11.

On 20 July, the weather is bad; the sky is overcast and visibility is poor. There is little to be seen of the enemy airmen. The Geschwader, however, makes an exception this one time, and sends its Staffeln into the ground conflict. Admittedly, this is not its responsibility, but rather the responsibility of the ground-support pilots. In the early afternoon hours, the red machines race away, right over the steel-helmeted soldiers. They leave a broad trail of death behind. Their machine guns lash the shell holes, marching columns fly in all directions in ruins, gun crews collapse by the dozens at their guns.

In the evening, around 6.00 p.m., a silent circle of officers and men stands in the military cemetery in Courcelles. Leutnants Kirschstein,

Bretschneider-Bodemer, and Markgraf are committed to the French earth. Words can scarcely express all that was associated with the name Kirschstein. He was an ideal fighter pilot, a perfect daredevil. Undying glory endured in his name.

On 21 July, the immortal honor roll continues: 8.15 p.m., a Sopwith by Oberleutnant von Wedel, his eighth victory. At the same minute, a Sopwith falls to Leutnant Wolfram von Richthofen, his third victory. At the same time, Leutnant Löwenhardt finishes off a Sopwith, his forty-second opponent.

On 22 July, at 4.20 p.m., Leutnant Richard Wenzl dispatches his fourth opponent, and in the same minute, Vizefeldwebel Hemer, his sixteenth; 7.10 p.m., Leutnant Koepsch, his fourth; 8.30 p.m., Leutnant Löwenhardt, his forty-third.

On 24 July, brave Vizefeldwebel Schumacher is severely injured and delivered to a field hospital.

On 25 July, finished off are: 7.30 p.m., a Spad by Leutnant Drekmann, his tenth victory; 7.50 p.m., a Sopwith by Leutnant Lothar von Richthofen, his thirtieth victory; 8.30 p.m., a Spad by Leutnant Just, his third victory; 8.50 p.m., a Spad by Leutnant Löwenhardt, his forty-fourth victory. With the downing of this airplane, the Jagdgeschwader Richthofen achieved its 500th victory.

Only after the achievement of this great combat record is the commander, who has fought continuously for many months on the major battle fronts, able to consider a little rest. On 26 July, the commander, Oberleutnant Göring, begins his truly well-deserved leave. Lothar von Richthofen assumes acting command of the Geschwader.

During the next few days, the enemy, with his vast superiority, continues his attacks in the air. Bombing squadrons fly over the Front in large formations. Even with all of their bravery and commitment, their numbers are too few to do anything against a superiority the likes of which they have never seen. The Jagdgeschwader shares the fate of the entire Army: the superior force facing them is beginning to grow so immense that even the bravest man's contempt for death can achieve little. In spite of this, they succeed in penetrating the enemy squadrons again and again. On 28 July, two airplanes are brought down, on 29 July, three.

The French and the Americans are pushing the Front ever further back. Monthussart Farm can no longer be held as an airfield. The airfield is moved back, to Puisieux Farm. From there, Leutnant Löwenhardt gets his forty-seventh and forty-eighth victories.

July was at an end. In this month, the final turning point of German destiny had come about, unrecognized by one and all. The German front was slowly withdrawn farther and farther; at the little river of the Vesle, they held fast. Everywhere on the horizon there stood towering clouds of smoke. The French ammunition dumps, which had been overrun and captured during the advance, were now blown up since they were unable to haul the munitions along with them. Terrible explosions thundered every-where in the sky, and whole forests of flame blazed.

The Staffeln of Jagdgeschwader Richthofen taking off on 1 August had a splendid overview of these countless, gigantic conflagrations. They didn't take much time to enjoy this spectacle, however, for there were more important matters at hand: the English, American and French squadrons swarming over the Front. By the evening of 1 August, the Geschwader had destroyed eleven enemy airplanes, an entire echelon, without the loss of a single man or machine of their own.

Leutnant Udet had returned from leave. Filled afresh with his cheerful, and crazy recklessness, on this day he increased his victory list to the numbers 41, 42, 43. Vizefeldwebel Hemer increased his to numbers 17 and 18, and Leutnant Lothar von Richthofen increased his to numbers 31 and 32. On 4 August, Leutnant Udet gets his forty-fourth.

During the night of 7 to 8 August, they heard heavy artillery fire and, since the true front-line soldier had a strange sense for extraordinary events, this heavy artillery barrage during the night seemed rather disturbing to the Jagdgeschwader Richthofen. There had to be something very wrong somewhere.

On the morning of 8 August, the acting commander of the Geschwader, Leutnant Lothar von Richthofen, was summoned to the Second Army by a radio message. Accompanied by Leutnant Löwenhardt, he flew over and when the two of them returned, they brought terrible news. The Geschwader was to fly by the quickest route to the Second Army where a catastrophe had occurred. The catastrophe of 8 August, the day of which Ludendorff writes: 'The eighth of August was the black day of the German Army in the history of the war.'

Early in the morning of this day, inside a protecting wall of fog, thickened even more by an artificial fog, the Canadians, Australians, and French attacked the German front between the Somme and the Luce Rivers with enormous swarms of tanks, and overran it totally. The English had penetrated deeply near Villers-Bretonneux. The High Command threw whatever they had at hand up against the tanks, and that included the Jagdgeschwader Richthofen.

They were sent into a veritable witch's cauldron. At the same low altitude as the scattered clouds which offered the English ground-support planes excellent cover, the English put into action an air operation, the like of which was totally unprecedented. At Löwenhardt's suggestion, only the old pilots who were experienced against the English flew in the afternoon, in order to avoid unnecessary losses. They flew the forty-minute route from Chambry to Peronne. On the Somme south of Peronne, they were struck by the peculiar smell in the air, originating from the English engines which were rich in castor oil. For the time being, however, there was nothing to be seen. When they went a little further, however, on the lower edge of the clouds, above them they could see the English pulling away, and it was a joy to see. It was just very difficult to get close to them. As soon as they attacked, the English disappeared into the clouds. Nevertheless, they fired anytime they got the chance.

The Richthofen pilots landed at a flying unit to take on fuel and ammunition, but unfortunately, the mechanics there set about it so ineptly that the pilots stood on the airfield and watched in a grim rage as the English flew around overhead. More than once, they were forced to dash right and left and throw themselves into shell holes as the Tommies came in low and raked the German machines with machine-gun fire. Six Bristol Fighters, for example, came down to 100 meters in order to empty their machine guns. Finally, everything was again ready and they could take off.

The Jagdgeschwader went to work in this witch's cauldron, and they did good work. Shortly after 5.00 p.m., the red machines turned up right in the midst of the enemy squadrons. At 5.30 p.m., Leutnant Udet opens the fight with the downing of an SE 5, his forty-fifth victory. An hour later, he gets his forty-sixth opponent. Leutnant Löwenhardt finishes off his forty-ninth, fiftieth, and fifty-first opponents; Leutnant Lothar von Richthofen his thirty-third, thirty-fourth, and thirty-fifth.

They were used to working on the English. The Geschwader had destroyed twelve opponents by that evening. The Geschwader returned to Puisieux Farm that night, in order to take off from there again the following day. One of the pilots spent the night with a flying unit near the Somme bridge at Brie. It was like an insane asylum there.

There now started quite an air operation! The air was buzzing continuously with Englishmen bombing the bridge. In the process, one time they hit a nearby munitions depot which then began to burn. All night long, one part of the depot after another went up, so that at any given moment you were jumping straight up in bed. At the same time, there were the constant impact of the bombs, the horrible noise of the columns, the moaning of the wounded, and the machine-gun fire of the bombers. English single-seaters flew continuously over our field. When our own bombers returned to their nearby fields from their work, the English were waiting for them. When our planes were then given the landing light, they were attacked along with the spotlights.

On the following day, 9 August, Jagdgeschwader Richthofen once again flew to the battlefield and early in the morning, around 7.00 a.m., the pilots again squeezed the triggers of their machine-guns. 7.25 a.m., a Sopwith by Leutnant Heldmann, his ninth victory; 7.30 a.m., a DH 9 by Leutnant Lothar von Richthofen, his thirty-sixth victory; 7.35 a.m., a Sopwith by Leutnant Just, his fourth victory; 7.40 a.m., a Sopwith by Leutnant Löwenhardt, his fifty-second victory; 8.00 a.m., a DH 9 by Leutnant Paul Wenzel, his tenth victory; 8.00 a.m., a DH 9 by Unteroffizier Reimers, his second victory; 4.20 p.m., a DH 9 by Leutnant Maushake, his sixth victory; 4.25 p.m., a Sopwith by Leutnant Udet, his forty-eighth victory; 6.40 p.m., a DH 9 by Leutnant Lothar von Richthofen, his thirty-seventh victory; 6.55 p.m., a Sopwith by Leutnant Löwenhardt, his fifty-third victory; 9.20 p.m., a Sopwith by Leutnant Udet, his forty-ninth victory.

That evening, the Geschwader returns to Puisieux Farm with the proud number of eleven aircraft downed. Vizefeldwebel Hemer has been lightly wounded in air combat, but he stays with the unit, and Leutnant Reinhardt, lightly wounded on both feet, remains in the field hospital. Leutnant Löwenhardt has been promoted to Oberleutnant. The pace at which he, Lothar von Richthofen, and Leutnant Udet have been scoring has been incredible.

On 10 August, a new airfield in Ennemain was finally prepared and the Geschwader moved in. It was a primitive, advance landing field. They slept on straw on the floor of a hastily erected hut, and their provisions consisted of bread they had brought along with them. On this day, Leutnant Udet almost caught up with Leutnant Löwenhardt's victory count; he shot down his fiftieth and fifty-first opponents. Oberleutnant Löwenhardt dispatched his fifty-fourth opponent. And then the God of Battle singled him out from the Geschwader and destroyed a brave man.

Shortly after Löwenhardt downed his fifty-fourth plane, at 12.15 p.m., the machines of Oberleutnant Löwenhardt and Leutnant Wentz collided in mid-air. Leutnant Wentz jumped from his machine with his parachute and landed smoothly; Oberleutnant Löwenhardt plunged to his death. Leutnant Wentz tells about this catastrophe:

> We were taking off three to four times a day, with a flight time of about an hour and a half at any given time. Each flight brought wild dogfights and losses on both sides, although the losses on the other side were always greater. For any comrade of ours who was shot down, there were at least three or more of theirs.
>
> On 10 August, at the noon hour, the engines were again cranked up. With our splendid Fokkers (DVII biplanes, the newest model on the Western Front) we quickly climbed to an altitude of about 5,000

meters, heading in the direction of the Front. Due to the scattered clouds, it was rather hazy at this altitude also, and very soon we had encountered a large English squadron. The usual dogfight began and everyone very quickly sought out and found one or more opponents. Already in the course of the next few minutes, here and there you saw burning airplanes shooting to earth with long trails of dark-red flame. Friend and foe, but mostly foe.

I watched as Löwenhardt sat behind an Englishman, but then suddenly broke off from him in a wide left-hand turn after a series of machine-gun bursts. There were certainly plenty of other opponents on hand. What's more, I believed he wanted to break off anyway since we were already pretty far on the other side of our lines. With this assumption in mind, with a short dive I got behind the Tommy who was maybe about 200 meters below me. I got him in my sights and my series of machine-gun bursts rained into his visibly cowering body from close range. Sticking tight to him in my machine, during my last rounds I was no more than 15 meters away from him, for in diving on him, I had reached a very high speed. Suddenly, just above me to the right and close enough to touch, I see Oberleutnant Löwenhardt's yellow machine and in the next instant, the wheels of his machine's under-carriage (probably the left wheel) strike my upper right wing.

While I was shooting at the Tommy from a horizontal direction, Löwenhardt, contrary to my assumption, had once again engaged him obliquely from above. I couldn't see Löwenhardt because I was firing, and he couldn't see me either because he had a limited view downwards due to the lower wing of his machine. So the collision had been unavoidable.

Somewhat stunned in that first moment, for just a few seconds I saw Löwenhardt's yellow machine shooting away over me in a jerky manner. A piece of fabric, almost the size of a tablecloth, tore away from my upper right wing. Instantly, my machine went over on its nose and went down. All of the controls failed. Several quick movements of the control stick had no effect on my crate. Spinning for a few seconds, it then plunged straight down at a rate of speed considerably higher than the maximum (at that time, top speed was about 200 km per hour), for in my poorly contained excitement, I forgot to throttle back the engine.

During this plunge, looking straight down to the far-distant ground, I was sitting on my parachute pack, fastened in by leg and shoulder straps which were supposed to prevent my being thrown out during loops and spins and so on. What to do? I certainly had no feeling of fear; I was young — twenty years old — my nerves were intact. At the moment, despite the altitude of more than 4,000 meters, I fancied myself still quite safe sitting there. I simply couldn't believe that it could all be over for me so quickly.

Unstable at that terrific rate of speed, my machine raced on towards the ground, straight towards the tumult of the shell positions on the Somme. At that moment I envied the infantry down below, to which I had belonged for three years.

A decision had to be made if I were to get out of this devilish situation. At first I made up my mind not to jump. Maybe the impact would result in nothing more than some broken arms and legs . . . but that was, of course, sheer nonsense. Anything that landed down there was pulp. So — out of the crate!

I pulled on the wire pin which would release the belts connected at my chest, but it was stuck too tightly. I tore at it once more, it released, and in the next second I was pulled out of the machine with a jerk. I was without any support. Below me, the plane, now left to its own devices, plunged on towards the ground. Suddenly I felt a strong jerk upwards. It felt to me as if someone above me wished to tear the flight suit from my body. The parachute had opened. I floated and swung slowly down towards the ground.

Due to the powerful jerk at the opening of the parachute, however, both the main harness around my body, which consisted of strong hemp cords about ten centimeters wide, as well as one leg strap, had broken. The straps slid up to my armpits. With one hand, I reached up to where they were connected to the parachute. I did that quite automatically because I had no real understanding that the straps breaking could have been my undoing. I was quite calm and waved happily to my comrades who were flying around watching me. I knew I was saved.

I did not know what had happened to Löwenhardt in the meantime, however.

Minutes passed during which I swung downward. They seemed like an eternity to me. Slowly, much too slowly, the ground drew nearer. I was then suddenly driven towards the east, in the direction of home, and that was my great good fortune because I was in enemy territory at the time of the crash.

I now saw more clearly what was going on down below and heard it as well — the hell on the Somme. I had been an infantryman for three years, at Verdun, Reims, Dixmude and so on. I knew what it was like. During my rough landing on the escarpment of a shot-up communication trench, I was greeted by the finest artillery barrage this region had to offer and the likes of which I had almost forgotten. I had landed scarcely 50 meters behind the shell positions of the forward line.

I saw no one at first, then an infantryman, muddy from head to foot like an infantryman in the true front lines usually is, came creeping slowly over to me. In the meantime I pulled my parachute, my life-saver (which I have today, still well-preserved), down into the trenches. A short conversation ensued with the soldier who had at first taken me for a Tommy, I then started towards the rear with the old, familiar bounds of an infantryman. Very soon I came to a badly battered field artillery emplacement, then to a howitzer battery. There they explained to me that they had observed everything with interest, and that three machines had crashed, another two besides mine. I assumed the last two had been Tommies. Later I got a car from the artillery commander which took me out to the Jagdgeschwader's airfield.

Up to that point, I hadn't gotten very excited. Neither the parachute jump, nor the long suspension in the air, nor the tricky landing on the ground in the midst of the heavy artillery barrage had particularly upset me. I was also looking forward to a jubilant reception at the airfield, but I saw only sorrowful faces. Lothar von Richthofen told me that Löwenhardt was down, too, but he was dead!

I cannot describe the emotional blow I took. I suffered over him a long time, and he returned in countless dreams. It was simply incomprehensible to me. I could not believe it. In my opinion, there hadn't even been a collision up there, but just a touch of my delicate right wing with the sturdy wheel on the undercarriage of Löwenhardt's machine! After all, his airplane had shot away over me with a jerk! I knew quite certainly that it was impossible for damage to my comrade's machine to have resulted from it.

But the fact remained: Löwenhardt was no longer with us. In combat with his fifty-fourth opponent, the fate of the fighter pilot had over-taken him. He went to his death undefeated. For some undetermined reason, he jumped from his machine but his parachute did not open. He fell to earth like a stone. It was the darkest day of my wartime life. If only it had never happened.

Only one single comfort helped me through the next few days: the assurance of my Staffel leader, Baron Lothar von Richthofen, that I was not to blame. 'Such things often just happen,' he said to me, calmly. 'It has already happened to others as well.'

The Commanding General of the Air Service telegraphs from Supreme Headquarters:

The news of Oberleutnant Löwenhardt's heroic death has affected me deeply. He will live on in our memory as one of our most successful and tenacious fighter pilots, and as an example of a daring and successful leader.

These are difficult days.

Opposite the notes for 11 August listing four aircraft downed, among them Leutnant Udet's fifty-second victory and Leutnant von Richthofen's thirty-eighth, there is another note: Leutnant Paul Wenzel, wounded in air combat, taken to field hospital, St Quentin; Leutnant von der Wense, Jasta 6, did not return from a flight (dead); Leutnant Festler, Jasta 11, did not return from a flight (dead).

On this day, the Geschwader moves once again, this time to Bernes. The airfield is very large and after getting rid of a few holes and trenches, it could be passable. Billeting was in the usual English corrugated-metal huts; the machines went into tents.

On 12 August, the Geschwader shoots down five enemy aircraft. With a blunt, taciturn monotony, the records report: 9.30 a.m., a Sopwith by Leutnant Wolfram von Richthofen, his fifth victory; 9.35 a.m., a Sopwith by Leutnant Just, his fifth victory; 9.35 a.m., a Sopwith by Leutnant Lothar von Richthofen, his thirty-ninth victory; 9.50 a.m., a Sopwith by Leutnant Lothar von Richthofen, his fortieth victory; 11.30 a.m., an SE 5 by Leutnant Udet, fifty-third victory. On 13 August, just as blunt:

> Due to the heavy losses of the last few days, Geschwader condensed to one Staffel. Collaboration with Jagdgeschwader III and Jagdgruppe Greim.

The Crown Prince telegraphs:

> Jagdgeschwader Richthofen is departing from my Army Group following glorious achievements. During its time with us, it has over-come 184 opponents. Under its active commander, it brought relief to the hard-fighting troops on the ground and, in so doing, achieved its 500th air victory. My thanks and my appreciation go with the Jagdge-schwader as it departs. With particular joy, I have taken note of the fact that, on the day the Geschwader changed bases, it was able to actively intervene on the new Front by downing 13 of the enemy. Together with the Geschwader, I mourn the loss of brave comrades, in particular the loss of Oberleutnant Löwenhardt, whose exemplary achievements will remain unforgettable.
>
> Wilhelm,
> Crown Prince of Germany
> and of Prussia

On 13 August, Leutnant Lothar von Richthofen is wounded in the thigh during air combat. It is his third wounding. Acting command of the Geschwader is assumed by Leutnant Udet, who on 14 August can enter his fifty-fourth opponent in his victory list.

With the wounding of Leutnant Lothar von Richthofen, the Geschwader suffers an almost indescribable loss. Within quite a short time, he had raised his list of victories to the proud number of forty. Cut from the same, hard wood as his fallen brother, Manfred, he was uncompromising in his soldierly virtues, and chivalrous as an opponent. He was a fine person and extremely good-looking. The two Richthofen brothers stuck together through thick and thin. They were bound by one of the rarest friendships and camaraderies ever known between two men. The one was worthy of the other.

On 14 August, Leutnant Laumann assumes the leadership of Jasta 10. He comes from Jasta 66 with a victory score of twenty-four. From this time on, the heroic struggle of the Jagdgeschwader Richthofen will be carried out as a singular, continuous, and sublime song of ultimate audacity, utmost devotion, and ultimate sacrifice. There is almost nothing else to be done. Hour after hour, the enemy now hurls at the Front the endless abundance of men and machines streaming in from around the world. On the ground and in the air, the sheer weight of this unparalleled numerical superiority gradually crushes any possibility of fighting it in a meaningful way. A swarm of squadrons of every kind: bombers, infantry-support planes, observation planes, artillery reconnaissance planes, ground-support planes, fighters. It is becoming more and more difficult to carve a piece from this vast wall of airplanes now and then.

Bit by bit, one after another, almost day by day, the Geschwader Richthofen threw its best fighter pilots into this hell, and gradually, one by one, they did not return. These geniuses of flying ability and marksmanship, these unbelievably cold-blooded, fearless, and tenacious young men know what is in store for them when after take-off, high in the French sky, they spot the enemy squadrons whose machines are of the finest materials, materials which have long since become a fairy tale for the Germans. It is with reverence and gnawing envy that they stand occasionally before a captured enemy machine with its nickel, copper, and rubber parts, with the costly fittings, with all of the refinements only an industry with unlimited materials at its disposal can produce.

Once again, they themselves have nothing else with which to oppose these machines but their own selves and the glowing hearts that beat for Germany within them. To be sure, whenever one of these hearts has ceased to beat and one of these young faces is now lifeless, there come other hearts afire with equal devotion to the struggle; there come other faces in which glowing eyes sparkle, but it is not like it is on the other side.

Over there, thousands upon thousands of fresh, well-nourished young Englishmen, Frenchmen, Canadians, Australians and Americans stand ready in vast multitudes to fill the gaps, with the certainty of a colossal force behind them. On the German side, however, they know that they must fight with their last remaining strength. Their Fatherland, bled white, can send no more vast multitudes of fresh, well-nourished young men into the field. All these thoughts are more than bitter, but whatever they can do, in the name of their homeland which is in such deadly peril, in the name of the great, fallen airmen who sacrificed their lives, in the name of the utmost, manly bravery, they do.

Day after day, they breach the walls of the enemy squadrons. On 19 August, Leutnant Matzdorf shoots down his second opponent, Leutnant Laumann downs his twenty-fifth, Leutnant Heldmann downs his eleventh, and Offizier Stellvertreter Aue downs his eighth. On 21 August, Leutnant Udet downs his fifty-seventh and fifty-eighth. On 22 August, Leutnant Udet downs his fifty-ninth and sixtieth, Leutnant Laumann downs his twenty-sixth and twenty-seventh, and Leutnant Kohlbach, his third. On this day, the commander, Oberleutnant Göring, returns from leave and resumes command of the Geschwader. At the same time, following the rotation, Leutnant Udet goes on four weeks' leave.

The fight continues against the enemy squadrons, with sacrifice after sacrifice. On 22 August, Leutnant Rolff, Jasta 6, is buried. On 23 August, Leutnant von Barnekow, Jasta 11, is wounded in both thighs during air combat, but remains with the unit. On 24 August, Oberleutnant Grosch, Jasta 4, is wounded by a shot in the arm during air combat. On the same day, the body of Oberleutnant Löwenhardt is laid out at the airfield, then transported home. On 27 August, Leutnant Wolff, Jasta 6, is badly injured during an emergency landing, and is delivered to the Auxiliary Field Hospital in Rouy.

The loss of machines is so great that the whole Geschwader possesses the strength of just one Staffel. The duty which the commander has to discharge in this difficult situation is now a completely new one. It is fundamentally different from the work of the earlier commanders. The numerical superiority of the enemy machines is increasing at an unbelievable rate. The Jagdgeschwader Richthofen throws itself up against this technologically superior force with an undiminished, even a growing rashness and contempt for death. The inevitable result is enormous losses.

Sometimes the Jagdgeschwader Richthofen is so depleted that it must be condensed into a half-Geschwader and even to a single Staffel at times. The commander is facing a completely new and unprecedented situation. It is no longer a matter of increasing his own victory list at a hellish pace. His own ambition must be immediately put aside in the face of a superhuman task: to pull, time and time again, the depleted ranks of the Geschwader together with an iron fist; to compensate everywhere; to direct deployment against the enemy with cunning skill; and by a fervent will to maintain and inspire the inner fighting strength of this dwindling little unit. The Geschwader commander, Oberleutnant Göring, with his incredible energy, his vitality, and his whole influential personality, discharged this superhuman duty splendidly.

During these days the new English offensive begins near Bapaume. Splendidly equipped, wonderfully provisioned, with brand-new divisions protected by a mighty artillery, guarded by a mighty air force, accompanied by brand-new tanks . . . in this way they come, onward against the emaciated faces of the German infantry, crouching in their trenches for weeks on end without relief, onward against the German artillery, grimly shooting off shell after shell with their worn-out guns . . . onward they come. They are in perfect condition. They are not suffering in the least from depressing thoughts. Their muscles do not sag, and their uniforms hang splendidly about their well-kept shoulders and are made of the finest material . . . onward they come.

Under the weight of this mighty machine, step by step, the German front gives way, but it does not give way entirely. From every shell hole, thin hands raise up to hurl hand grenades; gaunt faces peer intently over machine-gun sights; here and there, skinny figures in baggy uniforms throw themselves against the elegant attackers. The world knows little of the noble countenance of the front-line German soldiers of that day. In a hundred years, perhaps, the world will look up and, ashamed and dismayed, will realize what incredible accomplishments were achieved here by these modest, patient, heroic, exhausted, and drained men.

On 2 September, the Jagdgeschwader Richthofen also repairs farther back and occupies the airfield in Busigny. For the first time in a long time, it was a well-prepared field with hangars, work rooms and good quarters. The Geschwader did not vacate the old airfield at Bernes without taking several more victories with them. On 30 August, Leutnant Laumann shot down his twenty-eighth opponent, and Offizier Stellvertreter Aue, his ninth. On 31 August, Oberleutnant von Wedel downed his tenth, Leutnant Schulte-Frohlinde downed his first, and Leutnant Koepsch, his seventh.

On the last day of August, the Jagdgeschwader's modest wish for its own doctor is finally fulfilled. By order of the Second Army's doctor, Medical Officer Fisser is ordered to the Geschwader from Armee Flug Park II.

The commander's activity report for the month of August tells in terse words something of the superiority of the enemy's equipment.

... the enemy biplanes are very well-armed and fly extremely well in squadron formation, even if attacked by several German single-seaters together. They are equipped with either armored or fireproof fuel tanks ... On the Seventh and Second Army Fronts, quite often there were enemy captive balloons which were very often attacked repeatedly without managing to set them on fire ...

So, there is almost nothing more to be done. From now on, all their bravery, all their daredevilry, proves of no avail against the new equipment on the other side. From now on, what good does it do the German pilot to have the enemy aircraft within reach of his machine-gun fire, if his bullets just ricochet off the armor plating, if the fuel tank can no longer be shot to pieces, and if even the enemy airman himself sits behind an armored plate? What good does it do the coldblooded 'balloon killer' if he roars away right over the enemy balloon again and again, shooting his phosphorus ammunition into the gasbag, if the balloon's cover is so wonderfully impregnable that it will no longer burn?

All this would be enough to intimidate the Richthofen people ... if they would let themselves be intimidated. Oberleutnant Göring's face grows more stern in these days. Let them have their armor plating; we will get them anyway! Let them make their captive balloons impregnable; we will finish them off anyway!

Right! On 2 September, Oberleutnant von Wedel shoots down an armored infantry-support plane. It is his eleventh victory. On 4 September, Leutnant Just shoots down a captive balloon. It smokes, steams, then burns and rushes to earth like a big lump despite its fireproofing.

On 5 September, the sky was again full of very high cumulus clouds and as they flew over the Front, not one person was to be seen. Near Croisilles, however, three English captive balloons were standing there so impudently that Leutnant Richard Wenzl ignored their fireproofing and decided to attack. In a dive from an altitude of 5,000 meters with his engine throttled back, he pushed out over the balloons towards the English hinterland. His attack came as a total surprise. Because he took no flak and also because the observer, oddly enough, didn't jump out, Leutnant Wenzl feared a trap and so he very calmly flew around the balloon one time. He finally watched as two observers jumped at once. So! A staff balloon! He now shot a burst into it and, lo and behold, the balloon began to smoke and steam, slowly caught fire, and went down, enveloped in flame. At precisely the same minute, Leutnant Schliewen had ventured upon the next captive balloon and shot it down also, for the first victory of his life.

Those are the rays of hope. On the same day, Leutnant von Winterfeld falls to his death from out of his burning airplane.

On 6 September, Leutnant Wolfram von Richthofen shoots down his fifth opponent, and Leutnant Maushake, his seventh. On 7 September, four enemy airplanes are brought down. Among them are the sixth and seventh victories of Leutnant Wolfram von Richthofen and the twelfth victory of Oberleutnant von Wedel. On 15 September, the new leader of Jasta 6, Leutnant Neckel, gets his twenty-fifth opponent, and his twenty-sixth on 18 September.[1]

Towards the end of the month, the Jagdgeschwader Richthofen is sent to Metz when the Americans attempt a breakthrough west of there. When it arrives there in the course of the twenty-first and twenty-second of September, Jagdgeschwader II has actually already taken care of everything. The gentlemen of Jagdgeschwader II relate wonderful things about the splendid days they have experienced in the air over Metz. In just a few days, they (Jagdgeschwader II) had shot down eighty-nine American airplanes. The American pilots didn't have the slightest experience in air combat, and the tough, experienced, and wily German pilots had taken one American after another out of the air with ease.

There were still a few tidbits for the Jagdgeschwader Richthofen. Leutnant Udet shot down his sixty-first and sixty-second in the airspace over Metz. The situation in the air here was so desperate and so hopeless for the Americans that even Leutnant Udet was overcome by a certain emotion, and there was one time, after an entire American echelon had been wiped out, that he allowed one enemy pilot to fly home undisturbed 'so that at least one person can bear the sad tidings'.

On 29 September, Oberleutnant von Wedel, Leutnant Mohnicke,[2] and Leutnant Laumann received the Knight's Cross of the Hohenzollern House Order.

October approached with wintery weather everywhere and poor weather for flying. In the first few days of October, little happened. On 8 October, the Geschwader is transferred to Marville where the Fifth Army is locked in heavy defensive fighting against the Americans. On 10 October, there is finally some better weather and the Geschwader doesn't dally long: five victories are recorded on this day. Then there comes a long period of bad weather. On the enemy's side as well, there is not the slightest air activity. There is no one to be seen.

On 23 October, at 12.55 p.m., Leutnant Noltenius races over a captive balloon and brings it down; at 4.05 p.m., he shoots down a Spad, and at 5.35 p.m., he again races over a captive balloon and brings it down, scoring his

---

[1] Lt Ulrich Neckel, who came from Jasta 19, was given command of Jasta 6 on 1 September 1918.
[2] Lt Mohnicke had been posted out on 8 September 1918.

sixteenth, seventeenth, and eighteenth air victories on this day. Leutnant Neckel gets his twenty-seventh victory.

From out of the haze and fog, from out of the walls of clouds and rain, as soon as it is at all possible, the Jagdgeschwader streaks aloft. On 27 October, Leutnant Laumann receives the order *Pour le Mérite*.[1] This high decoration has become more rare; the prerequisites for it have now been raised. On 28 October, Leutnant Noltenius again gets a captive balloon. Despite their fireproofing, they still seem to burn now and then.

October's poor weather persists.

The Jagdgeschwader Richthofen hears precious little of the events back home and on the rest of the Front, nor are they particularly curious. They have enough problems of their own. They impatiently await every hour in which the weather clears a little. They sense quite clearly that on every front the scale of victory is tipping towards the other side, and all the more quickly the closer it gets to winter. But they are not there to rack their brains over it. They are there to give all that is humanly possible to the fight. In the relative isolation of their airfield, they hear less than the infantry, throughout whose ranks the wildest rumors are already being whispered, and yes, already being spoken and discussed above anything else. The same fog which lies over the landscape and which for a time makes any flying impossible, envelops the Jagdgeschwader Richthofen mentally as well. They know just little bits and pieces of what is brewing.

On 29 October, they again penetrate the American and English squadrons. They have just been waiting for the skies to clear somewhat, and in the afternoon, that time has come. Leutnant Richard Wenzl shoots down his ninth opponent; Leutnant Schliewen, his second; Leutnant Rieth, his first; and Leutnant Grassmann, his eighth. Leutnant Fischer does not return from a front-line patrol.[2]

On 30 October, the Jagdgeschwader's operating area is extended as far as the Aisne River. Just as the lines of defense are growing ever thinner for the infantry on the ground, and the enemy's concentrated divisions are growing ever more dense, it is exactly the same in the air. 'Operating area extended as far as the Aisne' means that, from now on, it is always one against a multitude. On this day, Leutnant Neckel gets his twenty-eighth, Leutnant Heldmann his thirteenth, and Leutnant Grassmann his ninth. On 31 October, Leutnant Neckel shoots down his twenty-ninth opponent.

How many men are actually still holding back the countless enemy squadrons as far as the Aisne River? The Geschwader's total ration strength, as of 31 October 1918, is sixty-three officers, including doctors and

---

[1] Lt Laumann was the last member of JG I to receive the *Pour le Mérite*.
[2] Killed in action near Montfaucon.

clerks, and 484 non-commissioned officers and enlisted men. A small unit!

The final, difficult, fateful month begins. From here and there, rumors are now reaching Marville as well. Something must be very wrong to the rear. They are well aware of this, but they do not get involved any further in any such thoughts or discussions.

From Grandpré to Dun, the American offensive with its enormous masses of men, artillery, and tanks again began like a review parade. The German infantry, however, spread out in countless shell holes and pitifully few in number, has pockets of a few soldiers here and there. The German infantry has seen to it that the splendidly matched, splendidly equipped, and incredibly cheerful Americans may very well have fallen in as if for a parade march, but that their elegant rhythm will be lost after their first foolish and cocky steps. The losses suffered by the attackers are enormous. From every dugout, from every remaining bit of wall, from every tree stump, from the edge of every hill, death spews forth.

High above the German soldiers, the Jagdgeschwader Richthofen roars into the squadrons hanging as thick as grapes in the sky overhead. It is 3 November, and a fine, clear day. And a bad afternoon for the others. 2.55 p.m., a Spad by Leutnant Richard Wenzl, his tenth victory; 2.55 p.m., a Spad by Leutnant Richard Wenzl, his eleventh victory; 3.15 p.m., a DH 9 by Leutnant Noltenius, his twentieth victory;[1] 3.50 p.m., a Spad by Leutnant von Köckeritz, his third victory; 4.05 p.m., an AR by Leutnant Gussmann, his fifth victory; 4.45 p.m., a Spad by Leutnant Hildebrandt, his first victory; 4.50 p.m., a Spad by Leutnant Geppert, his first victory; 4.50 p.m., a Spad by Leutnant Reinhardt, his first victory. Leutnant Maushake is severely wounded in air combat.

The spirit of Richthofen: in the face of a superior force that could disconcert even experienced pilots, three young officers score their first victories. This new generation of pilots comes from a good mold.

There is little rest for them now. The American ground attacks continue nonstop. As the waves of men are shot down, there come new waves of men. Behind these come new waves. Over and over again, new waves of men. And in the air, if some enemy squadrons turn back, in their places come others, and behind these still others, over and over again. When the machines of Jagdgeschwader Richthofen land, the pilots scarcely bother to look at the bullet holes in their wings. They return from each air engagement with a heightened sense of wonder that they have returned at all.

---

[1] Lt Noltenius had achieved the number of victories required for award of the *Pour le Mérite*, but the proposal was not acted upon before the Armistice. However, he did receive the Knight's Cross with Swords of the Royal Hohenzollern House Order on 8 November 1918.

On 4 November, they drive four enemy machines to earth: Leutnant Koepsch, his ninth; Leutnant Noltenius, who is working his way up to 'ace', his twenty-first; Leutnant Schulte-Frohlinde, his fourth; and Vizefeldwebel Niemz, his third. The fact that these few fighter pilots are able to roar around in the midst of the enemy squadrons and still come home with victories day after day without a single casualty of their own, gives them an unparalleled momentum. They turn their backs on the rumors and stories which are becoming ever more agitating, clamber into their fur flying boots, and slide in behind their machine guns. Nothing else concerns them.

On 5 November, their machine guns again rattle incessantly into the jumble of blue and red cockades. In just twenty-five minutes: 10.10 a.m., Leutnant Richard Wenzl, a DH 9 as his twelfth victory; 10.30 a.m., Leutnant Wolfram von Richthofen, a DH 9 as his eighth victory; 10.35 a.m., Oberleutnant von Wedel, a Spad as his thirteenth victory; 10.35 a.m., Leutnant Heldmann, who was with the Geschwader from its inception up until the very last moment, a Spad as his fourteenth victory; 10.35 a.m., Leutnant Bahlmann, a DH 9 as his first victory.[1] Leutnant Kirst crashes to his death following air combat.[2]

Their days in Marville are at an end. The Front slowly gives way. The Jagdgeschwader Richthofen shifts its airfield to Tellancourt, north of Longuyon. On 6 November, from out of Marville, Leutnant Neckel gets his thirtieth victory, Leutnant Grassmann his tenth, and Leutnant Heldmann his fifteenth. These were the Jagdgeschwader's final air combats.

On 7 November, in a pouring rain, they flew from Marville to Tellancourt right at tree level. It was the wildest flight any of them had ever lived through. The field at Tellancourt was unspeakably poor, and many a machine was lost here.

The weather is too bad for flying. They have some time to look around at what is being played out on the ground.

And there on the ground, an evil game has been played out. They stand as if thunderstruck there in Tellancourt when they hear what has happened. They hear it three times before they comprehend it. And then they grin rather uncertainly. That really is the craziest news the communications center has ever concocted. And then they are forced to believe it, whether they want to or not. There is revolution in Kiel. The Kaiser is to abdicate. There are riots in Berlin.

On 9 November, around noon, Oberleutnant Göring assembles his officers. The commander is icy. He outlines the situation at home and at the Front. With a few harsh words, he makes it clear where the Jagdgeschwader

---

[1] Aircraft listed as a DH 4 in the squadron log book.
[2] Last casualty of JG I.

Richthofen belongs in this dreadful mess. The Geschwader is ready for any deployment. *Any* deployment. Wherever it might be. Anywhere but there, where the empire is reportedly being destroyed from within. The order is issued for the officers to stay close together during the night of the ninth to the tenth. They post a watch. Each Staffel goes to sleep without leaving the others.

On 10 November, the order comes to take their airplanes to Darmstadt. Then there comes a counter-order to wait a while. Then another, remarkable order arrives. They are to plan on handing the Geschwader's airplanes over to the Americans. Not one feature changes on the commander's face, which is frozen with anger. He flat out rejects this order. He wouldn't dream of obeying it. The orders follow each other, cross each other, contradict each other. Order, counter-order, disorder.

The commander makes short work of it. He orders the Geschwader to fly as a unit to Darmstadt, irrespective of the orders still coming in. The adjutant is to follow with the supplies, spare parts, engines, equipment, and provisions on trucks.

Take-off was impossible for the time being. The fog was hundreds of meters high. On this day, they destroyed anything they were unable to take with them. As to luggage, only the absolute necessities could be kept. The officers stand around on the field all day and stare into the sky. The fog does not lift. When a bright patch somewhere in the clouds starts to spread, they push their machines out. They start the engines and inspect the airplanes down to the last screw. They are pale, bleary-eyed, and totally exhausted with strain, grief, and rage. They don't let their machines out of their sight for a moment.

Now and again, their eyes seek out the commander. He is stony-faced and absorbed within himself. And when his face lights up, one single thought is racing through his head: if the fog persists until the twelfth, the war will be over, and then the return flight will be impossible.

On 11 November, at noon, the Armistice goes into effect.[1] No one senses it, except as a particular sensation. The Front falls silent, and that is strange at best, after its having raged for four years like a continuous thunderstorm.

The Jagdgeschwader Richthofen waits for clear weather. The next morning, the fog has disappeared. At ten o'clock, the Geschwader takes off in flights. Airplane after airplane disappears over the horizon.

The adjutant, Oberleutnant Bodenschatz, crouches in silence on a truck, his coat collar upturned. He sets off with thirty-five trucks behind him. He has approximately 250 men in the convoy, traveling in a line to Worms, by

---

[1] German time; 11.00 a.m. Allied time.

way of Saarbrücken. They are never bothered *en route*, never. On the trucks, the enlisted men have written in chalk: 'Richthofen, the Red Battle Flyer!' (By this, however, they don't actually mean that inwardly they are 'red'.[1] They mean much more. *Here come Richthofen's red machines. Maybe this name still means something to you.*) Whenever they come upon bands of jeering soldiers who look at this loot with a great deal of interest and come nearer the trucks, the ruffians grow silent and fall back. And stand there in silence. Do they perceive a young cavalry captain in an Uhlan's uniform striding unseen in front of this column, with the *Pour le Mérite*, with his clear, pure eyes, and his quiet, calm gaze? The Jagdgeschwader Richthofen's convoy is not bothered anywhere on the whole, long way.

Their first stop is on the other side of the Rhine, past Worms. Only one single truck has been left behind, all the others are present. In Worms, the adjutant learns that the Geschwader has arrived in Darmstadt, where a brief, troublesome incident was immediately taken care of by the commander. One Staffel had lost their bearings and landed at the airfield there in Mannheim. The airfield was swarming with soldiers' councils.[2] The totally unsuspecting and defenseless officers had their weapons taken from them. A half hour later, the officers joined the Geschwader in Darmstadt, *sans* weapons. Oberleutnant Göring immediately took off with the entire Geschwader.

The red airplanes circle over the airfield at Mannheim. The Staffel whose officers had been disarmed here lands, and the officers proceed to the soldiers' council. They have an ultimatum to deliver from the commander of the Jagdgeschwader Richthofen: if the officers are not allowed to immediately take off again *with their weapons*, the field will be razed to the ground. Within just a few minutes, the horrified soldiers' council has surrendered the weapons, the Staffel takes off, and the Geschwader flies back to Darmstadt.

There an officer of the General Staff delivers the strict order to fly the planes to Strasbourg and hand them over to the French. The commander curtly replies that, if this order absolutely had to be carried out, then others could do it. He himself would not.

The officers of the Geschwader, having had a presentiment of similar orders, have already touched down in Darmstadt with landings that were not exactly flawless and not exactly gentle. The bulk of the airplanes were

---

[1] In the vernacular, the German word *rot* (red) carries the connotation of being rotten or foul; a veiled allusion to the communist sentiments sweeping the German Army.

[2] These revolutionary councils, made up largely of Army deserters, first sprang up in numerous industrial cities in northern Germany following the naval revolt in Kiel in October 1918, and then spread throughout Germany.

no longer really usable. The order to fly to Strasbourg is carried out to some extent, with considerable swearing. The French aviation officers who were awaiting these few German machines so expectantly were not at all pleased at how the machines were touched down during landing, and how they looked, both in general and in other respects.[1]

Following 16 November, the whole Geschwader is together in Aschaffenburg. While in Worms, Oberleutnant Bodenschatz received the order to travel directly through to this city.

These are the final days of the glorious Geschwader.

One day a communist town councilman from Nuremberg, Herr Baier, along with a large soldiers' council, shows up at the paper factory where the enlisted men are quartered. He asks the commander to allow him a speech. Oberleutnant Göring, who has shown up with his officers, permits it. He is curious as to what the man has to say, and how the enlisted men will react. The courtyard of the paper factory resounds with the formula for revolutionary incitement: '. . . You were in the front lines and you had it bad . . . your officers were behind the lines and they had it good . . . et cetera.'

Within the group of pilots, nobody bats an eye. They look absent-mindedly out over the councilman, over the enlisted men, and over the roofs of the factory. They see themselves shooting it out day after day in that inferno amid the enemy squadrons; they count their lists of victories; they recall the faces of their many dead comrades . . .

With cold eyes, the commander observes the effect of this speech on his men. Here and there, the councilman's speech seems to have made some impression. When the man is finished, the commander climbs up on a barrel. His clear voice fills the entire courtyard. *The enlisted men in front and the officers behind?* With one sweep of his hand, the commander brushes aside the councilman's entire speech. The men remember; they need only to think a little. Where were their officers while they themselves, the enlisted personnel, were lying in their huts on the airfield? Well then! Within a few minutes, his people are enthralled.

On 19 November, the officers are discharged. On that last, historic evening, they sit together one more time in the cellar of a monastery in Aschaffenburg.[2] The commander gives a farewell speech. What they heard would remain unforgettable for every one of them. One more time, the immortal deeds of the Geschwader pass before them. One more time, they

---

[1] This final act of defiance proved of little avail, as the Allies simply demanded that an equal number of undamaged machines be turned over to them in lieu of the damaged ones.

[2] For hundreds of years, religious orders were among the finest brewers of Germany, thus it was not unusual for a wine cellar or tavern to be located within the confines of a religious house.

hear the immortal names which will endure for ever in the military history of the German people. One more time, they hear the tension wires whistle, and the machine guns rattle; they see machines with blue and red rings rise up, burn, and crash. One more time, the deadly dance of days past goes through the room like a dream. Not one eye lifts its gaze from the commander's face. Scarcely a breath is to be heard. They are deeply moved. Their eyes fill with tears, whether they like it or not.

Then the commander speaks of his passionate faith in the future. Into an hour grey with hopelessness, this man projects a new faith and hope with his stirring words. In a moment when Germany was giving up its great struggle, bled white, utterly exhausted, powerless, and full of doubt, this man calls them to a new battle, a battle for the shaping of the German soul. And as for the proud Geschwader he commanded in the hellish last days of the war, he makes this promise to his comrades and to his Fatherland: that this Geschwader shall some day rise again. When he is finished, he smashes his wine glass on the wall, and a veritable hurricane of love and enthusiasm engulfs the commander. No one suspects that, in this minute, Oberleutnant Göring — bold, daring, and believing with his whole heart, mind and soul — has taken the first step into the darkness of that hard, hard climb which would lead to the deliverance of the German nation.

Beneath the heroic song of the Jagdgeschwader Richthofen, the commander places his final signature:

> The Geschwader has achieved 644 air victories since its founding. Casualties due to enemy action amounted to 56 officers and pilots, six enlisted men killed; 52 officers and pilots, seven enlisted men wounded.
>
> Hermann Göring, Oberleutnant
> and Geschwader Commander

CHAPTER TWO

SPRING 1935

I THE NEW JAGDGESCHWADER RICHTHOFEN

On 14 March 1935, at the suggestion of the Reichs Minister of Aviation, the Führer, as Commander-in-Chief of the Wehrmacht, issues a decree:

> The Reich's Luftwaffe is created as a new part of the Wehrmacht. It will take up the glorious aeronautical tradition of the World War. The name of Rittmeister Freiherr von Richthofen and his Jagdgeschwader will shine brightly within it.
>
> Through times of conflict and trouble, the last Geschwader commander, Reichs Minister of Aviation, General of Aviation Göring, faithfully and staunchly guarded Richthofen's will for battle and victory as a sacred legacy. It was his energy that allowed the first Jagdgeschwader to arise within the framework of the new Luftwaffe.
>
> Today I convey to this Jagdgeschwader the continuation of the tradition of the Jagdgeschwader Richthofen and I hereto order:
>
> Henceforth, the Jagdgeschwader will bear the designation:
>
> *Jagdgeschwader Richthofen*
>
> The officers, non-commissioned officers, and enlisted men shall wear a commemorative band on their coats with the name: *Richthofen*. The Reichs Minister of Aviation will issue further orders hereto.
>
> This distinction is intended to honor the undefeated victor of the air, our Manfred Freiherr von Richthofen. At the same time, it honors all the fallen heroes of our flying service.
>
> I am executing this decree in the certainty that the Jagdgeschwader Richthofen, imbued with the lofty significance of the tradition conveyed to it, will show itself ever equal to this tradition in spirit and the performance of its sacred obligation.
>
> Munich, 14 March 1935
> (signed) Adolf Hitler

A promise is kept, a legacy fulfilled.

II THE RICHTHOFEN SHRINE AT SCHWEIDNITZ

The quiet, solemn rooms are located on the second floor of the old house in Schweidnitz in Silesia. Out on the street, the life of a small city; over across the street, the greenery of the park where the young men of the Labor Service in their brown uniforms, the SA[1] men with their bright yellow Silesian collar patches and cap bands, and soldiers of the Reich's army stroll.

Upstairs here, amidst the silence, from every wall, from every cabinet, from every table, there roars the silent, harsh song of battle and death of the man who grew up here, who came here on holiday as a young cadet, a boy still as soft as cream and roses, who went to war as a young, unknown officer, and who now consecrates this house and these rooms with his immortal name.

The spoils of eighty downed aircraft. The spoils of a man's life. The spoils of a front-line soldier. Chivalrous spoils. Stretched upon the walls are the many, many insignia cut from the wings of those downed aircraft, those blue, white, and red rings that stared down upon the German front like murderous eyes. Now they gaze down here, lifeless and broken. English machine guns, flare pistols, steel helmets, Colt revolvers, machine-gun belts.

Countless photographs, portraits of the Rittmeister, photos of his comrades, a picture of Captain Ball, the most famous combat pilot of the English air service, who was shot down. Pictures of Manfred and Lothar, pictures of their father and mother, a picture of the Richthofen family tree.

A gallant photograph: Richthofen, shortly after bringing down an English pilot. The two of them stand together, the Englishman with his collar open, still flushed, still dazed, but already wearing once again the happy smile of the living on his excited face.[2] Opposite him, Richthofen's quiet, calm countenance.

In one corner hangs a long streamer. From it hung the bag containing the news of the Rittmeister's death that was dropped over the airfield. And then several tiny pieces of dark cloth, fabric from the airplane he flew on his last flight. The one came from a German prisoner of war who obtained it himself, and the other came the vast distance from Australia, sent to his mother in remembrance.

In the room furthest back, propped up between the flowers and the

---

[1] 'Sturm Abteilung', or storm troops.
[2] Lt F.A. Bird, 46 Squadron, RFC, shot down on 3 September 1917, Richthofen's 61st victory.

plants and the oleander trees, there stands something touching: a stark, wooden, black cross of the kind to be seen on all the graves of German soldiers in France. This cross stood on the grave dug for him by the English: *von Richthofen, Baron*. They buried him, as we know, and as is to be seen from the photographs, with all honors. A clergyman led the way, airmen carried his coffin, troops presented arms.

On velvet pillows lie the medals of the two brothers, Manfred and Lothar. Countless medals. Their broad chests would scarcely have been wide enough to wear them all. On each pillow, alone above all the other decorations, the blue cross of the order *Pour le Mérite*.

Oh, what this quiet house in this province had been able to place at the Fatherland's disposal in such sons as these! Now their mother stands in silence amid the undying remembrances. One is unable to say much in these rooms which exude the hot breath of battle.

A display case with many small silver cups, no bigger than a thumb. They were gifts from his comrades upon his individual victories, each cup bearing an engraved numeral.[1] All around the walls, framed telegrams from Supreme Headquarters, proud telegrams; that one, written in a telegraph clerk's hand, in which the Kaiser awards Rittmeister von Richthofen the order *Pour le Mérite*.[2] Other printed telegrams. Acknowledgements of the Commanding General of the Air Service. Further on, without number, framed, special edition newspapers with Army communiqués mentioning the names of the two Richthofen brothers. In a glass cabinet, Richthofen's uniforms, the colorful ones of peacetime, his flying furs from the field, his sword, his tschapka.[3] On every wall are propellers, both intact and shattered, taken from vanquished enemy airplanes.

He wanted to fill his rooms with these things after the war. It would have been a place in which he would have felt at home. Now these things are arranged in the rooms of the two brothers as they themselves would have arranged them. Only their physical presence is missing: their voices, their eyes, their gaits. But their immortal spirits remain.

Glory and honor to their memory!

---

[1] These cups were ordered by von Richthofen himself from a Berlin silversmith, until Germany's severe silver shortage forced an end to the collection. A total of 60 cups were made.
[2] von Richthofen was still a Leutnant when he received the *Pour le Mérite* on 12 January 1917.
[3] A distinctive helmet worn by the Uhlans.

CHAPTER THREE

THE WAR JOURNAL OF JAGDGESCHWADER NO. I

1917

24 June In accordance with telegram of Army Group Crown Prince Rupprecht (Ic 20706), Jagdgeschwader No. I is to be formed immediately from those Jagdstaffeln presently with the Fourth Army, numbers 4, 6, 10, [and] 11. The Geschwader is a closed unit. It is intended for the purpose of winning and securing dominance in the air in crucial combat sectors. It remains directly under the command of the Fourth Army High Command. The individual sections of the Geschwader are to assemble at one airfield if possible.

25 June Rittmeister Freiherr von Richthofen is appointed commander of the Jagdgeschwader (in accordance with Kogenluft 62880 Fl. II[1]).

25/26 June By order of the Chief of the General Staff of the Field Army of 23 June 1917 (Ic No. 58341 op.) Jagdgeschwader No. I is formed from Jagdstaffeln 4, 6, 10, [and] 11 (in accordance with Kogenluft No. 867 G. 2 of 26 June 1917).

27 June Instructions and authorization of the commander in accordance with Kogenluft 64683 Fl. II of 27 June 1917. Area south-west of Courtrai: Marcke, Marckebeke, Bisseghem, is assigned for the purpose of assembling the four Jagdstaffeln at one airfield. Move was carried out by the Staffeln on 2 July.

2 July Rittmeister Freiherr von Richthofen orders Leutnant Krefft (Jasta 11) to the staff of the Jagdgeschwader as technical officer for the time being (transfer applied for). Oberleutnant Bodenschatz of Jasta Boelcke is transferred to the Geschwader as adjutant under the date of 1 July. Rittmeister's 57th victory.

Marckebeke

4 July[2] Draft of a strength report for the staff, including, in addition to the three positions mentioned, still one doctor, one paymaster, and 62 (plus four posted) non-commissioned officers and enlisted personnel, submitted to Kogenluft for approval under the date of 4 July.

For the time being, staff business is being taken care of while sharing space

---

[1] 'Fl. II' (Flieger II) refers to that department of the German Air Service dealing with the organization of the Air Service itself.

[2] The following three dates appear exactly as they appear in the original text, with no entry for 3 July and two entries for 5 July. These were not changed because of the dates appearing within the text of the journal entries.

with Jasta 11. Telephone exchange and message center (housed together with those of Jasta 11) at a farm next to the Château Marckebeke. Observation stand with five-meter range-finder and stereo telescope; crew, with Jasta 11 until now, was taken over from this Jasta, ordered to the Jagdgeschwader for the time being. Quarters for the staff officers together with officers' quarters for Jasta 11 in Château Marckebeke.

Staff business divided into two sections: 1. General and Personnel matters and 2. Technical section.

5 July   In accordance with Army High Command order of 4 July, as of 12.00 noon on 5 July, Jastas 4, 6, 10, and 11 will pass over to Jagdgeschwader No. I in their new chain of command. As of 5 July, issuance of Geschwader orders to the subordinate Staffeln.

In accordance with Geschwader Order No. 1: As of 6 July, the order of the first daily take-off readiness (from daybreak on) Jastas 11, 10, 6, 4 in rotation; the daily afternoon take-off readiness (from 1.30 to 3.00 o'clock) Jastas 10, 6, 4, 11.

Of those officers requested or proposed as pilots for allocation among the four Staffeln since the order assembling the Geschwader, the following have arrived or have been assigned:

30 June Lt Stapenhorst from Park 10[1] to Jasta 11;
1 July Lt Joachim Wolff from Fl. Abt. (A) 216 to Jasta 11 (6 July);
1 July Lt Meyer from Fl. Abt. (A) 201 to Jasta 11 (14 July);
2 July Lt von Schönebeck from Fl. Abt. (A) 203 to Jasta 11 (7 July);
2 July Oblt Reinhard from Fl. Abt. 28 by way of Jastaschule, Geschwader Order of 14 July to Jasta 11 (7 July);
6 July Oblt Freiherr von Althaus from Jasta 14 to Jasta 10 as leader;
6 July Oblt Scheffer from Observers' School, Cologne, to Jasta 11 (12 July) for special duty;
8 July Lt Stock from Jasta 22 to Jasta 6 (13 July);
9 July Oblt Lischke from Fl. Abt. 39 to Jasta 6 for special duty;
11 July Oblt Weigand from Park 4; Geschwader Order of 11 July to Jasta 10;
15 July Oblt Müller[2] from Fl. Abt. 18 to Jasta 11 (19 July) by way of Armee Flug Park 4, Geschwader Order of 16 July.

Marckebeke
5 July
   Aircraft Downed:
   Oblt Dostler (Jasta 6) 6.20 p.m., north of Ypres, map quadrant K 43, captive balloon, as 13th. Partly cloudy.
6 July   As of 6 July, Staff orderly room, Marckebeke, Kortrijker Straat 74.
   Aircraft Downed:
   Lt Klein (Jasta 4) 3.25 p.m., Frezenberg, map quadrant A 45, small quadrant 7, Sopwith, as 13th.

---

[1] 'Park' is an abbreviated form of 'Armee Flugpark'.
[2] Rank should be Leutnant.

Lt Kurt Wolff (Jasta 11) 9.20 p.m., south-west of Ypres, RE, as 32nd.

Casualties: Rittmeister Freiherr von Richthofen, 11.30 a.m., near Wervicq, wounded in the back of the head by a machine-gun round (grazing shot) during attack upon a Vickers squadron. Taken to Field Hospital No. 76 (St Nicholas) in Courtrai.

Acting Geschwader Leader: Oblt von Döring, leader of Jasta 4. Oblt von Döring, slightly injured, discharging further duties.

Almost cloudless.

7 July

Aircraft Downed:

1. Lt Kurt Wolff (Jasta 11) 11.00 a.m., near Comines, this side of the lines, triplane, as 33rd.
2. Lt Krüger (Jasta 4) 11.05 a.m., near Wervicq, this side, triplane, as 1st.
3. Lt Niederhoff (Jasta 11) 11.10 a.m., near Bousbecque, this side, triplane, as 4th.
4. Vfw Krebs (Jasta 6) 11.35 a.m., near Zillebeke, other side, RE, as 6th.
5. Oblt Dostler (Jasta 6) 12.00 noon, near Deulemont, between the lines, Sopwith, as 14th.
6. Vfw Clausnitzer (Jasta 4) 2.30 p.m., Gheluvelt sector, other side, Nieuport, as 3rd.
7. Lt Klein (Jasta 4) 6.07 p.m., Houthem, this side, Sopwith, as 14th.
8. Vfw Lautenschlager (Jasta 11) 6.10 p.m., Wytschaete area, other side, Sopwith, as 1st.
9. Lt Anders (Jasta 4) 6.20 p.m., Hollebeke, other side, Sopwith, as 1st.

Decisions must first be made by a court of arbitration, consisting of Oblt von Althaus (Jasta 10), Oblt Dostler (Jasta 6), and Lt Krefft (Jagdgeschwader), concerning victory:

No. 2, in dispute between Lt Krüger (Jasta 4) and Vfw Lautenschlager (Jasta 11);

No. 3, in dispute between Oblt von Döring (Jasta 4) and Lt Niederhoff (Jasta 11);

No. 6, in dispute between Vfw Heldmann (Jasta 10) and Vfw Clausnitzer (Jasta 4);

No. 8, in dispute between Vfw Clausnitzer (Jasta 4) and Vfw Lautenschlager (Jasta 11).

Good, almost cloudless.

8 July No flight operations on account of rain.

9 July In accordance with Army Order (Army High Command 4, Ia No. 42/July of 2 July 1917), Jagdgeschwader No. I is transferred to the Army Group North for deployment under the Corps Headquarters of the Garde du Corps, for a planned operation in the land sector of the Army Group North.

In accordance with Division Order (3 Marine (Infantry) Division — Order Dr. 483 Ia of 7 July 1917), Operation 'Strandfest'[1] will take place on 9 July. Corresponding Geschwader Order No. 2 (Secret) of 8 July 1917 for 9, 10, and

---

[1] Operation 'Beach Party', (German attack on Nieuport) 10-11 July 1917.

11 July. On account of unfavorable weather, operation postponed till 10 July. Low clouds, rain at times.

10 July   The intended attack took place. Deployment of the Staffeln did not take place on account of uncertain weather. The attack was carried out, corresponding Geschwader Order (telephone message) of 11 July 1917. 'The attack in Sector N has succeeded as planned. Our infantry holds the east bank of the Yser [River], over 1,000 Englishmen captured up till now.' Low clouds, clearing in the evening.

11 July   The attack objective achieved and held. Jasta 10 took off for Jabbeke at 8.30 a.m.; Jastas 6, 11, and 4 on standby at the airdrome. Jasta 10 returned at 9.30 p.m. At 3.00 a.m., English bombing raid on the airfield of Jasta 6; three tent hangars and two machines slightly damaged.

   Casualties: Lt Kurt Wolff (Jasta 11) wounded in air combat, 10.20 a.m., (shot through left hand), taken to Field Hospital No. 76 (St Nicholas) in Courtrai.

   Aircraft Downed:
   Lt Klein (Jasta 4) 3.05 p.m., map quadrant Q 50, captive balloon, as 15th.
   Lt Klein (Jasta 4) 3.07 p.m., map quadrant Q 53, captive balloon, as 16th.
   Vfw Wüsthoff (Jasta 4) 3.10 p.m., map quadrant Q 56, captive balloon, as 3rd.
   Lt Mohnicke (Jasta 11) 9.15 p.m., Comines, triplane, as 3rd.
   Vfw Patermann (Jasta 4) 9.45 p.m., Houthem, Spad, as 2nd.

   Heavily overcast in the morning, clearing in the evening.

12 July   (Operation 'Strandfest') Jasta 11 (corresponding Geschwader Order No. 4 of 11 July 1917) was placed at the disposal of the Captain of Field Aviation and was to arrive at the Jabbeke airdrome at 8.00 a.m. (With Marine Feld Fl. 2.) On account of fog, it took off at 9.40 a.m., back at 10.15 p.m.

   Casualties: Vfw Patermann (Jasta 4) 11.00 a.m., shot down in air combat near Gheluvelt.

   Aircraft Downed:
   Oblt Dostler (Jasta 6) 11.50 a.m., near Houthem, Sopwith, as 15th.
   Lt Deilmann (Jasta 6) 11.50 a.m., map quadrant C 46, Nieuport, as 4th.
   Lt Adam (Jasta 6) 6.35 p.m., Dickebusch, Sopwith, as 4th.
   Lt Küppers (Jasta 6) 7.40 p.m., Wytschaete, Sopwith-1, as 4th.
   Vfw Marquardt (Jasta 4) 9.05 p.m., Zandvoorde, Sopwith, as 1st.
   Lt Hübner (Jasta 4) 9.20 p.m., Zuidschote, triplane, as 1st.
   Oblt Dostler (Jasta 6) 9.45 p.m., Zillebeke, Sopwith, as 16th.

   Hazy in the morning, clearing in the afternoon.

13 July   Casualties: Lt Klein (Jasta 4) wounded in air combat, 11.30 a.m., landed smoothly near Gistel.

   Aircraft Downed:
   Oblt Dostler (Jasta 6) 11.35 a.m., south of Becelaere, Sopwith, as 17th.
   Oblt Dostler (Jasta 6) 11.40 a.m., north of Zonnebeke, Nieuport, as 18th.
   Vfw Krebs (Jasta 6) 11.30 a.m., Polygon Wood, Sopwith, as 7th.
   Vfw Krebs (Jasta 6) 11.35 a.m., Zonnebeke, Sopwith, as 8th.
   Lt Adam (Jasta 6) 11.30 a.m., east of Ypres, Nieuport, as 5th.

Lt Deilmann (Jasta 6) 11.20 a.m., Zandvoorde, as 5th.

Army Order 4g (see enclosure).[1] Three-meter range-finder arrived. (Exchange for five-meter range-finder). Good flying weather, low clouds at times.

14 July Marckebeke. Nothing noteworthy. Cloudy at times.

15 July Nothing noteworthy. Variable cloudiness.

16 July Casualties: Vfw Clausnitzer (Jasta 4) missing since 5.35 p.m. attack on captive balloon.[2] Vfw Krebs (Jasta 6) 7.45 p.m., shot down in air combat north-east of Zonnebeke.

Aircraft Downed:

Vfw Wüsthoff (Jasta 4) 6.15 p.m., captive balloon, near Kemmel, as 4th.

Lt Adam (Jasta 6) 8.05 p.m., near Zonnebeke, Sopwith, as 6th.

In the evening hours, appearance of strong enemy squadrons. Variably cloudy.

17 July Casualties: Lt Meyer (Jasta 11) 8.55 p.m., wounded in air combat near Ypres (remained with the Staffel). Lt Krüger (Jasta 4) 1.15 p.m., severely wounded in air combat near Comines, died during the night in the field hospital.

Aircraft Downed:

1. Lt Tüxen (Jasta 6) 9.05 p.m., east of Comines, Sopwith, as 1st.

Victory No. 1 was in dispute at first between Lt Deilmann (Jasta 6), Lt Tüxen (Jasta 6), Vfw Wüsthoff (Jasta 4). Under revocation of the arbitration award of 18 July, following which it was decided for Lt Wüsthoff, victory was awarded to Lt Tüxen (Jasta 6) on 26 July by Rittmeister Freiherr von Richthofen as Geschwader Commander (Geschwader Order No. 13/2). A second victory, at first in dispute between Lt Niederhoff (Jasta 11) and Uffz Brettel (Jasta 10), decided by arbitration on 18 July. Decided by Kofl. for another Jasta.

Army Order 9g, concerning concentrating the Jastas in the Army more tightly. Geschwader Order of 17 July, regarding deploying all the Staffeln of the Geschwader simultaneously in the evening hours for the time being. Army Order 10g, concerning possible assignment of the Geschwader to the Sixth Army, choice of an airdrome in due course. Good, cloudy at times.

18 July Marckebeke. No flight operations on account of rain.

19 July Kofl. Order of the Day No. 26, numeral 2: Recognition on the part of the Commanding General of the pilots of the Fourth Army, above all, those pilots of the Jagdgeschwader, in the face of the superior strength of the enemy's combat pilots in recent days. Rain at times, clearing towards evening.

20 July

Aircraft Downed:

Lt Adam (Jasta 6) 7.40 a.m., south-west of Ypres, other side, lattice-tail, as 7th.

---

[1] Throughout the journal, references are made to enclosures, messages, and reports etc. that were once a part of the original Geschwader log book. Unfortunately, however, General Bodenschatz did not include the text of these enclosures in his book.

[2] Taken prisoner.

Lt Walter Stock (Jasta 6) 8.40 a.m., Armentières, other side, RE, as 1st.
Lt von Boenigk (Jasta 4) 9.00 a.m., north-west of Ten Brielen, Sopwith-1, as 1st.
Vfw Wüsthoff (Jasta 4) 9.20 p.m., Becelaere-Gheluvelt, Sopwith-1, as 6th.
Lt Niederhoff (Jasta 11) 9.10 p.m., Zonnebeke, Sopwith-1, as 6th (in dispute at first with Vfw Küllmer, Jasta 6).

Combating enemy captive balloons, Army Order 12g. Cloudy at times, ground haze, thunder showers in the afternoon, clear in the evening.

21 July
  Aircraft Downed:
    Fw Lt Schubert (Jasta 6) 8.25 p.m., west of Roubaix, Spad-1, as 2nd (still disputed at first with Lt Mohnicke, Jasta 11; decided on 26 July by Rittmeister Freiherr von Richthofen as Geschwader Commander, see Geschwader Order No. 13, numeral 2).

Enemy flight operations brisk in the evening; around 9.00 p.m., several enemy pilots advanced over our lines. Very hazy, clearing towards evening.

22 July Transfers: Lt Barth[1] posted to Jasta 10, in conformity with Kogenluft 63106; Lt Stapenhorst posted to Jasta 11, in conformity with Kogenluft 63018, (Geschwader Order No. 12 of 25 July).
  Aircraft Downed:
    Oblt von Döring (Jasta 4) 10.40 a.m., Mangelaar, this side, Spad, as 4th (still in dispute with Lt Adam, Jasta 6).
    Vfw Heldmann (Jasta 10) 10.40 a.m., Deulemont, this side, RE, as 1st.
    Lt Brauneck (Jasta 11) 11.25 a.m., east of Kortewilde, this side, Sopwith, as 9th.
    Lt Niederhoff (Jasta 11) 11.30 a.m., south-east of Zonnebeke, this side, Sopwith-2, as 7th.
    Oblt von Döring (Jasta 4) 8.50 p.m., Oosttaverne, forward lines, Nieuport, as 5th.
    Oblt Reinhard (Jasta 11) 11.30 a.m., Warneton, this side, Sopwith-2, as 1st. (At first disputed between Lt Deilmann, Vfw Küllmer, Jasta 6, and Oblt Reinhard, Jasta 11, decided on 26 July by Geschwader commander, see Geschwader Order No. 13, numeral 2.)

In the morning brisk enemy air activity. At midday, the enemy flight operations quieted down. In the evening very brisk air activity. Morning hazy, then clear.

23 July Enemy appears to have recognized the regularity of our joint appearance every evening; adapts himself to our flight times with his reconnaissance flights and also in ratio of forces, by holding superior numbers ready for crucial situations. Very hazy, clear in the evening.

24 July Enemy air activity moderate. Low-lying clouds, clearing in the evening.

25 July Rittmeister Freiherr von Richthofen, released from the hospital,

---

[1] Rank should be Vizefeldwebel.

resumes command of the Geschwader.

Aircraft Downed:

Lt Adam (Jasta 6) 6.20 p.m., near Nordhofwyk,[1] other side, Spad, as 8th.

Enemy air activity very low. Low-lying clouds, rain at times.

26 July　Casualty: Lt Brauneck (Jasta 11) 8.45 p.m., shot down in aerial combat south of Zonnebeke.

Only towards evening were there a few enemy airmen far behind the Front. Very hazy, clearing in the evening.

27 July　Enemy flight operations: low in the morning, in the afternoon, very brisk; reconnaissance and bombing squadrons flew far over our Front, since it was difficult to fire on them on account of darkness.

Aircraft Downed:

Vfw Wüsthoff (Jasta 4) 8.40 p.m., near Dadizeele, this side, a Sopwith forced to land, as 6th.

Lt von Schönebeck (Jasta 11) near Beythem, this side, triplane.[2]

Variable clouds, in the morning haze and poor visibility, clearing at times in the afternoon. Enclosure 17e.

28 July

Aircraft Downed:

Vfw Küllmer (Jasta 6) 11.50 a.m., north of Terhand, Nieuport, as 1st.

Lt Adam (Jasta 6) 12.10 p.m., north of Terhand, Sopwith, as 9th.

Lt Bockelmann (Jasta 11) 5.20 p.m., Merckem, Caudron lattice-tail, as 2nd.

Oblt Dostler (Jasta 6) 6.50 p.m., north-east of Courtrai, RDD-2,[3] as 19th.

Lt Czermak (Jasta 6) 6.50 p.m., Meulebeke, de Havilland, as 1st.

Lt Adam (Jasta 6) 6.55 p.m., Oostrozebeke, RDD-2, as 10th.

Lt Tüxen (Jasta 6) 6.55 p.m., east of Ingelmunster, de Havilland, as 2nd.

Oblt Dostler (Jasta 6) 7.00 p.m., Oostrozebeke, RDD-2, as 20th.

Lt Walter Stock (Jasta 6) 7.00 p.m., south of Deynze, RDD-2, as 2nd.

Lt Mohnicke (Jasta 11) 9.00 p.m., Becelaere-Moorslede, BE-1, as 4th.

Lt von Boenigk (Jasta 4) 9.00 p.m., Moorslede area, Sopwith-1, as 2nd.

Oblt Weigand (Jasta 10) 9.15 p.m., Loulers, Sopwith-1, as 1st.

Casualty: Lt Niederhoff (Jasta 11) 12.00 noon, west of Terhand, shot down in air combat.

Geschwader Order (telephone message, 7.45 p.m.): 'For the assault by our infantry in the Boesinghe region at 8.30 p.m., all machines still available will take off at 8.00 p.m. and will direct their attention mainly to this position.'

Enemy air activity very brisk; squadrons repeatedly advanced far over our lines. One bombing squadron of six English two-seater aircraft, which had advanced as far as Courtrai around 7.00 p.m., was destroyed under the leadership of Oblt Dostler of Jasta 6 (see above: Aircraft Downed).

---

[1] This may possibly refer to 'North' Vijfwege, a town located almost directly north of Ypres, as opposed to the town with the same name located further east, to the south of Roulers.

[2] Lt von Schönebeck's first victory, brought down at 8.40 p.m.

[3] 'Rumpf Doppeldecker'. Please see Glossary.

Night of the 28th to 29th, around 12.30 a.m., enemy airmen dropped three bombs between the railway embankment and the quarters of Jasta 11; several houses were unroofed and the windows in the surrounding area were shattered. No one was injured.

Slightly cloudy at times.

29 July

Aircraft Downed:

Vfw Heldmann (Jasta 10) 7.55 a.m., near Westhoek, Sopwith, as 2nd (at first still disputed with Vfw Wüsthoff (Jasta 4), decided by commander, 1 August 1917.

11.00 a.m., funeral services and conveyance of Lt Brauneck, St Joseph's Church, Aalebeeker Straat, Courtrai; the railway carriage departed at 12.36 p.m.

Enemy air activity very low. Heavily overcast, rain at times.

30 July   During the night of 30 July, around 1.00 a.m., an airplane gave an emergency signal over the airfields of the Geschwader, whereupon the men of the Staffeln shot off flare guns, and Jasta 4 set up the landing cross. The airplane departed in a south-westerly direction.

Transfers: Oblt Freiherr von Althaus, leader of Jasta 10, is transferred to Jastaschule II in conformity with Kogenluft 64550. Lt d. R. Voss, Jasta 14, is transferred to Jagdgeschwader No. I, in conformity with Kogenluft 64549, and appointed leader of Jasta 10.

Enemy air activity very low. Heavily overcast, rain at times.

31 July[1]

Aircraft Downed:

Lt Hübner (Jasta 4) 12.50 p.m., south of Zillebeke, Bristol-2, as 2nd.

Lt Meyer (Jasta 11) 1.00 p.m., west of Deimlingseck, RE, as 1st.

Lt von Schönebeck (Jasta 11) 1.00 p.m., Frezenberg, RE, as 2nd.

Oblt Dostler (Jasta 6) 2.05 p.m., west of Bellewaarde Lake, Nieuport, as 21st.

Vfw Wüsthoff (Jasta 4) 2.45 p.m., Verbrandenmolen, lattice-tail (FE), as 7th.

At 7.00 a.m., an enemy airman dropped a bomb on the railway embankment without causing any damage.

At 11.00 a.m., a report that an enemy attack is in progress near the Army Group Wytschaete. Infantry penetrated at several positions. Troops requesting air protection. Clouds 200 to 300 meters high. On the strength of that report, Geschwader order by telephone: Staffeln are to stand by, ready for take-off. Individual, small flights take off. See experiences of 31 July. Small flights of two, three and four aircraft flew over the Front the entire day. Despite low clouds, numerous air combats took place with enemy airmen.

At 3.00 p.m., Lt Niederhoff (Jasta 11) conveyed from St Joseph's Church, Aalebeeker Straat.

Low-lying clouds, hazy.

---

[1] Third Battle of Ypres began.

1 Aug No flight operations because of rain and storms.

2 Aug No flight operations because of rain and storms.

3 Aug No flight operations because of rain and storms.

4 Aug Few flight operations.

Aircraft Downed:

Lt Hübner (Jasta 4) 8.55 p.m., near Beningen, other side, as 3rd.

Transfers: Lt d. R. Graul from Park 4 (Kogenluft 64573) on 3 August to Jasta 4; Lt d. R. Koch from Park 4 (Kogenluft 64573) on 4 August to Jasta 6; Vfw Stumpf from Park 4 (Kogenluft 64574) on 4 August to Jasta 6.

Low-lying clouds, hazy, rain at times.

5 Aug

Aircraft Downed:

Lt Wüsthoff (Jasta 4) 3.00 p.m., Ypres, other side, Nieuport, as 8th.

Lt von Boenigk (Jasta 4) 3.15 p.m., west of Staden, this side, Sopwith-1, as 3rd.

Enemy flight operations brisk towards evening. Cloudy, hazy.

6 Aug No enemy flight operations. Low-lying clouds, very hazy.

7 Aug Enemy flight operations low. Low-lying clouds, very hazy.

8 Aug Jasta Boelcke is situated at the Bisseghem airfield and, as verbally agreed, placed tactically under the command of the Geschwader. Enemy flight operations fairly brisk. Cloudy at times, rather hazy.

9 Aug

Aircraft Downed:

Oblt Dostler (Jasta 6) Houthulst Forest, this side, Nieuport-1, as 22nd.

Transfer: Schirrmeister Seidl, in conformity with Kogenluft 64609 of 30 July, transferred to staff of Jagdgeschwader No. I.

Jasta Boelcke is already vacating the Bisseghem airfield again. Cloudy at times, clear visibility.

10 Aug Night of 9/10 August, between 3.00 and 4.00 in the morning, enemy airmen dropped five bombs, including one heavy one, on the airfield of Jasta Boelcke; seven machines were damaged, and two tent hangars were flattened. At Jasta 6, three telephone lines were disrupted by the bombing.

Very brisk enemy flight operations. 10.15 a.m., enemy FE squadron reported; order to attack with powerful forces then followed. 10.20 a.m., order deploying the Geschwader rescinded, since enemy squadrons had disappeared.

Aircraft Downed:

Lt Walter Stock (Jasta 6) 3.30 p.m., Dadizeele, this side, Sopwith, as 3rd.

Lt Voss (Jasta 10) 4.25 p.m., south of Dixmude, this side, Spad, as 35th.

Uffz Brettel (Jasta 10) 4.25 p.m., south of Dixmude, this side, Spad, as 2nd.

Wounded: Lt Rousselle (Jasta 4) 8.00 p.m., severely wounded in air combat, emergency landing near Artoishoek. See experiences of 10 August.

Variable clouds, good visibility.

11 Aug Night of 10/11 August, 4.00 a.m., during an enemy bombing raid, a dud [landed] near the telephone exchange.

In the evening, Lt Krefft, Jagdgeschwader staff, crashed while landing near the airfield at Marckebeke as a result of engine failure, slightly injured; machine, tail and wings heavily damaged.

Detailed: Lt d. R. Bellen ordered to Jagdgeschwader by Kogenluft 65069, Jasta 10. Lt d. R. von der Osten ordered to Jagdgeschwader by Kogenluft 65069, detailed to Jasta 11.

Very brisk enemy flight operations. Variable clouds, rain in places.

12 Aug   Enemy flight operations rather brisk.

Aircraft Downed:

Lt Stapenhorst (Jasta 11) 8.50 a.m., north of Bixschoote, other side, Sopwith, as 1st.

Oblt Dostler (Jasta 6) 3.55 p.m., Koelberg, this side, Sopwith, as 23rd.

Lt Adam (Jasta 6) 9.10 p.m., Poperinghe region, other side, RDD, as 11th.

Cloudy at times, rain in places, clear visibility.

13 Aug

Aircraft Downed:

Lt Bockelmann (Jasta 11) 9.20 a.m., near Schellebeke, this side, RDD, as 3rd.

Oblt Reinhard (Jasta 11) 10.45 a.m., Grotenmolen, this side, Sopwith, as 2nd.

Around 7.30, a report: large enemy flight operation over the Ypres salient. Geschwader Order: all Staffeln to take off immediately. Enemy flight operations very brisk at times. Cloudy at times, rain in places.

14 Aug

Aircraft Downed:

Lt Löwenhardt (Jasta 10) 10.15 a.m., Zillebeke Lake, other side, RE, as 2nd.

Oblt Reinhard (Jasta 11) 10.40 a.m., Boesinghe, other side, as 3rd.

Oblt Reinhard (Jasta 11) 10.45 a.m., two km north of Boesinghe, other side, Spad, as 4th.

Oblt Weigand (Jasta 10) 10.45 a.m., south-west of Dixmude, other side, Sopwith, as 2nd.

Lt Müller (Jasta 11) 5.35 p.m., north of Bixschoote, other side, Sopwith, as 1st.

Lt Meyer (Jasta 11) 6.40 p.m., Wytschaete, other side, Sopwith, as 2nd.

Lt Adam (Jasta 6) 7.30 p.m., Houthulst Forest, this side, Sopwith-2, as 12th.

Oblt Dostler (Jasta 6) 7.30 p.m., St Julien, over the lines, Sopwith, as 24th.

Casualty: Lt Hübner (Jasta 4) 8.35 p.m., shot down in air combat near Moorslede.

Wounded: Lt H. J. Wolff (Jasta 11) 9.20 a.m., Zillebeke Lake, wounded in air combat (shot to the thigh), delivered to Reserve Field Hospital 76 (St Nicholas) in Courtrai.

Cloudy, somewhat hazy.

15 Aug Upon Kofl. Order of 15 August, Staffeln 4 and 6 took off as cover for a bombing raid by Kagohl 1 on the battery nests west and north-west of Loos. The Staffeln met up with Kagohl 1 over Orchies. Weather conditions extremely unfavorable. On account of this, Jasta 6 made an emergency landing at Jasta 30 in Phalempin. Staffeln 4 and 6 returned around 10.00 in the evening.

Wounded: Uffz Brettel (Jasta 10) 7.20 p.m., wounded in air combat (shot to the arm), emergency landing near Moorslede, delivered to Base Hospital 34, St Eloois Winkel.

Aircraft Downed:
Lt Voss (Jasta 10) 7.10 p.m., Ypres, other side, FE, as 36th.
Enemy flight operations moderate. Cloudy at times, rain in places.

16 Aug
Aircraft Downed:
Rittmeister Freiherr von Richthofen, 7.55 a.m., south-west of Houthulst Forest, this side, Nieuport, as 58th.
Lt Groos (Jasta 11) 11.20 a.m., Zillebeke Lake, forward lines, triplane, as 4th.
Lt Mohnicke (Jasta 11) 12.20 p.m., Linselles, this side, Martinsyde, as 5th.
Lt Voss (Jasta 10) 9.00 p.m., area of St Julien, this side, Sopwith, as 37th.

Telephone message, 11.00 am., order from Kofl: Jagdgeschwader I will cover a bombing raid on Poperinghe with one Staffel. Further details will follow. As for the rest, the main area of attack for the other Staffeln will be Bixschoote–Ypres–Menin.

Telephone message 12.30 p.m., order from Kofl: one Staffel of the Jagdgeschwader will undertake to cover Kampfgeschwader I, which will assemble over Courtrai at 1.00 p.m. at an altitude of 3,000 meters, and begin the advance for the attack on the battery nests north of Zillebeke Lake.

Enemy Bombing Raid: At 6.15 a.m., an enemy aircraft dropped two bombs between the railroad embankment and the quarters of Jasta 11 without causing any damage. At 6.30 a.m., an enemy airman dropped a bomb on the airfield of Jasta 4; one tent hangar and two machines were heavily damaged. At 8.05 p.m., a bomb on the exit from Jasta 11's airfield to Marcke, causing no damage.

Shifting the airfield to Jabbeke west of Brugge has been under consideration for quite some time now. The Staffeln are preparing everything for the move. The present quarters and airfields will remain reserved for the Geschwader. All of the sheds and tent hangars will remain here.

Enemy flight operations very brisk. See experiences of 16 August. Cloudy.

17 Aug
Aircraft Downed:
Lt Groos (Jasta 11) 7.25 a.m., west of Passchendaele, this side, SE, as 5th.
Oblt Dostler (Jasta 6) 8.10 a.m., north of Menin, this side, Martinsyde, as 25th.
Lt Ohlrau (Jasta 10) 10.15 a.m., Becelaere, this side, Sopwith, as 1st.
Lt Deilmann (Jasta 6) 11.10 a.m., Zonnebeke, forward lines, FE, as 6th. (This victory was subsequently investigated and not awarded.)
Lt von der Osten (Jasta 11) 8.55 p.m., Staden, this side, Sopwith, as 1st.

This is the 200th victory of Jasta 11. Corresponding telegram about this to Kogenluft.

Bombing: 11.50 a.m., bombing raid on the airfields of Jastas 4, 10, and 11; at Jasta 4, two airplanes were heavily damaged on the wings, and at Jasta 11, a non-commissioned officer was slightly injured.

The squadron's maintenance technical sergeant[1] sent to Jabbeke with four non-commissioned officers and two men to set up the new airdrome and pitch the tents.

Enemy flight operations brisk towards evening. Variable cloudiness.

18 Aug

Aircraft Downed:

Oblt Dostler (Jasta 6) 8.15 p.m., Roeselare, this side, RDD, as 26th.

Detailed: Lt d. R. Galetschky, ordered to Jagdgeschwader I by Kofl. Order of the Day No. 45 of 16 August, numeral 3, and is detailed to Jasta 6.

Bombing: 8.00 a.m., enemy aircraft dropped bombs on the airfield of Jasta 6, no damage was caused.

Recognition by Kogenluft regarding the action of the pilots on 16 August, in particular the actions of Rittmeister Freiherr von Richthofen, who is not yet fully recovered but who has already flown, and who at the same time is admonished as to the responsibility of putting himself into action. Recognition by Kogenluft of the 200th victory of Jasta 11.

Enemy flight operations: brisk towards evening. Variably cloudy, hazy at times.

19 Aug 11.00 a.m., Ludendorff and his Staff at Jasta 11's airfield for discussions with Rittmeister Freiherr von Richthofen. Enemy flight operations moderate during the day, brisk at times in the evening. Cloudy at times, visibility very good.

20 Aug Protective air cover for the troop review at Courtrai (visit of His Majesty). Enemy flight operations low. Cloudy, good visibility.

21 Aug By order of the Army High Command, Jasta 4 deployed with the 6th Army. Jasta 4 flew there between 4.00-9.40 p.m. According to the report of the Staffel leader, enemy flight operations were extremely low there. Enemy air activity low on the whole.

Oblt Dostler (Jasta 6) has not returned from a combat flight since 12.00 p.m.

Kofl. Order (by telephone message): Enemy is evidently conserving his air forces. We must do the same as far as possible during the break in the fighting.

Recognition by the Commander-in-Chief of the 4th Army of Jagdstaffel 11's 200th victory. Cloudy at times, good visibility.

22 Aug Lt Adam is made leader of Jasta 6, as successor to the missing Lt Dostler.

Day of a major battle according to the announcement of the Army Group Ypres. Jastas deployed in the sector of the Army Group Ypres. A decrease in enemy air activity since 9.30 a.m. Brisk enemy flight operations towards evening. Cloudy, hazy at times.

---

[1] Schirrmeister Seidl.

23 Aug   Enemy flight operations: early, very brisk; in the evening, low.
   Aircraft Downed:
      Lt Groos (Jasta 11) 7.50 a.m., south of Poelcapelle, this side, Sopwith, as 6th.
      Oblt von Boenigk (Jasta 4) 9.05 a.m., Boesinghe, triplane, as 3rd.
      Lt Voss (Jasta 10) 10.10 a.m., south-west of Dixmude, other side, Spad, as 33rd.[1]

Rittmeister Freiherr von Richthofen was awarded the Imperial Austro–Hungarian Iron Crown Order, 3rd Class with War Decoration, by order of 8 August 1917.
   41 combat flights. Cloudy, clearing in the evening.

24 Aug   According to statements made by a captured Englishman, Oblt Dostler is said to have been taken prisoner by the English, uninjured.[2] No flying weather. Rain.

25 Aug   Enemy flight operations low.
   Aircraft Downed:
      Lt von der Osten (Jasta 11) 7.30 a.m., between Passchendaele and Langemarck, forward lines, triplane, as 2nd.
   Combat Flights: 18. Cloudy, somewhat hazy.

26 Aug
   Aircraft Downed:
      Rittmeister Freiherr von Richthofen, 7.30 a.m., between Poelcapelle and Langemarck, forward lines, Spad, as 59th.
      Oblt Reinhard (Jasta 11) 10.05 a.m., Bixschoote area, other side, RE, as 5th.
   Bombing Raid: 6.45 a.m., the airdrome of Jasta 6 attacked by six enemy RDDs (Sopwiths, Spads) using machine guns. One airplane slightly damaged. At 6.50 a.m., from a low altitude, enemy aircraft shot the airplanes standing ready for take-off, four of which were damaged, in part slightly and in part more seriously, by machine-gun hits.
   Combat Flights: 56. Enemy flight operations brisk. Cloudy, clear at times.

27 Aug   Flight operations low on both sides. Combat Flights: 13. Rain and storms.

28 Aug   Flight operations low on both sides. In the evening, Lt Voss (Jasta 10) test flies the newly arrived Fokker triplane. Combat Flights: 10. Rain and storms.

29 Aug   Weekly report of 21 to 28 August. No flights. Cloudy, rain at times.
   Detailed: Lt d. R. Drekmann, transferred to Jagdgeschwader I by Kogenluft 66043 Fl. I,[3] detailed to Jasta 4.

30 Aug   No special occurrences. Combat Flights: 7. Lt Adam (Jasta 6) appointed leader of Jasta 6 in conformity with Kogenluft 65985 Fl. I. Weather variable.

---

[1] This was Voss's 38th victory.
[2] Oblt Dostler had, in fact, been killed in action.
[3] 'Flieger I', the department of the German Air Service concerned with personnel matters. Lt Drekmann came to JG I from Jasta 26.

31 Aug
Aircraft Downed:
   Lt Adam (Jasta 6) 7.50 p.m., Zonnebeke, this side, Sopwith, as 13th.
   Posting: Lt Gerstenberg, ordered to Jagdgeschwader I in conformity with
Kofl. 4, 35062/7, is posted to Jasta 11.
   A complete radio telegraph receiving station (with accompanying person-
nel) located at Flieger Abteilung 3 will go into operation for Jagdgeschwader I
at 12.00 noon. See Kofl. Op. Order No. 4 of 27 August.
   Combat Flights: 35. Rain, clouds, clearing towards evening.
1 Sept
Aircraft Downed:
   Rittmeister Freiherr von Richthofen, 7.50 a.m., Zonnebeke, this side,
   forward lines, RE, as 60th.
   Oblt Reinhard (Jasta 11) 8.15 a.m., Zonnebeke, other side, Sopwith-1, as
   6th.
   Vfw Wawzin, transferred to Jagdgeschwader I in conformity with Kogenluft
66135 Fl. I, is posted to Jasta 10.
   Enemy air activity brisk in the morning. Combat Flights: 40. Clear, rain and
storms in the afternoon.
2 Sept   Experiences since founding of the Jagdgeschwader.[1] Combat Flights:
73. Relatively little enemy air activity. Changing weather, rain in the afternoon, clearing in the evening.
3 Sept
Aircraft Downed:
   Lt Mohnicke (Jasta 11) 7.30 a.m., south of Ten Brielen, this side, Sopwith,
   as 6th.
   Rittmeister Freiherr von Richthofen, 7.35 a.m., south of Bousbecque, this
   side, Sopwith-1, as 61st.
   Lt Wüsthoff (Jasta 4) 8.30 a.m., south of Ten Brielen, this side, Sopwith,
   as 9th.
   Lt Voss (Jasta 10) 9.52 a.m., north of Houthem, this side, Sopwith, as 39th.
   Lt von Schönebeck (Jasta 11) 10.00 a.m., Hollebeke, this side, triplane, as
   3rd.
   Lt Stapenhorst (Jasta 11) 10.18 a.m., Hollebeke, other side, triplane, as
   2nd.
   Oblt von Döring (Jasta 4) 12.10 p.m., north-west of Houthem, other side,
   RE, as 6th.
   Lt Wüsthoff (Jasta 4) 5.00 p.m., east of Zillebeke, other side, RE-2, as 10th.
   Lt Adam (Jasta 6) 7.50 p.m., Koelenberg, this side, Nieuport, as 14th.
   Oblt von Boenigk (Jasta 4) 8.00 p.m., Houthem, this side, Sopwith, as 4th.
   Oblt von Boenigk (Jasta 4) 8.15 p.m., Brielen, other side, Sopwith, as 5th.
   Wounded: Lt Bockelmann (Jasta 11) 2.30 p.m., near Bousbecque, severely
wounded in air combat (a shot to the lower leg), delivered to Bavarian Field
Hospital 133 near Courtrai.

---

[1] Probably a reference to a report that detailed these experiences.

Enemy air activity moderate. Combat Flights: 113. Clear, cloudy only in the afternoon.

4 Sept
　Aircraft Downed:
　　Lt Wüsthoff (Jasta 4) 8.05 a.m., north of Polygon Wood, this side, single-seater, as 11th.
　　Lt Mohnicke (Jasta 11) 8.40 a.m., Becelaere region, this side, Sopwith-1, as 7th.
　　Lt Wüsthoff (Jasta 4) 10.45 a.m., south of Ypres, other side, Sopwith-1, as 12th.
　Wounded: Oblt Reinhard (Jasta 11) 9.15 a.m., north of Houthulst Forest, badly wounded in air combat (machine-gun ricochet shot to the left thigh), delivered to Bavarian Field Hospital 133 near Courtrai.
　Congratulations [sent] to the Rittmeister on his 60th victory.
　Combat Flights: 98. Enemy air activity cautious. Sunny, no clouds.

5 Sept　Weekly report from 29 August to 4 September. Enemy air activity very brisk. Combat Flights: 100. Weather variable.
　Aircraft Downed:
　　Lt Wüsthoff (Jasta 4) 10.00 a.m., north of Zillebeke Lake, other side, Sopwith, as 12th.
　　Lt Löwenhardt (Jasta 10) 3.50 p.m., St Julien, other side, Sopwith Pup, as 3rd.
　　Lt Voss (Jasta 10) 3.50 p.m., St Julien, other side, Sopwith Pup, as 40th.
　　Lt Voss (Jasta 10) 4.30 p.m., Bixschoote, other side, Caudron, as 41st.

6 Sept
　Aircraft Downed:
　　Lt Voss (Jasta 10) 4.35 p.m., St Julien, other side, FE, as 42nd.
　Transfer: Lt d. R. Meyer transferred to Jasta 4 from Adlershof Aircraft Production Office in conformity with Kogenluft 65396 Fl. I, as officer for special duty.
　The Rittmeister began four weeks' convalescent leave. Oblt von Döring (Jasta 4) acting Geschwader leader for the duration of the Rittmeister's leave. Oblt von Boenigk (Jasta 4) [assumes] acting command of Jasta 4. Lt Groos [assumes] acting command of Jasta 11 in place of the wounded Oblt Reinhard.
　Enemy air activity brisk. Combat Flights: 72. Fog, haze, cloudy.

7 Sept　Little enemy air activity. No flights of our own. Haze and ground fog.
　Order: Lt d. R. Hertz, ordered to Jagdgeschwader I by Kogenluft 65709 Fl. I, is posted to Jasta 4.

8 Sept　Little enemy air activity. No flights of our own. Fog and haze.

9 Sept
　Aircraft Downed:
　　Lt Stapenhorst (Jasta 11) 12.50 p.m., Frezenberg region, forward lines, Spad, as 4th.
　　Oblt von Boenigk (Jasta 4) 7.05 p.m., Poelcapelle, this side, Sopwith, as 5th.
　　Lt Löwenhardt (Jasta 10) 8.55 p.m., Alveringhem, other side, captive balloon, as 4th.

Detailed: Vfw Rüdenberg, Park 4, Jastaschule, is ordered to the Jagdge-schwader in conformity with Kogenluft 66592 Fl. I, detailed to Jasta 10.

The technical officer of the Geschwader is ordered to the Pfalz Works in Speyer until further notice, in accordance with Kogenluft telephone message 36573 Fl. III[1] of 8 August 1917.

Enemy air activity brisk in the afternoon. Combat Flights: 71. Fog, clearing in the afternoon.

10 Sept

Aircraft Downed:

>   Lt Voss (Jasta 10) 5.50 p.m., Langemarck, other side, Sopwith, as 43rd.
>   Lt Voss (Jasta 10) 5.55 p.m., Langemarck, other side, Sopwith, as 44th.
>   Lt Voss (Jasta 10) 6.15 p.m., Langemarck, other side, FE, as 45th.

Detailed: Vfw Hemer, Vfw Burggaller, both Jastaschule I, in conformity with Kogenluft 66669 Fl. I, under transfer to Park 4, ordered to Jagdge-schwader: Vfw Hemer with Jasta 6, Vfw Burggaller with Jasta 10.

Enemy air activity brisk. Combat Flights: 38. Weather variable.

11 Sept

Aircraft Downed:

>   Lt Wüsthoff (Jasta 4) 10.20 a.m., St Julien, other side, Sopwith, as 13th.
>   Oblt Weigand (Jasta 10) 10.20 a.m., Bixschoote, other side, Spad, as 3rd.
>   Lt Voss (Jasta 10) 10.30 a.m., Langemarck, this side, new type,[2] as 46th.
>   Lt Voss (Jasta 10) 4.25 p.m., St Julien, this side, Sopwith, as 47th.

At 5.30 p.m., order from Kofl. 4: Jagdgeschwader I will hold its forces back, in order to be able to appear in the Houthulst Forest–South Ypres sector with strong forces from 7.00 p.m. on. From 7.00 p.m. onwards, the Geschwader, with 34 aircraft, flew in the prescribed sector.

Bombing Raid: At 1.30 p.m., enemy airmen dropped four bombs on the airfield of Jasta 6. Sheds and tent hangars, as well as one machine, damaged by bomb fragments.

Enemy air activity increasing in the evening. Combat Flights: 85. Cloudy.

12 Sept

Aircraft Downed:

>   Lt Wüsthoff (Jasta 4) 8.00 p.m., Deulemont, other side, Sopwith, as 14th.

Weekly report from 5 to 12 September.

Bombing Raid: At 7.30 p.m., enemy airmen dropped bombs on Jastas 6 and 10, without causing any damage.

Lt Wolff (Jasta 11) was promoted to Oberleutnant by His Majesty. Lt Voss (Jasta 10) received a portrait with a handwritten dedication from His Majesty.

Enemy air activity increasing in the evening. Combat Flights: 32. Somewhat hazy.

13 Sept

Aircraft Downed:

>   Lt Wüsthoff (Jasta 4) 8.30 a.m., south of Wervicq, this side, a triplane forced to land, as 15th.

---

[1] 'Fl. III' was the department of the German Air Service concerned with technical matters.
[2] Aircraft was a BF2b.

Combat Flights: 66. Enemy air activity brisk. Weather variable.
14 Sept   The appearance of enemy aircraft in the morning hours on 14
September is to be reckoned with according to the tactical situation. The
Staffeln will stand by for deployment should the need arise. (Geschwader
order, telephone message.)

Wounded: Lt Groos (Jasta 11) 9.40 a.m., near Ypres, slightly wounded in air
combat, remains with the Staffel. Oblt Weigand (Jasta 10) 5.25 p.m., slightly
wounded, remains with the Staffel.

Combat Flights: 93. Enemy air activity low in the morning and afternoon,
brisk in the evening. Heavily overcast, moderate visibility.

15 Sept

Aircraft Downed:

Lt von der Osten (Jasta 11) 12.45 p.m., Frezenberg, other side, Sopwith,
as 3rd.

Lt d. L. Adam (Jasta 6) 7.00 p.m., Ypres, Sopwith, as 14th.

Lt d. R.Wüsthoff (Jasta 4) 7.30 p. m., north-west of Wervicq, Sopwith, as
16th.

Casualty: Oblt Wolff (leader of Jasta 11) 5.30 p.m., north of Wervicq, shot
down in air combat. Aircraft: Fokker triplane FI 102 totally consumed.

Combat Flights: 54. Enemy air activity: none in the morning, brisk in the
afternoon, very brisk in the evening. Heavily overcast, moderate visibility.

16 Sept   Lt Groos (Jasta 11) has taken over acting command of Jasta 11.

Aircraft Downed:

Oblt von Döring, leader of Jasta 4, 12.45 p.m., west of Staden, this side,
Sopwith, as 7th.

Lt d. R. Wüsthoff (Jasta 4) 12.45 p.m., west of Staden, this side, Sopwith,
as 17th.

Telegram of condolence from Kogenluft on the downing of Oblt Wolff.
Telephone report from Lt Adam (Jasta 6) concerning the fate of Oblt Dostler,
who did not return from a flight.[1]

Combat Flights: 61. Enemy air activity in the morning 1:1, moderate in the
afternoon, in the evening 3:1 in favor of the enemy. Slightly cloudy, visibility
good.

17 Sept

Aircraft Downed:

Vfw Bachmann (Jasta 6) 7.20 a.m., south of Zillebeke Lake, other side,
Sopwith, as 1st. Ground observation lacking.

Lt d. R. Hertz (Jasta 4) 8.40 a.m., Houthulst Forest, other side, Nieuport,
as 1st. Ground observation lacking.

Combat Flights: 40. Enemy air activity very light. Slightly cloudy, good
visibility.

18 Sept   11.00 a.m., Oblt Wolff conveyed from St Joseph's Church in Courtrai
to the train station, and from there to Memel.

Detailed: Lt d. R. Joschkowitz, Jastaschule I, detailed to Jasta 4; Lt d. R.

---

[1] Missing in action on 21 August 1917.

Just, Jastaschule I, detailed to Jasta 11, ordered to Jagdgeschwader I, in conformity with Kogenluft 67170 Fl. I of 17 Sep 1917 (Kofl. Order of the Day 7, Numeral 1).

Combat Flights: 39. Enemy air activity moderate. Unbroken cloud cover, rain at times.

19 Sept Obituary for Oblt Wolff. Weekly report from 13 to 19 September.

Aircraft Downed:

Lt Adam (Jasta 6) 10.00 a.m., west of Ypres, other side, RE, as 16th.

Lt Galetschky (Jasta 6) 10.05 a.m., Houthulst Forest, this side, Sopwith, in flames, as 1st.

Wounded: Offz Stellv Aue (Jasta 10) wounded in air combat near Roulers at 10.00 a.m. (a shot through the lower left leg), smooth emergency landing near Roulers; delivered to Military Hospital 13, Courtrai.

Combat Flights: 100. Enemy air activity picking up in the morning, brisk in the afternoon, low in the evening. Slightly cloudy.

20 Sept Day of major battle.[1] Combat report.

At 8.30 a.m., an English Sopwith-1, swooping out of the clouds, dropped one bomb apiece on Jasta 4 and Jasta 11 from a very low altitude. Resulting damage at Jasta 4: three airplanes totally destroyed, five airplanes heavily damaged, one airplane slightly damaged. At Jasta 11: window panes broken in the enlisted men's quarters. The Geschwader's depot which is under construction and the Jasta's car sheds damaged by bomb fragments.

Casualties: One non-commissioned officer and three men of Jasta 4 dead due to the bombing, one man of Jasta 4 wounded by machine-gun fire from the air. In addition, of that machine-gun sharpshooter detail ordered to the airfield from the Army Group Wytschaete for anti-aircraft defense purposes, one gunner dead (died in hospital), two badly wounded, two slightly wounded.

Aircraft Downed:

Lt Adam (Jasta 6) 9.40 a.m., west of Bellewaarde Lake, other side, Sopwith-1, as 17th.

Lt Adam (Jasta 6) 9.50 a.m., Becelaere region, this side, Sopwith-1, as 18th.

Lt K. Stock (Jasta 6) 9.50 a.m., Becelaere region, this side, triplane, as 1st.

Lt Wüsthoff (Jasta 4) 12.15 p.m., near Amerika, this side, Spad, as 18th.

Oblt von Döring (Jasta 4) 12.30 p.m., south of Ypres, other side, Spad, as 8th.

Vfw Bachmann (Jasta 6) 2.00 p.m., near Kemmel, other side, captive balloon, as 2nd.

Lt Wüsthoff (Jasta 4) 2.30 p.m., west of Langemarck, other side, Spad, as 19th.

Wounded: Lt Löwenhardt (Jasta 10) 11.10 a.m., slightly wounded, smooth emergency landing near Roulers.

Casualty: Lt Just (Jasta 11) made an emergency landing near Becelaere following air combat on account of a shot through the gas tank.

---

[1] The Battle of the Menin Road Ridge (20 to 25 Sept), during the Third Battle of Ypres.

Combat Flights: 101. Enemy air activity 2:1 in favor of the enemy in the morning, in the afternoon very brisk, moderate in the evening. Light rain, clearing later.

21 Sept   Detailed: Lt Römer transferred to Jagdgeschwader I by Kogenluft 61189 Fl. I., detailed to Jasta 10.

Aircraft Downed:

Lt Bellen (Jasta 10) 2.45 p.m., north-west of Ypres, other side, map quadrant S42, captive balloon, as 1st.

Lt Löwenhardt (Jasta 10) 7.25 p.m., map quadrant 51, captive balloon, as 5th.

Combat Flights: 75. Enemy air activity moderate in the morning, picking up in the afternoon, brisk at times in the evening. Sky almost cloudless, hazy later.

22 Sept

Aircraft Downed:

Lt Wüsthoff (Jasta 4) 2.10 p.m., Langemarck, other side, Sopwith, as 20th.

One man was severely wounded by machine-gun fire at 1.00 p.m. when a Pfalz at Jasta 4 was strafed.

Combat Flights: 47. Enemy air activity very moderate early, low in the afternoon, moderate in the evening. Cloudy, high ground haze.

23 Sept   Vfw Niess, Uffz Beschow, Uffz Werkmeister transferred to Jagdgeschwader I in conformity with Kogenluft 67394 Fl. I.

Detailed: Vfw Niess, Uffz Beschow to Jasta 6; Uffz Werkmeister to Jasta 10. (All arrived on 23 Sept.)

Aircraft Downed:

Lt Voss (Jasta 10) 9.30 a.m., south of Roulers, this side, de Havilland in flames, as 48th.

Lt Adam (Jasta 6) 10.45 a.m., north of Ypres, other side, RE, as 19th.

Oblt von Döring (Jasta 4) 11.30 a.m., Langemarck, other side, Sopwith, as 9th.

Casualties: Lt Voss (Jasta 10) 6.05 p.m., took off with his Staffel, did not return from this flight. Probably crashed fatally on the other side of the enemy lines following air combat. Airplane: Fokker triplane.[1]

Combat Flights: 75. Enemy air activity low in the morning, brisk in the afternoon, in the evening a lot of enemy single-seater action, mostly on the other side. Almost cloudless sky, ground haze.

24 Sept   Jasta 10 reports that, according to statements by Lt Wendelmuth (Jasta 8), while in air combat with a Sopwith, Lt Voss was shot down from behind by a second Sopwith. He is said to have crashed just north of Frezenberg (other side).

Arrival of a radio telegraph test unit from Döberitz (four officers, five pilots, six non-commissioned officers, 42 men; quarters and rations with Jastas 4 and 11). Set up at Jasta's airdrome.

Lt Pastor, ordered to the Jagdgeschwader by Kogenluft 67389, is detailed to

---

[1] Fokker Triplane FI 103/17.

Jasta 11. Oblt Weigand assumes acting command of Jasta 10 until further notice.
Aircraft Downed:
Lt Wüsthoff (Jasta 4) 4.50 p.m., Moorslede, this side, Sopwith, as 21st.
No enemy air activity in the morning, slight on the whole in the afternoon.
Fighter patrols at high altitudes. Between 2.00 and 3.00 o'clock, a couple of
squadrons up as far as the Menin–Roulers line. In the evening, brisk single-
seater action at 5,000 to 6,000 meters.
Heavy fog in the morning, clearer in the afternoon.
25 Sept Submission of the action report requested by Kogenluft Op. Order
No. 9 of 9 Sep 1917. Report concerning hints for recognizing and combating the
different enemy airplane types.
Lt Freiherr von Richthofen (Lothar) appointed leader of Jasta 11 in conformity with Kogenluft 67259.
Telegram from Kogenluft on the occasion of the loss of Lt Voss.
Casualties: Oblt Weigand (Jasta 10) 5.40 p.m., Houthulst Forest, crashed in
flames following air combat, dead. Uffz Werkmeister (Jasta 10) 5.42 p.m.,
broke up and crashed in flames following air combat over Houthulst Forest.
Almost cloudless, heavy ground haze, clear in the afternoon, good visibility.
Combat Flights: 75. Enemy air activity picking up at times in the morning,
moderate in the afternoon, brisk in the evening.
26 Sept Large-scale attack.[1] Combat report. Lt d. R. Kühn acting leader of
Jasta 10. Aircraft Downed:
Lt K. Stock (Jasta 6) 7.20 a.m., north-west of Dadizeele, this side, Spad,
as 2nd.
Lt Wüsthoff (Jasta 4) 10.40 a.m., Becelaere, this side, Spad, as 22nd.
Lt Joschkowitz (Jasta 4) 10.40 a.m., Becelaere, this side, Spad, as 1st.
Weekly report from 20 to 26 September.
Low hanging clouds, poor visibility, unfavorable weather conditions.
Combat Flights: 62. Enemy air activity low in the morning; from 10.00 on, very
brisk at low altitude, very brisk on the other side of the lines during the evening.
27 Sept Lt d. R. Hans Klein appointed leader of Jasta 10 in conformity with
Kogenluft 67799. No enemy flight operations.
Combat Flights: 76. Enemy air activity: none in the morning. From 11.00 on,
more single-seater activity; in the evening heavy single-seater activity above
and behind the lines. Hazy, rain.
28 Sept No enemy flight operations. Heavy fog in the morning, then hazy.
Combat Flights: 79. Enemy air activity low, none in the evening.
29 Sept Jagdgeschwader deployed for temporary short, limited, combat
action with the 6th Army. (In accordance with Army Order of 27 Sep 1917, see
enclosure.)
11.00 a.m., Oblt Weigand and Uffz Werkmeister (Jasta 10), who fell in air
combat on 25 September, conveyed from St Joseph's Church, Courtrai.
Combat Flights: 51. Enemy air activity low, heavy in the evening, mostly on
the other side of the lines. Heavily overcast, hazy.

---

[1] Battle of Polygon Wood, during Third Battle of Ypres.

30 Sept   No aircraft downed; enemy flight operations mostly on the other side of the Front.

Vfw Stumpf (Jasta 6) slightly injured as a result of overturning during landing, remains with the unit.

Heavy fog in the morning, clearing up at noon, good visibility in the afternoon, heavy mist at higher altitudes in the evening. Combat Flights: 66. Enemy air activity low in the morning, especially brisk at higher altitudes in the afternoon; in the evening a few single-seaters at higher altitudes, otherwise almost no flight operations.

1 Oct   Transmission of information to Jagdgeschwader I concerning the breakthroughs of enemy squadrons (Army Order of 16 Sep 1917), see enclosure. Outline of Jagdgeschwader I's telephone system, see enclosure. No airplanes downed. Enclosures 45, 46.

2 Oct   Lt d. R. Koepsch, ordered to Jagdgeschwader I in conformity with Kogenluft 67947 Fl. I of 30 Sep 1917. Detailed: Jasta 4.

Rittmeister Freiherr von Richthofen was awarded the Lübeck Hanseatic Cross on 22 September, and the Brunswick War Merit Cross on 24 September.

Aircraft Downed:

Lt d. R. Klein (Jasta 10) 10.40 a.m., Meulebeke, this side, de Havilland, as 17th.

Casualties: Lt Römer (Jasta 10) 9.30 a.m., took off on a combat patrol and did not return. Postscript: crashed in flames at 10.30 a.m., near West Roosebeke, this side, dead. Lt d. R. Rüdenberg (Jasta 10) made an emergency landing near Arsele following air combat, uninjured; machine totally destroyed.

3 Oct   No flight operations.

4 Oct   On 23 September, Rittmeister Freiherr von Richthofen was given by His Majesty a bronze bust with the engraved dedication: 'To The Glorious Fighter Pilot Rittmeister Freiherr von Richthofen. His Grateful King. 10 Sept 1917.'

No flight operations on account of low clouds and rain. Enemy air activity etc. of the last week, see weekly report of 27 Sept to 3 Oct 1917.

Large-scale attack, see telephone message of Kofl. 4.

5 Oct   Situation following large-scale attack of 4 October,[1] see telephone message (enclosure).

Aircraft Downed:

Lt d. R. Wilde (Jasta 4) 7.45 a.m., Dadizeele, this side, triplane, as 1st.

6 Oct   11.00 a.m., in Courtrai, burial of Lt Römer (Jasta 10) who fell in air combat. No enemy flight operations.

7 Oct   On account of continuous rain, almost no flight operations.

Aircraft Downed:

Lt Galetschky (Jasta 6) 8.10 a.m., map quadrant W 46, other side, RE, as 2nd.

A second radio telegraph station set up with sending and receiving apparatus. Further orders concerning the purpose of the station still to follow.

8-14 Oct   Enemy flight operations very low.

---

[1] Battle of Broodseinde Ridge, during Third Battle of Ypres.

15 Oct   No special occurrences.

The Cross for Faithful Service 1914 of Schaumberg–Lippe was conferred upon Rittmeister Freiherr von Richthofen, under the date of 10 Oct 1917.

Combat Flights: 72. Enemy air activity moderate in the afternoon, low in the evening. Broken clouds, good visibility.

16 Oct   No special occurrences. Unbroken clouds, rain at times; good visibility in the morning. Combat Flights: 39. Enemy air activity low.

17 Oct   Weekly report from 11 to 17 Oct 1917.

18 Oct

Aircraft Downed:

9.45 a.m., a Bristol-2 biplane forced to land near Château Ardooie by Lt Löwenhardt, this side, as 7th.

9.55 a.m., a Bristol-2 biplane forced to land in the Staden region by Lt Klein (Jasta 10) as 20th.

Combat Flights: 65. Enemy air activity brisk in the morning, low in the afternoon.

Hazy, poor visibility.

19 Oct   No flight operations. Rain, heavily overcast. No enemy air activity.

20 Oct   Wounded: Lt Gerstenberg (Jasta 11) 12.00 noon, severely wounded (shot in the lung), in air combat near Vassenmolen and forced to land, machine totally demolished. Delivered to Medical Company 40, in Rollegem Capelle. Uffz Hardel (Jasta 10) 1.10 p.m., wounded in air combat (shot in the leg). Broken leg and concussion during landing near Potteribrug, machine totally destroyed.[1] Delivered to Bavarian Field Hospital 49, Courtrai.

Combat Flights: 55. Enemy air activity low, none in the afternoon. Hazy, poor visibility.

21 Oct

Aircraft Downed:

4.00 p.m., SE 5 near Moorslede by Oblt von Döring (Jasta 4) as 9th.

Casualties: Vfw Bachmann (Jasta 6) missing since 11.20 a.m., following air combat.[2]

Decoration: Rittmeister Freiherr von Richthofen was awarded the Princely Lippe War Honor Cross for Heroic Act under the date of 13 Oct 1917.

Bombing Raid: Around 7.00 in the evening, an enemy airman dropped a large bomb between the airplane hangar and quarters at Jasta 6, without causing any damage.

Good in the morning, but misty; good visibility in the afternoon. Combat Flights: 68. Enemy air activity low in the morning, brisk in the afternoon, moderate in the evening.

22 Oct   No flight operations.

Bombing Raid: Around 7.00 in the evening, an enemy airman dropped a bomb in the vicinity of Jasta 11's airdrome. Five machines in one hangar were damaged by bomb fragments. In addition, several billets as well as the

---

[1] No town found with this name; the town of Potijze is one possibility.
[2] Killed in action near Ypres.

Geschwader's office were unroofed.

Rain. Combat Flights: 4. No enemy air activity all day long, low activity in the evening.

23 Oct Rittmeister Freiherr von Richthofen resumes command of the Geschwader today, from noon on.

Detailed: Lt Zwitzers, ordered to Jagdgeschwader I in conformity with Kogenluft 69295, assigned to Jasta 4.

Overcast, rainy. Combat Flights: 33. Enemy air activity low, only single-seater fighters at high altitude on the other side of the lines.

24 Oct No special occurrences. Good visibility, variable cloudiness. Combat Flights: 73. Enemy air activity moderate, several artillery-spotting and single-seater fighter squadrons.

25 Oct Weekly report from 18 to 24 Oct 1917.

26 Oct No special occurrences. Rain. Combat Flights: 7. Enemy air activity low.

27 Oct Casualties: Lt Müller (Jasta 11) crashed fatally on the field in front of the airdrome during a test flight with a Fokker biplane. Machine demolished.

Aircraft Downed:

9.30 a.m., a triplane, near Poelcapelle-Hooge, by Lt Wüsthoff (Jasta 4) other side, as 22nd.

2.20 p.m., RE2, north of Gheluvelt, by Vfw Hemer (Jasta 6) this side, as 1st.

Bombing Raid: At 9.30 in the evening, an enemy airman dropped a bomb directly in front of the telephone exchange of Jagdgeschwader I. A telephonist was killed by bomb fragments. The telephone system was heavily damaged to some extent. No further damage resulted. At 2.00 a.m. during the night, an enemy airman dropped a bomb on the airfield at Jasta 4, no damage.

Clear in the morning, good visibility, misty at times in the afternoon, misty in the evening, poor visibility. Combat Flights: 79. Enemy air activity moderate in the morning, brisk in the afternoon, very low in the evening.

28 Oct No special occurrences. Heavy ground haze, fog. Combat Flights: 28. Enemy air activity very moderate the whole day.

29 Oct Vfw Lautenschlager (Jasta 11) 10.45 a.m., shot down in Fokker Dr. I north of Houthulst Forest, this side of the lines, as a result of shots fired by mistake by one of our own airplanes.

In the afternoon hours, several flights of the Geschwader flew in the sector of the Army Group Ypres, in order to keep the enemy from getting a look at the troop displacement.

Good visibility in the morning, clouds in the afternoon at an altitude of 2,000 m. Enemy air activity low morning and afternoon.

30 Oct Rittmeister and Lt Freiherr von Richthofen made emergency landings at 9.50 [a.m.], near Zilverberg, both uninjured. The Rittmeister's machine (Fokker Dr. I 114/17) totally demolished, the other machine undamaged.

Service instructions for the radio telegraph unit.

Day of major battle.[1] Rain, heavily overcast. Combat Flights: 6. Enemy air

---

[1] The Battle of Passchendaele, Third Battle of Ypres.

activity very low in the morning, none in the afternoon.

31 Oct
   Aircraft Downed:
      12.30 p.m., an SE 5, north of Bellewaarde Lake, by Lt Wüsthoff (Jasta 4) other side, as 23rd.
   Casualties: Lt d. R. Pastor (Jasta 11) 3.20 p.m., one km north of Moorseele, crashed fatally with Fokker Dr. I 121/17, machine totally demolished.
   16 unsuccessful air combats, one successful. Good visibility, cloudy at times. Combat Flights: 95. Enemy air activity low.

1 Nov   No special occurrences. Weekly report from 25 to 31 October. Report as to ration strength on 1 November. Personnel strength report, status as of 31 October. Good visibility, cloudy. Combat Flights: 29. Enemy air activity low.

2 Nov   No special occurrences. Very foggy, rain at times.

3 Nov   No special occurrences. Vfw Lautenschlager's funeral, 3.00 p.m. Information concerning the downing of Lt Voss (Jasta 10). Lt Müller and Lt Pastor conveyed from St Joseph's Church in Courtrai, 11.00 a.m. Very hazy. Combat Flights: 10. No enemy air activity.

4 Nov   Afternoon visit to the Geschwader by the Turkish General Izet Pascha and the Swiss Colonel Egli.
   Radio telegraph test unit entrained at 3.00 p.m. in Wevelghem, Transport No. 26999. Tests concluded. Report as to practical experience with radio telegraph equipment in single-seater fighters.
   Award: The Turkish Crescent awarded to Rittmeister Freiherr von Richthofen.
   Foggy, overcast, no visibility.

5 Nov
   Aircraft Downed:
      12.45 p.m., a Sopwith near Poelcapelle, above the lines, by Lt Wüsthoff (Jasta 4) as 24th.
      1.00 p.m., a Sopwith in the Staden region by Lt Wüsthoff (Jasta 4) this side, as 25th.
   Five unsuccessful air combats, two successful. Combat Flights: 33. Enemy air activity fairly brisk between 12.30 and 2.00. Squadrons of single-seater fighters at high altitude. Very hazy, unbroken cloud cover.

6 Nov   Casualty: 8.30 a.m., Lt Löwenhardt (Jasta 10) made an emergency landing near St Eloois Winkel, as a result of wings breaking. Machine totally demolished, passenger unhurt.
   Aircraft Downed:
      8.45 a.m., a Nieuport near Zonnebeke, by Vfw Stumpf (Jasta 6) as 1st.
      8.50 a.m., a Sopwith-1, west of Passchendaele, by Lt Adam (Jasta 6) as 21st.
   Two unsuccessful air combats, two successful, on the other side of the lines.
   Day of major battle.[1] Heavily overcast, rain, ceiling 800 m. Combat Flights: 70. Enemy air activity low.

---

[1] Battle of Passchendaele. The village of Passchendaele taken by the Canadian Corps.

7 Nov   No special occurrences. Weekly report from 1 to 7 November.

Heavily overcast, rain, clearing at times. Combat Flights: 58. Enemy air activity from 8.30-9.00 a.m., strong blockade on the other side, low activity on this side; very low in the afternoon and evening.

8 Nov   Casualty: Flieger Riensberg (Jasta 10) overturned as a result of setting down too short while landing; machine wrecked, pilot: fracture of the right radius bone.

Somewhat hazy, unbroken cloud cover in the afternoon, good visibility in part. Combat Flights: 95. Enemy air activity low in the morning; in the afternoon mostly brisk on the other side, moderate on this side; in the evening brisk on the other side of the lines and moderate on this side.

9 Nov

Aircraft Downed:

> 10.30 a.m., a Bristol-2 north-west of Zonnebeke, by Lt Lothar Freiherr von Richthofen (Jasta 11) as 25th, other side.
>
> 10.30 a.m., an RE north of Bellewaarde Lake by Lt Wüsthoff (Jasta 4) as 26th, other side.

18 unsuccessful air combats, two successful. In the morning good, clear visibility; cloudy at times in the afternoon, good visibility; in the evening good visibility. Combat Flights: 85. Enemy air activity brisk, artillery spotters mostly on the other side, low in the afternoon till 2.30, brisk from 4.00-5.00 p.m., moderate towards evening.

10 Nov   No special occurrences. Rain.

11 Nov   Casualties: Lt Tüxen (Jasta 6) 2.00 p.m., crashed while banking over the airfield with training machine Fokker DV 2642/16; machine totally demolished, passenger unhurt.

Three unsuccessful air combats.

3.00 p.m., protective flight by Jasta 6 for a Kampfstaffel of Kagohl 1 for a bombing run in the direction of Ypres.

Instructions for operating the radio telegraph system.

Cloudy in the morning, visibility to 2,000 m, hazy in the afternoon, cloudy. Combat Flights: 76. No enemy air activity in the morning, activity quite low in the afternoon, quite low in the evening.

12 Nov

Aircraft Downed:

> 10.35 a.m., an RE north-east of Ypres in map quadrant V 43, other side, by Vfw Hemer (Jasta 6) as 2nd.

Ten unsuccessful air combats, one successful. Enemy air activity conspicuously low, and mostly on the other side.

Transmission of information concerning the fighter units in the air when enemy squadrons break through.

Ground fog, heavy mist. Combat Flights: 59. Enemy air activity fairly brisk between 8.00 and 9.00 a.m., low later on.

13 Nov   No special occurrences. Hazy, clouds at an altitude of 800 m. Combat Flights: 36. No enemy air activity in the morning, little activity in the afternoon.

14 Nov   No special occurrences. Weekly report from 4 to 14 November.

15 Nov Casualty: Lt d. L. I Adam (Jasta 6) 9.20 a.m., Albatros DV 5222/17, shot down to his death in air combat north-west of Kortewilde. Aircraft totally destroyed.

Nine unsuccessful air combats. Hazy. Combat Flights: 47. Enemy air activity low.

16 Nov No special occurrences. Fog, poor visibility. Combat Flights: 19. No enemy air activity.

17 Nov No special occurrences.

18 Nov

Aircraft Downed:

> 9.25 a.m., a Spad, in flames, north of Ypres, other side, by Vfw Wawzin (Jasta 10) as 1st.

19 Nov No special occurrences. Fog.

20 Nov 11.00 a.m., Lt Adam conveyed from the Carmelite Chapel, Field Hospital 38, Courtrai.

At 12.18 p.m., a Sopwith-1 pushing down out of the clouds fired on the airdrome of Jasta 11 with machine guns, causing no damage. He flew off in the direction of Wevelghem.

21 Nov In conformity with Kofl. Order II of 20 November, No. 1a 619/20 op., Jagdgeschwader hastily transported to the 2nd Army. Airdromes: Staff and Jasta 11, Avesnes le Sec; Jastas 4 and 6, Lieu St Amand; Jasta 10, Iwuy. The airplanes are to go by air as soon as possible to the Jastaschule airdrome at Valenciennes. Station for entraining Jagdgeschwader I: Lauwe. Preparations for entraining.

Clouds at an altitude of 800 m, hazy. Combat Flights: 32. Enemy air activity very low.

22 Nov The Staffeln move by air to the La Briquette airdrome (near Valenciennes). The Jagdgeschwader will remain in Marckebeke until further notice since entraining not possible before 23 November, due to a lack of railway cars and to heavy bombarding of the train stations near the 4th Army.

Airplane crews will occupy quarters located partly in La Briquette and in Valenciennes. With assistance from the mechanics of Jastaschule I and small detachments of the Staffeln, flight operations can be maintained.

Clouds at an altitude of 600 m., very hazy. Combat Flights: 7. Almost no enemy air activity.

23 Nov Enemy air activity: large groups of enemy airmen appeared at times, especially between 1.00 and 2.00 o'clock (single- and two-seaters) at lowest altitude over Bourlon Wood. Almost all of the air combats [were] at the lowest altitudes.

Aircraft Downed:

> At 2.00 p.m., a DH5 near Bourlon in the forward lines, by Rittmeister Freiherr von Richthofen, as 62nd.
>
> A Bristol-2 biplane, two km west of Seranvillers, by Lt Lothar Freiherr von Richthofen (Jasta 11) this side, as 26th.
>
> At 3.00 p.m., Sopwith biplane west of Cambrai by Lt d. R. Küppers (Jasta 6) this side, as 5th.

Special occurrences: Lt H. J. Wolff (Jasta 11) overturned during landing near Avesnes le Sec, slightly injured, remained with the unit. Lt von Schönebeck made an emergency landing near Epinoy, machine and passenger unhurt.

Staff and Jasta 11 entrained at 4.00 in Lauwe.

Clouds at 500 m, downward visibility hazy during the morning; in the afternoon mostly good visibility, clouds at 300 m and 1,000 m. Combat Flights: 48. No enemy air activity in the morning, activity low in the afternoon and mostly far on the other side, brisk air combat (unsuccessful) with Sopwith-2s [during] main operation.[1]

Hazy, cloudy, no rain. Combat Flights: 37. Enemy air activity very brisk in the afternoon hours.

24 Nov Enemy air activity conspicuously low, occasional airmen far on the other side of the lines. The reserve machines located with the 4th Army were flown to Briquette in part by pilots of the 4th Army. Staff and Jasta 11 arrived in Haspres at 12.00 noon. Jastas 6 and 10 entrained at 8.00 in Lauwe.

Combat Flights: 33. Enemy air activity conspicuously low, and mostly on the other side.

Avesnes le Sec

25 Nov All the Staffeln occupy their airdromes during the course of the day. Evening report to Kofl. 2. Jasta 6 arrived in Bouchain at 9.30, Jasta 10 in Iwuy at 10.20. Jasta 4 is entrained at Lauwe at 4.00.

Lt Klein (Jasta 10) overturned while landing on the Iwuy airfield. Machine heavily damaged, pilot unhurt.

Low clouds, rain at times. Combat Flights: 21. Almost no enemy air activity.

26 Nov No flight operations. Jasta 4 arrived in Bouchain at 9.00 a.m. Oblt Reinhard appointed leader of Jasta 6. Low clouds, rain. Combat Flights: 37. Enemy air activity very low.

27 Nov No flight operations. Lt d. R. Wüsthoff (Jasta 4) decorated with the *Pour le Mérite* according to a radio message from Kogenluft.

Lt Bahr and Lt von Hartmann, Lt von Schweinitz and Lt von Linsingen are transferred to Jagdgeschwader I in conformity with Kogenluft 70831 and 71025 Fl. I respectively. Lt von Hartmann is posted to Jasta 4, the others to Jasta 11. Lt von Alvensleben (Jasta 4) is transferred to Jasta 21 in conformity with Kogenluft 70937 Fl. I.

Low clouds, rain. Combat Flights: 18. No enemy air activity.

28 Nov No flight operations. Order from Army Group (see enclosure 69). Rain. Enclosure 69.

29 Nov Jasta 10 moves from Iwuy to Avesnes le Sec (east).

Aircraft Downed:

> 9.45 a.m., an SE 5 forced to land near Wambaix by Fw Lt Schubert (Jasta 6) this side, as 3rd.
>
> Around 10.00 a.m., a Sopwith near Crevecoeur by Lt d. R. Klein (Jasta 10) over the lines, as 21st.

---

[1] The British capture Bourlon Ridge during Battle of Cambrai, 20 Nov – 7 Dec 1917.

Around 10.00 a.m., a Sopwith near Crevecoeur by Lt d. R. Heldmann (Jasta 10) this side, as 3rd.

Preparations for the attack ordered for 30 November, Army Order for the attack.[1]

Lt d. R. Bouillon (Jasta 4) is transferred to Armee Flugpark 4 in conformity with Kogenluft 2339 Personnel Fl. I.

Hazy, clouds at 1,000 m. Combat Flights: 69. Enemy air activity: isolated reconnaissance squadrons in the morning, later almost no activity.

30 Nov   Day's occurrences: see evening report, telephone message no. 535 (see enclosure). Order concerning employment of aviation forces on 1 December. Situation at 10.00 a.m., 12.40 p.m., and 2.00 p.m.

Aircraft Downed:

12.30 p.m., a captive balloon (English), in flames, west of Ribecourt by Lt Klein (Jasta 10) as 22nd.

1.45 p.m., a DH 5, south of Bourlon Wood by Lt von der Osten (Jasta 11) as 4th.

2.30 p.m., an SE 5, in flames, near Moevres by Rittmeister Freiherr von Richthofen, this side, as 63rd.

2.45 p.m., a DH 5, in flames, between Moevres and Bourlon Wood by Lt Gussmann (Jasta 11) as 2nd.

3.45 p.m., a Sopwith-1 over Bourlon Wood by Lt Löwenhardt (Jasta 10) as 8th.

A Sopwith four km south-west of Marcoing by Lt Janzen (Jasta 6) as 2nd.[2]

Casualties: 11.35 a.m., Lt Schultze (Jasta 4) crashed fatally following a collision with an Albatros near Fontaine Notre Dame, this side. Lt Demandt (Jasta 10) did not return from a pursuit flight at 4.00 p.m.[3]

Clouds at low altitude. Combat Flights: 103. Enemy air activity: see evening report.

1 Dec   Situation at 2.00 p.m. (see enclosure). Activity report.

Lt d. R. Meyer (Jasta 11) is ordered to Jasta 4 until further notice.

Rittmeister Freiherr von Richthofen's report concerning the downing of his 63rd aircraft.

Heavily overcast, rain at times. Combat Flights: 56. Enemy air activity moderate all day long.

2 Dec   No special occurrences. Overcast at times, heavy ground fog. Combat Flights: 62. Enemy air activity very low.

3 Dec   No special occurrences. Army Order of 3 [December].

Clear visibility, some ground haze, strong west wind. Combat Flights: 53. Enemy air activity very low.

4 Dec   Seven unsuccessful air combats.

Albatros DV No. 2161 (Lt von Linsingen), No. 5313 (Lt von Schweinitz) and No. 4628 (Lt Gussmann) damaged during landing, No. 4628 totally demolished.

---

[1] Massive counterattack by the German Second Army under General von der Marwitz.
[2] Victory achieved at 3.45 p.m.
[3] Killed in action near Cambrai.

Cloudless, high ground haze. Combat Flights: 55. Enemy air activity moderate.

5 Dec

Aircraft Downed:

11.20 a.m., a Bristol north of Cambrai by Vfw Barth (Jasta 10) this side, as 1st.

12.35 p.m., a Sopwith near Graincourt on the Bapaume–Cambrai road, by Lt Koepsch (Jasta 4) as 1st.

14 unsuccessful air combats, two successful.

Lt d. R. Klein (Jasta 10) was decorated with the *Pour le Mérite* according to a radio message from Kogenluft.

Almost cloudless, light ground haze. Combat Flights: 76. Enemy air activity: from 10.00-12.00 a few reconnaissance and bombing squadrons at high altitude, increasing from 3.00-4.00 p.m., otherwise moderate.

6 Dec No special occurrences. Seven unsuccessful air combats. Cloudless, heavy ground haze. Combat Flights: 58. Enemy air activity somewhat more brisk than in the last few days.

7 Dec No special occurrences. Order for air cover for Operation 'Wintersport'. Sky overcast, heavy ground haze. Combat Flights: 39. Enemy air activity low.

8 Dec No special occurrences. Overcast, rain at times, clearing from 2.00 p.m. on. Combat Flights: 18. Enemy air activity low.

9 Dec No special occurrences. Sky overcast, rain.

10 Dec

Aircraft Downed:

1.20 p.m., an SE 5 south-east of Gonnelieu by Lt Janzen (Jasta 6) this side, as 3rd.

One successful, seven unsuccessful air combats.

During an air combat, Lt Mohnicke flew into Oblt von Boddien's machine from behind. Lt Mohnicke crashed; machine totally demolished, passenger unhurt. Oblt von Boddien flew back to the Staffel's airfield without elevators and landed smoothly.

Clear, heavy ground haze. Combat Flights: 64. Enemy air activity more brisk at times.

11 Dec No special occurrences. Partly overcast, slight ground haze.

12 Dec Rittmeister Freiherr von Richthofen is ordered to the Pfalz Aircraft Works in Speyer for a period of eight to ten days. During this time, Rittmeister von Döring[1] will assume acting command of the Jagdgeschwader.

Aircraft Downed:

1.20 p.m., a captive balloon, in flames, near Ruyaulcourt by Lt d. R. Just (Jasta 11) as 1st.

Partly overcast, slight ground haze. Combat Flights: 45. Enemy air activity low.

13 Dec No special occurrences. Partially overcast, slight ground haze.

14 Dec No special occurrences. Partially overcast, slight ground haze.

15 Dec Aircraft Downed: 10.25 a.m., an SE 5 near Havrincourt by Lt von der

---

[1] Promoted to Rittmeister on 28 Nov 1917.

Osten (Jasta 11) other side, as 5th.

Five unsuccessful air combats, one successful. Slightly cloudy, moderate visibility. Combat Flights: 81. Enemy air activity low.

16 Dec No special occurrences. Heavily overcast, hazy. Combat Flights: 17. No enemy air activity.

17 Dec No special occurrences. Heavily overcast, hazy, driving snow.

18 Dec No special occurrences. Partially overcast, ground haze, strong wind.

19 Dec No special occurrences. Air cover for the Court train and employment of the Staffeln for this purpose. Five unsuccessful air combats. Combat Flights: 60. Enemy air activity low.

20 Dec No special occurrences. Rittmeister Freiherr von Richthofen resumes command of the Jagdgeschwader. Fog, no visibility.

21 Dec No special occurrences. Fog, no visibility.

22 Dec No special occurrences. Protective flights for the Kaiser's Troop Review near Solesmes. Clearing, visibility from 12.00 noon; heavy ground haze. Combat Flights: 74. Enemy air activity low.

23 Dec No special occurrences. Five unsuccessful air combats. Cloudless, high ground haze. Combat Flights: 34. Enemy air activity low.

24 Dec No special occurrences. Foggy, rain increasing from 11.00 a.m.

25 Dec No special occurrences. Clear visibility, heavy clouds and snow. Combat Flights: 7. No enemy air activity.

26 Dec No special occurrences. Clear visibility, heavy ground haze from 10.00 a.m. Combat Flights: 13.

27 Dec Casualties: Lt von Schweinitz (Jasta 11) crashed with Albatros DV 5313 at 2.35 p.m. due to breakage of fuselage and wings. Airplane and pilot incinerated. Vfw Hecht (Jasta 10) did not return from a flight.

Overcast, very foggy. Combat Flights: 4.

28 Dec No special occurrences. Clear, ground haze, overcast from 12.00 noon, snow. Combat Flights: 28. Enemy air activity very low.

29 Dec No special occurrences. Cloudless, high ground haze and fog. Combat Flights: 3. No enemy air activity.

30 Dec No special occurrences. Sky overcast, heavy ground haze.

31 Dec No special occurrences. Sky overcast, heavy ground haze, clearing somewhat from 4.00 p.m.

1918

1 Jan No special occurrences. Two unsuccessful air combats. Ration strength, and personnel strength report. Cloudless, heavy ground haze. Combat Flights: 34. Enemy air activity brisk between 2.00 and 3.00, otherwise low on the average.

2 Jan No special occurrences. Foggy, clear for a short time.

3 Jan No special occurrences. Almost cloudless, heavy ground haze in the morning. Combat Flights: 52. Enemy air activity brisk over the noon hour, otherwise low on the average.

4 Jan Aircraft Downed: 12.30 p.m., a Bristol biplane, in flames, 500 m south of Niergnies, by Oblt Reinhard (Jasta 6) this side, as 7th. Combat Flights: 30. Enemy air activity brisk over the noon hour, otherwise moderate.

5 Jan
  Aircraft Downed:
    4.05 p.m., a captive balloon, in flames, near Attilly, west of St Quentin, by Lt Löwenhardt (Jasta 10) other side, as 9th.
  Sky overcast, heavy ground haze. Combat Flights: 13.

6 Jan No special occurrences. Two unsuccessful air combats. Practical experiences with regard to combating enemy squadrons that have broken through. Almost cloudless, heavy ground haze. Combat Flights: 46. Enemy air activity brisk at noon, otherwise moderate.

7 Jan No special occurrences. Rain, heavily overcast, heavy ground haze.

8 Jan No special occurrences. Overcast, heavy ground haze, snow fall from 11.00 a.m. Combat Flights: 11. Enemy air activity very low.

9 Jan No special occurrences. Combat Flights: 41. Enemy air activity low.

10 Jan No special occurrences. Sky cloudy, clearing at noon, strong wind. Combat Flights: 5. Enemy air activity very low.

11 Jan No special occurrences. Fairly heavily overcast, strong wind, rain in the afternoon.

12 Jan No special occurrences. One unsuccessful air combat. Overcast, strong wind. Combat Flights: 37. Enemy air activity: brisk from 9.00 to 10.30 a.m., otherwise low.

13 Jan Three unsuccessful air combats, one successful.
  Aircraft Downed:
    4.37 p.m., a captive balloon, in flames, near Heudicourt by Lt Steinhäuser (Jasta 11) as 2nd.
  Casualty: Lt Stapenhorst (Jasta 11) did not return from an attack on a balloon.[1]
  Cloudless sky, ground haze. Combat Flights: 68. Enemy air activity brisk at noon, otherwise low.

14 Jan No special occurrences. Rain at times in the morning, partially clearing in the afternoon.

15 Jan No special occurrences. Rain at times in the morning, continuous rain in the afternoon with increasing wind.

16 Jan No special occurrences. Storms in the morning, rain at times; cloudy in the afternoon, some visibility at times.

17 Jan No special occurrences. Sky overcast, ground haze, rain at times. Combat Flights: 1.

18 Jan Casualties: Flieger Riensberg (Jasta 10) 10.30 a.m., crashed fatally with Pfalz D III 4059/17 following air combat.
  Aircraft Downed:
    10.23 a.m., a Bristol near Le Petit Priel Farm, other side, by Lt Löwenhardt (Jasta 10) as 10th.
    10.30 a.m., a Sopwith forced to land on the other side, around Hargiscourt, by Lt von Breiten-Landenberg (Jasta 6) as 5th (not recognized as a victory).[2]

---

[1] Taken prisoner.
[2] This victory was credited later.

Overcast, slightly cloudy. Combat Flights: 32. Enemy air activity brisk in the morning, otherwise low.

19 Jan No special occurrences. Two unsuccessful air combats. Rittmeister Freiherr von Richthofen ordered to Berlin–Adlershof until further notice. Rittmeister von Döring has command of the Jagdgeschwader during this time. Cloudy, slight ground haze, strong wind. Combat Flights: 54. Enemy air activity brisk in the morning, otherwise low.

20 Jan No special occurrences. Cloudy, slight haze. Combat Flights: 56. Enemy air activity brisk at noon, otherwise low on the average.

21 Jan No special occurrences. Cloudy, slight ground haze, strong wind, rain at times. Combat Flights: 25. Enemy air activity very low.

22 Jan No special occurrences. Cloudy, ground haze. Combat Flights: 66. Enemy air activity very low, a little more brisk in the afternoon between 2.00 and 4.00 p.m.

23 Jan No special occurrences. Cloudy, hazy, rain at times. Combat Flights: 1. No enemy air activity.

24 Jan Casualty: Lt von Linsingen (Jasta 11) 3.35 p.m., crashed with Pfalz DIII 4223 on the road to Iwuy. Lt von Linsingen seriously injured and taken to the military hospital in Noyelles.

Overcast, clearing in the afternoon. Combat Flights: 29. Air activity very low.

25 Jan No special occurrences. Eight unsuccessful air combats. Slightly cloudy, heavy ground haze. Combat Flights: 62. Enemy air activity low, somewhat more brisk in the early afternoon hours.

26 Jan No special occurrences. Heavy fog, clearing later. Combat Flights: 9.

27 Jan No special occurrences. Heavy fog, clearing in the afternoon. Combat Flights: 2.

28 Jan No special occurrences. Slightly cloudy, heavy ground haze. Combat Flights: 65. Enemy air activity low, somewhat more brisk in the afternoon hours.

29 Jan No special occurrences. 14 unsuccessful air combats. Slightly cloudy, heavy ground haze. Combat Flights: 71. Enemy air activity mostly low, somewhat more brisk in the afternoon hours.

30 Jan Casualty: Vfw Barth (Jasta 10) did not return from a flight to the Front with Albatros DV 4565; shot down to his death near Anneux.

Two unsuccessful air combats. Clear visibility, ground haze. Combat Flights: 74.

31 Jan No special occurrences. Activity report for the time period from 1 to 31 December. Heavy fog.

1 Feb No special occurrences. Total ration strength. Heavy fog.

2 Feb

Aircraft Downed:

    3.40 p.m., an SE 5 forced to land near Bouchain by Lt Kühn (Jasta 10) this side, as 3rd.

12 unsuccessful air combats. Slightly cloudy, ground haze. Combat Flights: 85. Enemy air activity: none in the morning, brisk at noon and in the afternoon, low towards evening.

3 Feb No special occurrences. Six unsuccessful air combats.

Lt H. J. Wolff (Jasta 11) had to make an emergency landing with Fokker Dr. I 155/17 near Villers Outreaux, as a result of the spars and ribs of his uppermost wing breaking.

Slightly cloudy, ground haze. Combat Flights: 50. Enemy air activity low, more brisk at midday.

4 Feb   No special occurrences. Cloudy, hazy, clearing somewhat from 3.30 p.m. on. Combat Flights: 3.

5 Feb   No special occurrences. Two unsuccessful air combats. Overcast, visibility good. Combat Flights: 58. Enemy air activity very low.

6 Feb   No special occurrences. Overcast in the morning, decreasing cloudiness in the afternoon. Combat Flights: 26. Enemy air activity.

7 Feb   No special occurrences. Overcast, strong wind.

8 Feb   No special occurrences. Rain.

9 Feb   No special occurrences. Clear, somewhat cloudy later. Combat Flights: 55. Enemy air activity low.

10 Feb   No special occurrences. Sky overcast, strong wind. Combat Flights: 29. Enemy air activity low.

11 Feb   No special occurrences. Sky overcast, ground haze. Combat Flights: 28. Enemy air activity low.

12 Feb   Lt Bender (Jasta 10) made an emergency landing near Brussels. Sky overcast, clearing from 1.00 p.m. Combat Flights: 21. No enemy air activity.

13 Feb   No special occurrences. Rain.

14 Feb   No special occurrences. Overcast, fog.

15 Feb   No special occurrences. Overcast, fog. [Enemy air activity] very low.

16 Feb   Three unsuccessful air combats, one successful.

Aircraft Downed:

    1.45 p.m., a Bristol-2, in flames, west of St Quentin near Fayet, other side, by Oblt Reinhard (Jasta 6) as 8th.

Clear, good visibility. Combat Flights: 45. Enemy air activity low.

17 Feb   Casualty: Lt Lübbert (Jasta 11) 12.30 p.m., wounded (by a shot through bone of upper arm) in air combat with an SE 5 near Rumilly.

Four unsuccessful air combats. Cloudless sky, heavy ground haze. Combat Flights: 48. Enemy air activity brisk towards noon, otherwise low.

18 Feb   No special occurrences. Almost cloudless, sky hazy. Combat Flights: 35. Enemy air activity more brisk in the early afternoon hours, otherwise low.

19 Feb   Casualty: Lt Klein (Jasta 10) with Pfalz DIII 4283/17, wounded in air combat at 1.00 p.m. Index finger of right hand shot off, a glancing shot to the right arm. In Field Hospital 253 for treatment.

Five unsuccessful air combats. Cloudless, hazy. Combat Flights: 21. Enemy air activity low.

20 Feb   No special occurrences. Overcast, heavy ground haze.

21 Feb   No special occurrences. Overcast, hazy, clearing later. Combat Flights: 29. Enemy air activity low.

22 Feb   No special occurrences. Overcast, rain from 9.00 a.m. on, strong wind.

23 Feb   No special occurrences. Overcast, strong wind, hazy. Combat Flights: 3. Almost no enemy air activity.

24 Feb   No special occurrences. Overcast. Combat Flights: 8. Almost no enemy air activity.

25 Feb   No special occurrences. Overcast, clearing to some extent. Combat Flights: 4. Almost no enemy air activity.

26 Feb   No special occurrences. Five unsuccessful air combats. Report concerning the capture of Lt Stapenhorst. Overcast, hazy. Combat Flights: 36. Enemy air activity brisk in the afternoon hours, otherwise low.

27 Feb   Poor visibility, rain at times. Combat Flights: 11. Almost no enemy air activity.

28 Feb   Work commencing on the intermediate landing field in Awoingt. Construction of necessary quarters. Overcast, hazy, clearing later, hail at times. Combat Flights: 19. Enemy air activity low.

1 March   Casualties: Lt Mohnicke (Jasta 11) wounded in air combat, bullet wound in the left thigh, with Fokker Dr. I 155/17. Machine undamaged, pilot in Field Hospital 243 for treatment. Lt Just (Jasta 11) wounded in air combat, bullet wound in the left hand, with Fokker Dr. I 110/17. Machine undamaged, pilot will remain with the Staffel.

Four unsuccessful air combats.

Personnel strength report for the time period of 1 January to 1 March. Radio Telegraph Station No. 92 handed over for a new assignment near Akonach.

Hazy. Combat Flights: 30. Enemy air activity brisk between 10.00 and 12.30, otherwise low.

2 March   No special occurrences.

3 March   No special occurrences. Army Order I attached to Kofl. 414.

4 March   No special occurrences.

5 March   Inspection of Jagdstaffeln 10 and 11 by the Commander-in-Chief.[1] Three unsuccessful air combats. Good visibility. Combat Flights: 23. Enemy air activity low, somewhat more brisk in the evening hours.

6 March   Casualties: Lt Bahr (Jasta 11) shot down in Fokker Dr. I 106/17 at 10.40 a.m., in air combat between Nauroy and Atricourt.

17 unsuccessful air combats. Visibility: hazy. Combat Flights: 38. Enemy air activity brisk between 9.00 and 11.00 a.m. on the other side, and also between 11.00 a.m. and 12.00 noon on this side, persisted until 2.00 p.m. on the other side, only then was the activity less.

7 March   No special occurrences. Combat Flights: 7. No enemy air activity.

8 March   Casualties: Lt Skauradzun (Jasta 4) severely wounded in air combat in Pfalz DIII 4042/17.

Aircraft Downed:

12.20 p.m., a French biplane near Fresnoy le Grand by Lt Heldmann[2] (Jasta 10).

Three unsuccessful air combats, one successful. Combat Flights: 42. Enemy air activity was brisk until the afternoon hours, low in the evening.

9 March   No special occurrences. Two unsuccessful air combats.

---

[1] General Georg von der Marwitz, Commander in Chief of the Second Army.
[2] Victory no. 4.

Order of the Commander of Aviation[1] concerning assigning two Staffeln to the 6th Army. Safeguarding the transmission of information.

Combat Flights: 36. Enemy air activity low on the average.

10 March   Casualties: Sgt Beschow (Jasta 6) slightly wounded in air combat by a bullet lodged in the left thigh.

Aircraft Downed:

2.20 p.m., a Sopwith near Montbrehain by Vfw Hemer (Jasta 6) as 3rd.

Nine unsuccessful air combats, one successful.

Arrival and assembly of the field receiving station. Order concerning deployment of aerial forces with [Operation] Michael.

Combat Flights: 18. Enemy air activity low during the day, picking up only during the afternoon hours.

11 March

Aircraft Downed:

1.10 p.m., a Bristol-2, north-east of Fresnoy le Petit by Lt Lothar von Richthofen (Jasta 11) as 27th.

1.10 p.m., an SE 5 in Honon Wood by Vfw Scholtz (Jasta 11) as 2nd.

14 unsuccessful air combats, one successful. Combat Flights: 17. Enemy air activity very brisk between 11.00 a.m. and 3.00 p.m.

12 March

Aircraft Downed:

11.00 a.m., a Bristol-2, in flames, near Maretz by Lt Lothar von Richthofen (Jasta 11) as 28th.

11.00 a.m., a Bristol-2, near Cléry by Lt Lothar von Richthofen (Jasta 11) as 29th.

11.00 a.m., a Bristol-2, near Beauvais by Lt Steinhäuser (Jasta 11) as 4th.

11.15 a.m., a Bristol-2, north-east of Nauroy in map quadrant 2858 by Rittmeister Freiherr von Richthofen, as 64th.

1.05 p.m., an SE 5 between La Bassée and Béthune by Lt Wüsthoff (Jasta 4) (6th Army at this time).[2]

7.45 p.m., a captive balloon, in flames, west of La Bassée by Lt Löwenhardt (Jasta 10) (6th Army at this time) as 11th.

7.45 p.m., west of La Bassée, a captive balloon, in flames, by Lt Bohlein (Jasta 10) (6th Army at this time) as 1st.

Combat Flights: 25. Enemy air activity brisk in the morning, squadron activity far this side of the lines at high altitude.

13 March   Casualty: Lt Lothar Freiherr von Richthofen (Jasta 11) 10.30 a.m., crashed near Awoingt following air combat.

Aircraft Downed:

10.35 a.m., an enemy single-seater in the weather ravine in map quadrant 1853 by Rittmeister Freiherr von Richthofen, as 65th.

---

[1] Hauptmann Wilhelm Haehnelt, Commander of Aviation of the Second Army.

[2] Lt Wüsthoff's twenty-seventh victory, its inclusion on this date is in dispute. Please see *Above The Lines* (Franks, Bailey and Guest) and *Nachrichtenblatt der Luftstreitkräfte*, page 233.

10.40 a.m., a Sopwith-1, in flames, between Les Rues des Vignès and Vaucelles by Vfw Scholtz (Jasta 11) as 3rd.

10.40 a.m., an SE 5, in flames, at an altitude of over 4,000 m, south of Cambrai by Vfw Hemer (Jasta 6) as 4th.

Lt Löwenhardt (Jasta 10) and Lt Wüsthoff (Jasta 4) recalled, both with the 6th Army at this time.

Combat Flights: 17. Enemy air activity brisk in the morning, squadron activity far this side of the lines.

14 March   No special occurrences. Combat Flights: 8. No enemy air activity.

15 March

Aircraft Downed:

7.05 p.m., a captive balloon near Villers Faucon by Lt Löwenhardt (Jasta 10) as 12th.

Five unsuccessful air combats, one successful. Combat Flights: 38. Enemy air activity: spirited action by single-seater fighters and two-seaters over the Front and on this side of the lines, less only towards evening.

16 March   Lt Wüsthoff (Jasta 4) is ordered to the Geschwader staff until further notice. Lt von der Osten (Jasta 11) will assume acting command of Jasta 4. Lt von Breiten-Landenberg (Jasta 6) assumes acting command of Jasta 11 (in accordance with Geschwader Order No. 43, personnel, of 16 March).

Casualties: Lt Bohlein (Jasta 10) 11.00 a.m., crashed to his death following air combat near Marcq.

Five unsuccessful air combats. Combat Flights: 34. Enemy air activity brisk between 11.00 a.m. and 12.00 noon, several SE and reconnaissance squadrons this side of the lines.

17 March   Casualties: Lt Steinhäuser (Jasta 11) made an emergency landing at Jasta 3 as a result of a gunshot wound to the foot.

The Commanding General of the Air Service inspecting the Geschwader on the airfield of Jasta 11.

Three unsuccessful air combats. Combat Flights: 56. Enemy air activity: brisk single-seater and reconnaissance activity at the Front at all altitudes in the morning.

18 March

Aircraft Downed:

11.00 a.m., a Bristol Fighter near Joncourt, this side, by Lt Gussmann (Jasta 11) as 3rd.

11.05 a.m., a Bristol Fighter near St Souplet by Oblt Reinhard (Jasta 6) this side, as 9th, (plane broke up in the air).

11.05 a.m., a Sopwith Camel forced to land near Vaux Andigny, this side, by Lt Kirschstein (Jasta 6) as 1st.

11.10 a.m., a Bréguet, in flames, by Lt Löwenhardt (Jasta 10) south of Le Cateau, this side, as 13th (plane broke up in the air).

11.15 a.m., a single-seater fighter, in flames, near Escaufourt by Lt H. J. Wolff (Jasta 11) this side, as 1st.

11.15 a.m., a Sopwith Camel on the Molain-Vaux Andigny road by Rittmeister Freiherr von Richthofen, this side, as 66th.

11.20 a.m., a Sopwith biplane near la Vallée Mulâtre by Vfw Scholtz, this side, as 4th.

11.22 a.m., a Sopwith Camel near Honnechy by Vfw Scholtz (Jasta 11) this side, as 5th.

11.25 a.m., a Sopwith Camel near Awoingt by Lt Friedrichs (Jasta 10) this side, as 1st.

Three Staffeln took off together under the leadership of the commander, Rittmeister Freiherr von Richthofen. Only as a large formation was it possible to successfully combat the numerous, strong English squadrons.

Three unsuccessful air combats, nine successful. Combat Flights. 31. Air activity: brisk squadron activity far this side of the lines during the morning.

19 March   No special occurrences.

Avesnes le Sec — Awoingt

20 March   Secret orders disclosed to the Staffel leaders.

Move to the advance landing field at Awoingt during the afternoon. Billeting of officers and enlisted personnel in huts. Airplanes in tent hangars. Landing field good. The old airdromes in Avesnes le Sec and Lieu St Amand will remain as home fields. All unnecessary luggage and small detachments left behind. (The Staffeln equipped with one C-type airplane.)

Rain in the morning, haze, clearing towards noon. No enemy air activity.

Awoingt

21 March   Division of the fighter pilots of the 2nd Army: Pursuit Region North: Jagdgeschwader I and Jagdgruppe 2 (Staffeln 5 and 46) under command of Rittmeister Freiherr von Richthofen. Pursuit Region South: Jagdgruppe 9 (Staffeln 3, 37, 54, 56) and Jagdgruppe 10 (Staffeln 16, 34), Oblt Kohze, leader.

Due to unfavorable weather conditions, the deployment of the fighter pilots ordered by the Commander of Aviation[1] on 19 March 1918 could not be carried out. On account of heavy ground fog, flight operations were not possible until 12.00 noon.

12.15 p.m., report from Kofl. 2 that there are captive balloons near Ruyaulcourt and Fins. As a result, Jastas 4 and 10 take off at 12.30 p.m. Both balloons were shot down. Lt Friedrichs (Jasta 10) shot down the balloon near Ruyaulcourt at 1.55 p.m.,[2] and Lt Löwenhardt (Jasta 10) shot the one near Fins down in flames at 1.10 p.m.

Around 3.00 p.m., the weather cleared up somewhat. Individual Staffeln deployed in connection with quite moderate enemy flight operations.

Quartering of officers and enlisted personnel in wooden huts. Billeting very tight. Rations from storage depot.

Fog, clearing up in the afternoon. Visibility: very hazy. Combat Flights: 52.

---

[1] Hauptmann Wilhelm Haehnelt, Commander of Aviation of the Second Army.

[2] This time may be a typographical error in the original book as Bodenschatz asserts in the main text that both balloons were brought down at almost precisely 1.00 p.m. From the entry's position ahead of the victory at 1.10 p.m., there is a possibility that this was meant to read 12.55 p.m.

Enemy air activity very low, only isolated enemy aircraft on the other side of the lines sighted and driven off.

22 March   Heavy fog in the morning. Clear weather in the afternoon from 2.00 p.m. on. At 4.30 p.m., the Geschwader took off as a unit for the area of the attack.

Enemy air activity extremely low at all altitudes. Several unsuccessful air combats. Hazy visibility. Combat Flights: 35. Enemy air activity low.

23 March   Ground fog over the entire area of the 2nd Army until 9.30 a.m. Only single Staffeln were deployed in the morning. During the afternoon, fighter patrols in Staffel and Geschwader formation. Enemy air activity was again extremely low.

The radio telegraph field station assembled and set up. Using the radio telegraph transmitter station, air defense officer in Belle Etoile receives an order for the 183rd Infantry Division in the Fins region to advance.

Hazy visibility, clear from 1,000 m upwards. Combat Flights: 80. Enemy air activity very low.

24 March
> Aircraft Downed:
> 2.45 p.m., an SE 5 over Combles (on the other side during the battle, now on this side) by Rittmeister Freiherr von Richthofen, as 67th.

Casualty: Lt Keseling (Jasta 10) did not return from a flight, take-off at 9.30 a.m.

15 unsuccessful air combats, one successful. Good visibility. Combat Flights: 103. Air activity brisk at times.

25 March
> Aircraft Downed:
> 3.55 p.m., a Sopwith-1, in flames, on the Bapaume–Albert road, this side, in the area of Contalmaison by Rittmeister Freiherr von Richthofen, as 68th.

Preparations for the move to the English airdrome at Lechelle.

Two unsuccessful air combats, one successful. Good visibility. Combat Flights: 39. Enemy air activity moderate in general.

26 March
> Aircraft Downed:
> 4.45 p.m., a Sopwith-1, in flames, near the little wood south of Contalmaison, this side, by Rittmeister Freiherr von Richthofen, as 69th.
> 5.00 p.m., a Sopwith Camel, north of Albert by Lt Gussmann (Jasta 11) as 4th.
> 5.00 p.m., an RE 2, old type, in flames, two km north-east of Albert, this side, by Rittmeister Freiherr von Richthofen, as 70th.[1]

The move was carried out with great difficulty. The Geschwader's trucks were not sufficient; only by commandeering a motor transport column was it possible to manage the transfer. The move was finished around 6.00 p.m. in the evening. Flight operations could be maintained. The airfield must have been

---

[1] Aircraft was an RE 8 from 15 Squadron, RFC.

vacated by the English in quite a hurry. Four airplane hangars were still standing (wood construction with canvas roofs), which were only partly useable. The landing field is bumpy, numerous shell craters had to be levelled out by the infantry first. Quarters for the pilots and men in very pleasant corrugated-iron huts which hadn't been destroyed. In the way of fuel, only 1,500 litres of petrol were found. The airplanes of the Staffeln were stored in part in those hangars which were still serviceable, but for the most part in tents. Jastas 6, 10 and 11 on the southern edge of the airfield, and Jasta 4 on the northern edge.

Communications: The most essential incoming lines were laid; connection made with the 39th Reserve Corps (cantonment at the crossroad north of Etricourt). Radio telegraph field station was ready to receive at 2.00 p.m. The air defense officer assigned to the 54th Reserve Division had his observation post on Hill 155 east of the Fourreaux Wood[1] between Martinpuich and Longueval. Flight reports were transmitted by radio-telegraph. Enemy air activity brisk especially at low altitudes. Connections to the rear to Army headquarters and Kofl.; connections to the Jagdgruppen were not possible. Corps Headquarters of the 39th Reserve Corps gave information concerning the progress of the foremost lines. The Staffeln were kept continuously up-to-date.

Rations: On the day before departure, provisions for six days were received. The lack of water made itself felt quite unpleasantly. Water barrels which had been brought along provided some relief. The existing water lines were destroyed.

Billeting of officers and enlisted personnel in wooden and corrugated-iron huts which were quickly made habitable. Plenty of materials in the way of stoves, blankets and tarpaulins available.

Good visibility. Combat Flights: 63. Enemy air activity especially brisk at low altitude.

Lechelle

27 March Numerous low-flying Englishmen were harassing our fighting troops. It was mainly these planes which were being fought.

13 aircraft downed, specifically:

7.50 a.m., a Bristol south-east of Albert by Vfw Hemer (Jasta 6) as 5th.

7.50 a.m., a DH 4 in flames west of Miraumont, this side, by Lt Löwenhardt (Jasta 10), as 15th.

9.00 a.m., near the Ancre [River], one km north-east of Aveluy by Rittmeister Freiherr von Richthofen, this side, in flames, as 71st.[2]

9.20 a.m., an RE 8 south of Aveluy Wood by Lt Janzen (Jasta 6) as 4th.

10.30 a.m., an SE 5 north of Pozières by Lt Friedrichs (Jasta 10) this side, as 3rd.

11.40 a.m., an RE 8 south of Morcourt by Hauptmann Reinhard (Jasta 6) this side, as 10th.

---

[1] Also known as 'High Wood'.
[2] A Sopwith Camel from 73 Squadron RFC.

11.50 a.m., an RE 8 south of Albert by Lt Udet (Jasta 11) this side, as 22nd.

12.05 p.m., a Bristol Fighter, in flames, one km south of Albert by Vfw Scholtz (Jasta 11) this side, as 6th.

3.20 p.m., an Armstrong,[1] in flames, three km south-west of Albert by Lt Kirschstein, as 2nd.

3.25 p.m., a Sopwith Camel, in flames, five km north-east of Albert by Lt Kirschstein (Jasta 6) as 3rd.

3.25 p.m., an RE8, in flames, five km east of Albert by Jasta 6, this side, as 96th.[2]

4.30 p.m., a Bristol Fighter, in flames, near Foucaucourt by Rittmeister Freiherr von Richthofen, this side, as 72nd.[3]

4.35 p.m., a Bristol Fighter, in flames, north-east of Chuignolles by Rittmeister Freiherr von Richthofen, this side, as 73rd.[4]

13 successful air combats, 39 without success. Good visibility in the morning, misty and hazy in the afternoon. Combat Flights: 118. Enemy air activity brisk.

28 March

Aircraft Downed:

9.10 a.m., a Sopwith Camel between Thiépval and Courcelette by Lt Udet (Jasta 11) as 23rd.

9.30 a.m., an SE, in flames, near Suzanne on the Somme by Lt von Rautter (Jasta 4) as 1st.

11.15 a.m., a Bristol-2 near Sailly by Lt Weiss (Jasta 10) as 13th.

12.30 p.m., an Armstrong, in flames, near the small wood east of Méricourt by Rittmeister Freiherr von Richthofen, as 74th.

Ten unsuccessful air combats, four successful.

Reports concerning enemy flight operations did not arrive. The air defense officer is moving forward. New observation post south-west of Pozières. Radio text in clear.

Casualty: Lt von der Osten, acting leader of Jasta 4, crashed during air combat and was severely injured. Flying Albatros DV 4566, aircraft totally destroyed. Lt Janzen assigned as acting leader of Jasta 4.

Clear visibility, low visibility. Combat Flights: 54. Enemy air activity low.

29 March With stormy weather, low clouds and rain, no enemy flight operations of any kind! Work on the camp. Our planned attack was postponed. Misty. Combat Flights: 11. Enemy air activity low.

30 March 12.00 noon, attack from the Ancre River to Marcelcave.[5] Geschwader ordered into action in Staffel formation. Execution of order not possible due to rain and storms.

---

[1] Armstrong-Whitworth FK8.

[2] No individual pilot credited.

[3] Variously identified as either a BF2b, possibly of 11 Squadron RFC, or an AWFK8 of 2 Squadron RFC.

[4] Long thought to be a BF2b of 11 Squadron RFC, this victory is listed as a Sopwith Dolphin in *Above The Lines*, op cit.

[5] As part of Operation 'Michael' (1918 Battle of the Somme, Second Battle of Picardy).

Congratulations from His Excellency von Hoeppner: 'To Kofl. 2 for Rittmeister Freiherr von Richthofen. I congratulate you on your new successes, dear Richthofen, the most successful embodiment of the fighter pilots' confident spirit. Your Commanding General von Hoeppner.'

Promotion: Kogenluft 15592 A1 of 26 March. In accordance with Army HQ [Order] 6 of 22 March 1918, Oblt Reinhard is promoted to Hauptmann.

Transfers: Lts Hübner and Karjus are transferred to Jagdgeschwader I. Lt Hübner was posted to Jasta 4, Lt Karjus to Jasta 11. Pilot Flieger Nitsche transferred to Jagdgeschwader I, detailed to Jasta 10 (Kogenluft of 27 March 1918).

Deployment and use of the fighter pilots.

Stormy in the morning, heavy rain in the afternoon. Combat Flights: 49. Enemy air activity low.

31 March Situation unchanged.

Transfers: Lt Stoy is transferred to Jagdgeschwader I in accordance with Kogenluft 1934 (personnel), is assigned to Jasta 10.

Good visibility, rain at times. Combat Flights: 57. Enemy air activity low.

1 April Situation unchanged. Total personnel strength of Jagdgeschwader I.

Departures: Lt d. R. Joschkowitz (Jasta 4), Vfw Delang, and Vfw Burggaller, (both Jasta 10), ordered to Armee Flugpark 2.

Congratulatory telegram from His Excellency von Hoeppner to Major von Richthofen.

Lt d. R. Weiss (Jasta 10) is ordered to Jasta 11.

Aircraft Downed:

8.00 a.m., a Sopwith Camel, one km south-east of Fouilloy by Lt Siempelkamp, other side, as 1st.

8.00 a.m., a Bristol Fighter, in flames, near Achiet le Petit, by Vfw Hemer (Jasta 6), other side, as 6th.

9.00 a.m., a DH 4, in flames, near Grevillers by Lt H. J. Wolff (Jasta 11) as 2nd.

1.05 p.m., this side, an SE 5 near Martinpuich by Hptm Reinhard (Jasta 6) as 11th.

5.00 p.m., an SE 5, over the woods north-east of Moreuil, by Lt H. J. Wolff (Jasta 11) as 3rd.

Activity report for the time period from 1 February to 31 March 1918.

Good visibility. Combat Flights: 106. Enemy air activity very brisk on the left flank of the Army,[1] moderate on the right flank, heavy blockade by single-seaters far on the other side.

2 April Scouting for an airdrome. Lt Steinhäuser is released to Jasta 11 from the hospital.

Aircraft Downed:

12.35 p.m., an RE, in flames, on Hill 104 north-east of Moreuil by Rittmeister Freiherr von Richthofen, as 75th.

4.50 p.m., a Bristol Fighter on the Roman road between Morcourt and Framerville by Lt H. J. Wolff (Jasta 11) as 4th.

---

[1] The German Second Army.

5.00 p.m., a Bristol Fighter on the Roman road to Morcourt and Harbonnières by Lt Weiss (Jasta 11) as 14th. (Airplane broke up.)

6.05 p.m., a Bristol Fighter, in flames, north-east of Bray by Lt Paul Wenzel (Jasta 6) as 1st.

6.20 p.m., an SE 5, two km west of Harbonnières by Lt Kirschstein (Jasta 6) as 4th, burned on impact.

Ten unsuccessful air combats, five successful.

The Geschwader was placed directly under the command of the Army High Command. Deployed at the focal point of the battle.

Heavily overcast in the morning, good visibility in the afternoon. Combat Flights: 89. Enemy air activity brisk on the left flank of the Army.

3 April Scouting for an airdrome behind the center of the Army was very difficult. Airfields were partially in bombarded terrain, roads for advancing were inadequate, no billets. The single airfield on that fork in the road open to the south-west between the Roman road and the Harbonnières–Proyart road, was situated only eight km behind the forwardmost lines and came into consideration solely as an advance landing field.

The air defense officer receives orders to radio general information concerning the start of enemy flight operations, heavy enemy air activity, [and] squadrons which have broken through 'to whomever it may concern'.

With little favorable weather, the number of combat patrols was limited.

Aircraft Downed:

10.05 a.m., an Armstrong-2 which burned on impact, one km east of Blangy–Tronville by Lt von Rautter (Jasta 4) as 2nd.

The advance detail departed in the afternoon for the advance landing field north of Harbonnières. Quarters in English peaked [bell] tents. Leveling and repair of the landing field.

Lt Udet (Jasta 11) is delivered to Military Hospital 7 in Valenciennes when taken ill. Clouds, rain at times. Combat Flights: 44. Enemy air activity moderate in the morning, none in the afternoon.

4 April Lt Wolfram von Richthofen arrived at Jagdgeschwader I and was detailed to Jasta 11.[1]

Tactical Situation: Attack on both sides of the Roman road up to the left flank of the 2nd Army. The advance landing field could not be occupied on account of heavy rain. Staffeln 4 and 10 each undertook a combat patrol in the attack sector. Brisk enemy flight operations despite low clouds and rain at times. Carrying out of air combats impossible.

Sergeant Schumacher taken ill and delivered to Field Hospital 69.

New assignment of the aviation units during the XI Corps Headquarters' move to the Front on the evening of 2 April.

Low clouds, rain. Enemy air activity brisk at times in the attack sector.

5 April Tactical situation: Attack is continuing along almost the entire Army front. During the night of 4 April 1918, aircraft tents for two Staffeln were transported to the advance landing field. No flight operations at all on account of unfavorable weather conditions.

---

[1] Cousin to Manfred and Lothar von Richthofen.

Cloudy, rain. No enemy air activity.

6 April Tactical situation unchanged. Take-off from the advance landing field on the Roman road. The enemy's flight operations, which were very brisk at times, could be accurately observed and deployment regulated.

Aircraft Downed:

2.15 p.m., Lt Udet (Jasta 4), a Sopwith Camel, in flames, forest south of Hamel, this side, as 23rd.

3.00 p.m., Lt H. J. Wolff (Jasta 11), a Bristol Fighter, in flames, north-east of Vauvillers, this side, as 5th victory.

3.25 p.m., Lt d. R. Kirschstein (Jasta 6), a Sopwith Camel forced to land, this side, two km north-east of Wartisse, 5th victory.

3.45 p.m., Rittmeister Freiherr von Richthofen, a Sopwith Camel, in flames, north-east of Villers-Bretonneux, Hamel Wood, this side, 76th victory.

3.55 p.m., Lt H. J. Wolff (Jasta 11), a Sopwith Camel, in flames, east of Lamotte, this side, as 6th victory.

4.00 p.m., Lt d. R. Weiss (Jasta 11), a Sopwith Camel, demolished, south edge of Marcelcave, this side, as 15th victory.

4.05 p.m., Vfw Scholtz (Jasta 11), a Sopwith Camel, in flames, near Cérisy, as 7th victory.

4.10 p.m., Lt d. R. Just (Jasta 11), a Sopwith Camel, in flames, near Méricourt, other side.[1]

5.15 p.m., Vfw Hemer (Jasta 6), a Sopwith Camel, landed smoothly, Hill 102 south of Demuin, this side, as 7th victory.

5.50 p.m., Lt Weiss (Jasta 11), a Sopwith Camel, demolished, crossroad three km north-east of Sailly le Sec, this side, as 16th victory.

The advance landing field was situated approximately eight km from the Front. Housing of enlisted personnel in peaked [bell] tents. Eight tents were pitched for housing the triplanes in case of a sudden change of weather.

Transmittal of reports by telephone. Connections to the 51st Corps in Framerville and the 1st Corps in Proyart.

Congratulatory telegram from His Excellency von Hoeppner to Rittmeister von Richthofen on the occasion of his being awarded the Order of the Red Eagle, 3rd Class with Crown and Swords.

7 April Situation unchanged. With favorable weather conditions, the intermediate landing field is now ready for action. The English airmen were noticeably cautious.

Four successful air combats:

11.30 a.m., Rittmeister Freiherr von Richthofen, an SE 5 near Hangard, as 77th victory.[2]

11.45 a.m., Lt Kirschstein (Jasta 6), a Sopwith south of the crossroads of the Roman road and the Proyart–Harbonnières road, as 6th victory.

---

[1] This was Lt d. R. Just's second victory.

[2] Various identifications have been suggested for this victory, among them either an SE 5a of 24 Squadron, or a Sopwith Camel of 73 Squadron, RAF.

11.50 a.m., Lt H. J. Wolff (Jasta11), an SE 5 north of Dammard as 7th victory.

12.05 p.m., Rittmeister Freiherr von Richthofen, a Spad 500 m east of Hill 104, north of Villers-Bretonneux, as 78th victory.

Casualty: Lt Gussmann slightly wounded (shot in the right calf). Delivered to Field Hospital 69, Etricourt.

By order of Kogenluft, Jagdgeschwader I assigns a captive balloon flight to the 6th Army for a short length of time. Lt Löwenhardt, with his Staffel, reported to the Commander of Aviation during the course of the afternoon.

Somewhat hazy later. Combat Flights: 110. Enemy air activity very restrained.

8 April No enemy flight operations on account of rainy weather. Rainy weather. No activity.

9 April No flight operations as a result of the rainy weather. Army Order No. 14/April regarding Kofl's thanks for the successful air combats of 3 to 7 April.

A new airdrome was scouted out one km south-east of Cappy. An advance detail from the advance landing field on the Roman road was transported to the new airdrome. Repairs to the landing field by English prisoners and a machine gun company.

Hazy. Clouds at low altitude. No enemy air activity.

10 April No flight operations. Preparations for the move. Repairs made to the new airdrome. Housing huts and peaked [bell] tents transported. Construction of telephone connections.

Departure: Lt Siempelkamp (Jasta 4), Vfw Delang, and Vfw Burggaller (both Jasta 10) transferred to Armee Flugpark 2.

Weather good at times. Enemy air activity low.

11 April With favorable weather conditions, conspicuously low enemy air activity. As to single-seaters, mainly SE 5s and fewer Sopwith Camels were observed. Cover flights for Bombing Geschwader No. 7 could not be carried out because the bombers came several hours too late. Improvements made to the new airdrome. Move begun with the help of commandeered trucks.

Lt Kortüm (Jasta 10) ordered to Park 2.

South of Cappy
12 April The new airdrome occupied. The move was carried out by evening with a great deal of difficulty. The detail from the advance landing field on the Roman road was withdrawn. After slight preliminary work, the landing field was good, ground soft and covered with grass. Housing was not available. Officers and enlisted men quartered in English peaked [bell] tents, machines in tent hangars. Construction of English huts. Readiness for action was maintained despite the move.

With favorable weather, brisk enemy air activity by the hour. The English were conspicuously cautious, however. An enemy bombing raid met with no success.

Aircraft Downed:

12.25 p.m., a Sopwith Camel north-west of Peronne by Lt Löwenhardt

(Jasta 10), this side, as 16th victory.

1.30 p.m., a Spad north of Roye by Hptm Reinhard (Jasta 6) this side, as 12th victory.

2.00 p.m., a Spad near Bayonvillers by Lt Hübner (Jasta 4) this side, as 1st victory.

2.00 p.m., a Spad near Bayonvillers by Lt von Pressentin[1] (Jasta 4) as 3rd victory.

Wounded: Lt Wolff III[2] (Jasta 6) wounded by two machine-gun rounds, admitted to Field Hospital 397, Peronne.

Casualty: 3.10 p.m., Uffz Eiserbeck (Jasta 11) crashed on the hill south of Méaulte following air combat.

Good visibility, cloudless skies. Combat Flights: 89.

13 April   Dispatched to the 6th Army by order of the Army Group Crown Prince Rupprecht of Bavaria. Lomme airdrome west of Lille. Advance details of mechanics to the 6th Army by fast truck. Machines are to reach the new airdrome by air. Rain, dreary.

Cappy — Lomme

14 April   Move to the 6th Army. A large part of the Staffeln accomplished the transfer by the land route with our own trucks. The rest were entrained onto the railway in Cattenières. The airplanes were unable to take off because of unfavorable weather conditions.

Departure: Lt Kortüm (Jasta 10) is transferred to Park 19. Rain.

15 April   The ground transport arrived in Lomme. Setting up and improvement of this very poor airdrome. Officers and enlisted personnel accommodated in roomy houses. Shortly before the Geschwader's take-off at Cappy, order for transfer back to the 2nd Army. Rain.

Cappy

16 April   Transport back by way of the ground. Those being transported by train were diverted en route. Rain, clearing up at times.

17 April   Arrival of the transports. No special occurrences.

Promotion: In conformity with Kogenluft 16326 A1 of 13 April 1918, Army HQ of 7 April 1918, Vfw von Raffay (Jasta 6) promoted to Lt d. R. of the Air Service.

18 April   With variable weather conditions, improvements made to the camp.

Sgt Beschow (Jasta 6) ordered to Park 2.

Added to Strength: Lt Udet and Lt Weiss were transferred to Jagdgeschwader I in conformity with Kogenluft No. 175640 of 5 April and are posted to Jasta 11.

Rain in the area at times.

---

[1] All other victories listed under the name of Lt von Rautter. His full name was Lt Viktor von Pressentin gen. von Rautter.

[2] Lt Wolff of Jasta 6 was designated as 'Wolff III' in the records to differentiate him from Lt Kurt Wolff ('Wolff I') and Lt H. J. Wolff ('Wolff II'), both of Jasta 11.

19 April   No special occurrences. Action by fighter forces. Communications concerning enemy flight operations.

Tactical Situation: No combat engagements. Some single English aircraft over the Front during the morning hours.

Construction work on the camp and the telephone system.

Casualty: Lt d. R. Wolff (Jasta 6) slightly wounded. Delivered to the hospital in Peronne.

Added to Strength: Lt d. R. Bretschneider transferred to Jagdgeschwader I and detailed to Jasta 6.

Staffel Leader: Lt Löwenhardt was assigned as leader of Jasta 10 in accordance with Kogenluft 175803 Fl. I of 10 April.

Cold, rain and snow at times. Combat Flights: 14. No enemy air activity.

20 April   No special occurrences.

Aircraft Downed:

A Sopwith Camel, south-west of Hamel Wood by Lt Weiss (Jasta 11) this side, as 17th victory. Aircraft burned.

6.40 p.m.,[1] a Sopwith Camel, south-west of Hamel Wood by Rittmeister Freiherr von Richthofen, this side, as 79th victory. Aircraft burned.

6.43 p.m., a Sopwith Camel, in flames, north-east of Villers–Bretonneux by Rittmeister Freiherr von Richthofen, this side, as 80th. Aircraft burned.

Departure: In accordance with Kogenluft 175899 Fl. I of 15 April, Sgt Beschow (Jasta 6) is transferred to Park C.

Rainy weather. Combat Flights: 30. Enemy air activity very low.

21 April   Rittmeister Freiherr von Richthofen did not return from a combat patrol. According to irreproachable testimony, he landed smoothly in the area of Hill 102 north of Vaux sur Somme while in pursuit of an Englishman.

Aircraft Downed:

11.50 a.m., a Sopwith Camel south of Hamelet by Lt H. J. Wolff (Jasta 11) as 8th victory.

22 April

Aircraft Downed:

11.50 a.m., a Sopwith Camel by Lt H. J. Wolff (Jasta 11) south of Hamelet, as 8th victory.[2]

11.58 a.m., a Sopwith Camel, in flames, in the large wood north of Moreuil by Lt Weiss (Jasta 11) this side, as 18th victory.

12.00 noon, a Sopwith Camel north of Moreuil Wood by Lt H. J. Wolff (Jasta 11) this side, as 9th victory, aircraft disintegrated on impact.

Casualties: Offz Stellv Aue and Flieger Nitsche (Jasta 10) have not returned from a flight up to this time.

Order: Hptm Reinhard (Jasta 6) ordered to staff as Geschwader commander.

---

[1] Rittmeister von Richthofen's seventy-ninth and eightieth victories are erroneously listed as occurring in the morning in the original book.
[2] Since this same entry is given for Wolff's victory of 21 April 1918, it would appear to be a proofing error in the German edition; Bodenschatz notes just two successful combats on 22 April.

Three unsuccessful air combats, two successful. Hazy, clouds at low altitudes. Combat Flights: 57. Enemy air activity brisk at times.

23 April Flieger Nitsche (Jasta 10) landed here at 9.15 a.m. following an emergency landing at an advance landing field near Bapaume as a result of disorientation. Offz Stellv Aue (Jasta 10) landed here at 11.00 a.m. following an emergency landing at Jasta 26 due to a lack of fuel.

Aircraft Downed:

> 6.55 a.m., an SE 5 north of Sailly Laurette by Lt Koepsch (Jasta 4) this side, as 4th.
>
> 8.30 a.m., a Bristol Fighter forced to land near Morisel by Lt Löwenhardt (Jasta 10).

According to a Reuters news report, Rittmeister Freiherr von Richthofen was killed in action and buried with honors in a cemetery in the area of his landing.

Added to Strength: Oblt von Wedel arrived at Jagdgeschwader I and was detailed to Jasta 11.

Hazy, poor visibility, clearing up later. Enemy air activity: heavy enemy air blockade on the other side. The enemy behaving cautiously.

24 April Tactical Situation: German assault in the sector on both sides of the Roman road. With heavy fog, several combat patrols had to be aborted. Improvements made to the camp, construction of housing huts.

Added to Strength: Pilot Uffz Biewers arrived at the Jagdgeschwader and was detailed to Jasta 10. Lt d. R. Krüger, Lt von Winterfeld and Lt Skowronski were transferred to Jagdgeschwader I, and are detailed as follows: Lt Krüger (Jasta 4), Lt von Winterfeld (Jasta 4), Lt Skowronski (Jasta 6). Lt d. R. Laumann transferred to Jagdgeschwader I in conformity with Kogenluft 175052 Fl. I of 21 April 1918 and detailed to Jasta 10.

Special aviation wire-communication network in the 14th Army Corps' sector.

Fog. No enemy air activity.

25 April No special occurrences. Improvements to the camp. Telephone system. Poor visibility, low clouds. Combat Flights: 37. No enemy air activity.

26 April No air activity. Practical experiences with regard to the advance, and change of airfield.

Departures: In conformity with Kogenluft 176023 Fl. I of 24 April, Lt Lothar Freiherr von Richthofen, leader of Jasta 11, is placed at the disposal of Id. Flieg. Lt von Breiten-Landenberg (Jasta 6) is placed at the disposal of Id. Flieg., in conformity with Kogenluft 17597 of 24 April 1918. Lt von der Osten (Jasta 11) is placed at the disposal of Id. Flieg. in conformity with Kogenluft 176022 Fl. I of 23 April 1918. Lt d. R. Gussmann (Jasta 11) is placed at the disposal of Id. Flieg., Kogenluft 176020 of 23 April 1918. Lt Joschkowitz (Jasta 4) is placed at the disposal of Id. Flieg., Kogenluft 176012 of 23 April 1918.

Telegram from Major Freiherr von Richthofen. 'My proud son must live on as your example. Signature — Father Richthofen.' Telegram to Major Freiherr von Richthofen from Hptm Reinhard.

Fog. No enemy air activity.

27 April   No combat engagements. Only occasional low-flying Englishmen.

Appointment: Hauptmann Reinhard, leader of Jasta 6, is appointed commander of Jagdgeschwader I.

Order: Lt d. R. Fischer (Jasta 4) is ordered to Park 2.

Sincere condolences of the Commanding General von Hoeppner on the loss of Rittmeister Freiherr von Richthofen.

Low-lying clouds, poor visibility. Combat Flights: 43. Enemy air activity — all solitary enemy aircraft.

28 April   No combat engagements. Low-lying clouds, poor visibility. Combat Flights: 2. No enemy air activity.

29 April   No combat engagements.

Departure: Lt von Conta (Jasta 11) is placed at the disposal of Id. Flieg., in conformity with Kogenluft 176094 of 25 April.

Poor visibility. Combat Flights: 28. No enemy air activity.

30 April   No special occurrences. Hptm Lischke (Jasta 6), Lt H. J. Wolff (Jasta 11), Lt Freiherr [Wolfram] von Richthofen (Jasta 11) were ordered to Berlin to attend the memorial service for Rittmeister Freiherr von Richthofen.

Total strength of Jagdgeschwader I: Jasta 4: 13 non-commissioned officers, 117 enlisted men; Jasta 6: 13 non-commissioned officers, 124 enlisted men; Jasta 10: 11 non-commissioned officers, 115 enlisted men; Jasta 11 (Staff): 16 non-commissioned officers, 155 enlisted men. All together, 53 non-commissioned officers, 511 enlisted men.

Poor visibility, low clouds. No enemy air activity.

1 May   No special occurrences. Obituary notice as to the hero's death of Rittmeister Freiherr von Richthofen. Visibility: misty. No enemy air activity.

2 May

Aircraft Downed:

Lt Löwenhardt (Jasta 10) shoots down an SE 5 north of Montanbau, 12.30 p.m., this side, as 18th victory. Aircraft smashed to pieces on impact.

Casualties: Lt Weiss (Jasta 11) crashed with Fokker Dr. I 545 south of Etachern.[1] Aircraft heavily damaged. Lt Stoy (Jasta 10) made an emergency landing two km west of Peronne due to an arm wound, will remain with the unit. Vfw Scholtz (Jasta 11) crashed to his death at 5.50 p.m., shortly after take-off with Fokker Dr. I 591, as a result of the machine stalling. Aircraft heavily damaged.

One successful air combat, seven unsuccessful. Hazy in the morning, clearing up later, slightly cloudy. Combat Flights: 66. Enemy air activity brisk, a few long-range reconnaissance squadrons at high altitudes.

3 May

Aircraft Downed:

11.00 a.m., Lt Hübner (Jasta 4) shoots an Armstrong two-seater down in flames between Buire and Morlancourt, as 2nd victory.

12.15 p.m., Offz Stellv Aue (Jasta 10) shoots down a Bristol Fighter near Proyart, this side, as 6th victory.

---

[1] Killed in action. No town by this name could be located; possibly the town of Etinehem.

12.20 p.m., Lt d. R. Bretschneider (Jasta 6) shoots down a Spad between Cayeux and Caix, this side, as 1st.

12.50 p.m., Lt d. R. Kirschstein (Jasta 6) shoots down a Spad west of Pozières, this side, as 7th victory.

5.50 p.m., Lt von Rautter (Jasta 4) a Bréguet near Chuignes, this side, as 4th victory.

6.50 p.m., Lt Friedrichs (Jasta 10) a DH 9 near Fontaine lès Cappy, this side, as 3rd victory.

8.05 p.m., Lt von Winterfeld (Jasta 4) shoots down an Armstrong west of Villers, this side, as 1st victory.

Casualty: Lt Just (Jasta 11) was wounded in air combat in the Proyart region, glancing shot left side of the neck; he was delivered to the hospital.

Order: Lt Kühn (Jasta 10) is ordered to Armee Flugpark 2, Kogenluft 176196 of 28 April.

Staffel Command: Lt d. R. Janzen (Jasta 6) is appointed as leader of Jasta 6 in conformity with Kogenluft 176196 of 28 April.

Eight unsuccessful air combats, seven successful. Ground haze, clear visibility up above. Combat Flights: 118. Enemy air activity mostly brisk, particularly several bombing squadrons at high altitude.

4 May Transfer: Lt d. R. Wüsthoff (Jasta 4) is placed at the disposal of Id. Flieg. in conformity with Kogenluft 176180 of 29 April.

At 2.00 p.m., the burial of Lts Weiss and Scholtz, both Jasta 11, took place in the military cemetery in Cappy.

Aircraft Downed:

5.50 p.m., Lt Bretschneider (Jasta 6) shoots down a Bréguet, 200 m south of Champien, as 2nd victory.

7.30 p.m., Lt Heldmann (Jasta 10) shoots down an SE 5 near Mametz, as 5th victory.

7.55 p.m., Lt Janzen (Jasta 6) shoots down a Spad south of Etinehem, as 5th victory.

Three unsuccessful air combats, three successful. Cloudy at times. Combat Flights: 58. Enemy air activity: very strong enemy squadrons at times above the lines and several bombing squadrons at high altitude far this side of the lines.

5 May No special occurrences. Rain, low clouds. Combat Flights: 16. No enemy air activity.

6 May With little favorable weather, the number of combat patrols was restricted.

Aircraft Downed:

Lt von Rautter (Jasta 4) shoots down an RE 8 south of Méricourt, as 5th victory.

Detailed: Transferred to Jagdgeschwader I in conformity with Kogenluft 176309: Lt d. R. Schröder and Lt Otto, both are detailed to Jasta 10.

Order: Hptm Lischke (Jasta 6) is ordered to Armee Flugpark 2.

One successful air combat. Heavily overcast, rain at times. Combat Flights: 81. Enemy air activity moderate.

7 May No special occurrences. Hptm Lischke, Lt [H. J.] Wolff, and Lt

[Wolfram] Freiherr von Richthofen back from Berlin. Six unsuccessful air combats. Rain, somewhat hazy. Combat Flights: 28. Enemy air activity very low.

8 May No special occurrences. Order for impending removal to the 7th Army. Hazy. Combat Flights: 5. No enemy air activity.

9 May

Aircraft Downed:

12.30 p.m., an RE east of Cachy by Vfw Hemer (Jasta 6) as 8th victory.

1.15 p.m., Lt von Rautter (Jasta 4) shoots a DH 9 down in flames near Wiencourt, this side, as 6th victory.

7.50 p.m., Lt Löwenhardt (Jasta 10) shoots down an SE 5 near Hamel, as 19th victory.

8.00 p.m., Hptm Reinhard, commander of Jagdgeschwader I, shoots down a Sopwith Camel west of Morlancourt, as 14th victory.

Four successful air combats. Scouting for airdromes near the 7th Army. Visibility good. Combat Flights: 94. Enemy air activity brisk during the evening.

10 May Towards evening, a very successful combat patrol in Geschwader formation.

Aircraft Downed:

Lt von Rautter (Jasta 4) a Bristol near Chuignes, this side, as 7th victory.

Lt Paul Wenzel (Jasta 6) a Sopwith Camel, this side, south-west of Caix, as 2nd victory.

Lt von Winterfeld (Jasta 4) a Sopwith Camel between the lines north of Hamel, as 2nd victory.

Vfw Hemer (Jasta 6) a Sopwith Camel this side of Chérisy, as 9th victory.

Lt Kirschstein (Jasta 6) a Sopwith Camel this side of Chipilly, as 8th victory.

Oblt von Wedel (Jasta 11) a Sopwith Camel, this side, in the area of Chérisy, as 1st.

Lt Steinhäuser (Jasta 11) a Sopwith Camel north of Chérisy, this side, as 5th victory.

Lt H. J. Wolff (Jasta 11) a Sopwith Camel two km south of Sailly-Laurette, this side, as 9th victory.

Lt von Rautter (Jasta 4) a DH 9 this side of Pozières, as 8th victory.

Lt Paul Wenzel (Jasta 6) a DH 9, this side of Vrély–Chaulnes, as 3rd victory.

Lt Löwenhardt (Jasta 10) a DH 9, this side of Chaulnes, as 20th victory.

Seven unsuccessful air combats, eleven successful.

Code for the weather reports of the front-line weather stations.

Expressions of sympathy on the hero's death of Rittmeister Freiherr von Richthofen.

Visibility: misty. Combat Flights: 47. Enemy air activity brisk in the evening hours.

11 May No combat engagements.

Departures: Placed at the disposal of Id. Flieg.: Lt Kühn (Jasta 10) in conformity with Kogenluft No. 176343 of 6 May; Sgt Schumacher (Jasta 10) Kogenluft 176342; Lt Wolff (Jasta 6) Kogenluft 176344.

Added to Strength: Lt Mohnicke was transferred to Jagdgeschwader I in conformity with Kogenluft 176400, and was detailed to Jasta 11; likewise Sgt Jagla to Jasta 11.

Order: Lt Krüger (Jasta 4), Oblt Karjus (Jasta 11) and Lt Matthies (Jasta 4) are ordered to Armee Flugpark 2.

Visibility: hazy. Combat Flights: 6. Enemy air activity low.

12 May Army communiqué: In the last few days, 19 enemy airplanes were shot down in air combat; 11 of them brought down by the Jagdgeschwader, which was previously led by Rittmeister Freiherr von Richthofen. Lt Löwenhardt achieved his 20th and 21st air victories. Rain at times, heavily overcast. Combat Flights: 18. Enemy air activity low.

13 May No special occurrences. Rain, heavily overcast. Combat Flights: 13. Enemy air activity low.

14 May No special occurrences. Activity report for the time period from 1 to 30 April, inclusive.

Detailed: Lt d. R. Rademacher was transferred to the Geschwader in conformity with Kogenluft 175492, is detailed to Jasta 10.

Rain, low clouds. Combat Flights: 63. Enemy air activity low all day long, somewhat more brisk in the evening.

15 May Ten unsuccessful air combats, 13 successful.

Aircraft Downed:

8.15 a.m., a Sopwith Camel by Lt Friedrichs (Jasta 10) as 4th.

10.30 a.m., a DH 4 by Lt Paul Wenzel (Jasta 6) as 4th.

11.15 a.m., a Bréguet by Lt Gluszewski (Jasta 4) as 1st.

12.05 p.m., a Sopwith Camel by Lt Kirschstein (Jasta 6) as 9th.

12.10 p.m., a Sopwith Camel by Sgt Schmutzler (Jasta 4) as 1st.

12.15 p.m., a Sopwith Camel by Lt von Rautter (Jasta 4) as 9th.

12.50 p.m., a Bristol Fighter by Lt Janzen (Jasta 6) as 6th.

1.25 p.m., a DH 9 by Lt Löwenhardt (Jasta 10) as 21st.

3.10 p.m., a Bristol by Lt H. J. Wolff (Jasta 11) as 10th.

3.15 p.m., a Bristol by Lt Kirschstein (Jasta 6) as 10th.

3.15 p.m., a Bristol by Oblt von Wedel (Jasta 11) as 2nd.

6.05 p.m., a Bréguet by Lt von Rautter (Jasta 4) as 10th.

6.20 p.m., a Bristol by Lt Kirschstein (Jasta 11) as 11th.

Cloudy, good visibility. Combat Flights: 137. Enemy air activity was brisk up till noon and kept to moderate levels during the remaining hours.

16 May Three unsuccessful air combats, four successful.

2.40 p.m., a Bristol by Lt Kirschstein (Jasta 6) as 12th.

3.45 p.m., a Spad by Lt Löwenhardt (Jasta 10) as 22nd.

7.30 p.m., an SE 5 by Lt Richard Wenzl (Jasta 6)[1] as 3rd.

9.10 p.m., an SE 5 by Lt Kirschstein (Jasta 6) as 13th.

Casualties: 8.20 a.m., Lt H. J. Wolff (Jasta 11) shot down north of Lamotte,

---

[1] Transferred from Jasta 11.

this side, two bullets below the heart. Sgt Schmutzler (Jasta 4) crashed at 8.00 p.m. near Proyart following combat flight, severely injured, died. Lt Hübner (Jasta 4) did not return from a combat flight, take-off 4.15.

Bombing Raid: 3.50 p.m., attack on airdrome by seven enemy bombers, numerous bombs in the middle of the camp, four men slightly injured. Slight property damage. All aircraft and tents undamaged.

Orders arrive concerning the further utilization of the Geschwader.

Cloudy, good visibility. Combat Flights: 77. Enemy air activity brisk in the afternoon and evening hours, strong enemy squadrons appearing.

17 May   Eight unsuccessful air combats, four successful.

　　11.10 a.m., a Bréguet by Lt Kirschstein (Jasta 6) as 14th.

　　11.15 a.m., a Bréguet by Lt Janzen (Jasta 6) as 7th.

　　12.30 p.m., a Spad by Lt Drekmann (Jasta 4) as 2nd.

　　5.05 p.m., an SE 5 by Lt von Rautter (Jasta 4) as 11th.

Bombing Raid: During the night from 10.50 to 11.10 p.m., enemy airmen dropped numerous bombs on the airdrome. Property damage slight, no casualties, aircraft and tents undisturbed. Two of the aircraft were shot down.

Transfers: Lt Heidenreich transferred to Jagdgeschwader I in conformity with Kogenluft 176564, is detailed to Jasta 6. Lt d. R. Brocke transferred to the Jagdgeschwader in conformity with Kogenluft 176630, is detailed to Jasta 6. Vfw Gabriel, of Schlachtstaffel 15, transferred to Jagdgeschwader I, is detailed to Jasta 11. Vfw Degen transferred to Jagdgeschwader I and detailed to Jasta 6.

Cloudy, good visibility. Combat Flights: 70. Enemy air activity brisk in the morning, low in the afternoon.

18 May   With little favorable weather, number of combat patrols curtailed.

Aircraft Downed:

　　7.00 a.m., a Bréguet by Lt Kirschstein (Jasta 6) as 15th.

　　7.30 a.m., a balloon by Lt Friedrichs (Jasta 10) as 5th.

　　7.45 a.m., a Sopwith by Lt Löwenhardt (Jasta 10) as 23rd.

　　12.40 p.m., a DH 9 by Lt von Rautter (Jasta 4) as 12th.

One unsuccessful air combat, four successful.

At 11.00 a.m., the burial of Lt H. J. Wolff (Jasta 11) took place in the military cemetery in Cappy.

Transfer: Oblt Hartmann was transferred to Jagdgeschwader I in conformity with Kogenluft 176628 and is detailed to Jasta 6.

Telegram from His Excellency von Hoeppner: Congratulations as to the successes of 10 May, by which the 300th air victory of the Geschwader was scored.

Cloudy, good visibility, thunderstorms in the afternoon. Combat Flights: 48. Enemy air activity low.

19 May   Nine unsuccessful air combats, five successful.

　　11.30 a.m., a Bristol by Lt Steinhäuser (Jasta 11) as 6th.

　　7.40 p.m., a Spad by Vfw Hemer (Jasta 6) as 10th.

　　8.00 p.m., a Spad by Oblt von Wedel (Jasta 11) as 3rd.

　　8.10 p.m., a DH 9 by Vfw Gabriel (Jasta 11) as 2nd.

　　8.10 p.m., a DH 9 by Lt Steinhäuser (Jasta 11) as 7th.

Good visibility. Combat Flights: 66. Enemy air activity was low all day, and picked up during the evening hours.

20 May
   Aircraft Downed:
      7.30 a.m., a balloon by Lt Löwenhardt (Jasta 10) as 24th victory.
      9.30 a.m., a Sopwith Camel by Lt Janzen (Jasta 6) as 8th.
      9.30 a.m., an SE 5 by Lt Bretschneider (Jasta 6) as 3rd.
      11.25 a.m., a Bristol by Lt von Rautter (Jasta 4) as 13th.
   Telegram from His Excellency von Hoeppner: Jagdgeschwader I will carry the name of Jagdgeschwader Freiherr von Richthofen No. I.
   Move to Guise by way of the ground. Rail transport (two trains to Puisieux Farm, 7th Army).
   Good visibility. Combat Flights: 48. Enemy air activity low.

Guise
21 May   Rest billets.
   Transfers: Lt von Conta and Lt Förster were transferred to Jasta 11, the latter as officer detailed for special duties. Lt d. R. Udet of Jasta 11 is ordered to Jasta 4 as of today, as acting Staffel leader.
   Airfields of the Staffeln: Staffel 4 on the road to Longchamps; Jasta 6, Guise; Jasta 10 on the road to Etreux; Jasta 11, Lamotte Farm.
   Good visibility.
22 May   Rest billets. Machines overhauled. Improvements to the new airdrome with the 7th Army. Very good visibility.
23 May   As on previous day. Thunderstorms, slightly cloudy.
24 May   As on previous day. Rain.
25 May   As on previous day. Slightly cloudy, good visibility.
26 May   Rest billets. Occupation of the airdrome near Puisieux Farm, five km north-east of Laon. Tents pitched at dusk. The airplanes arrived at 9.15 p.m. Quartering of officers and enlisted personnel in huts near the farm. Landing field near the farm (east of the crossroads) for three Staffeln, Jastas 6, 10 and 11. Landing field for Jasta 4 just north of the farm. Both fields good.
   Attack orders, deployment of the fighter pilots, communications. Guaranteeing of adequate reserves of fuel, aircraft and radio telegraph equipment. Army order for deploying the pilots on the first day of the attack.
   Recognition of the [Geschwader's] splendid achievements by His Excellency von Gontard with the 2nd Army.
   Order for deployment of the fighter forces.
   Low clouds, poor visibility.

Puisieux Farm
27 May   First day of attack,[1] no enemy air activity.
   Aircraft Downed:
      11.25 a.m., a Bristol by Lt von Rautter (Jasta 4) as 13th.

---

[1] Operation 'Blücher' (Battle of the Aisne, 1918, Third Battle of the Aisne).

6.15 p.m., a Bréguet by Lt von Rautter (Jasta 4) as 14th.

One unsuccessful, two successful air combats.

Visit by the Commanding General of the Air Service.

Transfer: Lt Matthies was placed at the disposal of Id. Flieg.

Slightly cloudy, good visibility. Combat Flights: 84. Enemy air activity low.

28 May Light enemy air activity. Attack making good progress.

Aircraft Downed:

5.30 p.m., a balloon by Lt Friedrichs (Jasta 10) as 6th victory.

Four unsuccessful air combats, one successful.

Scouting for new airdromes in the area south of Braine.

Transfer: Lt Krüger (Jasta 4) is placed at the disposal of Id. Flieg. in conformity with Kogenluft 154976.

Commander-in-Chief von der Marwitz wishes the Jagdgeschwader further great successes. Site sketch of the Geschwader's airfields.

Good visibility. Combat Flights: 74. Enemy air activity low.

29 May No enemy flight operations in the morning. Towards 5.00 p.m., advances by powerful enemy aviation forces.

Two unsuccessful air combats.

Transfer: Oblt Karjus (Jasta 11) is transferred to Park 2 in conformity with Kogenluft 176.

Good visibility. Combat Flights: 28. Enemy air activity low.

30 May The enemy was very cautious. The French airfield just south of the Beugneux–Cramaille Road was scouted out. An advance detail with a strength of around 100 men departed for the airfield. Order of Kofl. 7 No. 1a/1195 of 29 May.

Transfers: Lt Bender (Jasta 10) transferred to Jasta 4. Lt Hofmann transferred to Jagdgeschwader I, detailed to Jasta 11. Lt d. R. Matzdorf, Lt Jessen and Lt von Puttkammer transferred to the Jagdgeschwader; latter two detailed to Jasta 4, the former to Jasta 6. Lt Feige transferred to the Jagdgeschwader, detailed to Jasta 10.

Good visibility. Combat Flights: 53. Enemy air activity moderate.

31 May Advance landing field near Beugneux could not be occupied yet on account of artillery fire.

Advance landing field east of Regny Farm and east of Beugneux. Takeoffs from the airfield south-east of Arcy-Regny until 2.00 p.m.

Good visibility. Combat Flights: 93. Enemy air activity fairly brisk on the other side.

The Beugneux airfield was a French airdrome for night-flying aircraft. All hangars except for three were burned, as were all the aircraft (ten Voisins, a Bréguet, and 12 Spad single-seaters). Field good, only slight improvements necessary. Enemy flight operations could be observed from the field. In the evening, return flight to home field.

Order concerning deployment of the Jagdgeschwader.

Aircraft Downed:

12.55 p.m., a Bréguet south-west of Soissons by Lt von Rautter (Jasta 4) as 15th.

1.00 p.m., a Bréguet by Lt Udet (Jasta 4) as 24th.

2.35 p.m., a Bréguet by Lt Kirschstein (Jasta 6) as 16th victory.

7.40 p.m., a Bréguet by Lt Skowronski (Jasta 4)[1] as 1st.

7.45 p.m. a Spad by Hptm Reinhard, as 14th.

Casualties: Lt von Rautter (Jasta 4) did not return from a front-line patrol.[2]
Lt Rademacher (Jasta 10) did not return from a front-line patrol.[3]

Beugneux–Cramaille

1 June   The attack went well. With favorable weather conditions, enemy very active on the other side of the lines. One successful air combat: 5.10 p.m., a Spad by Vfw Gabriel (Jasta 11) as 3rd. The French showed themselves to be skillful, but cautious pilots.

The Staffeln moved with their own trucks without any assistance by the Army. Consequently, [obtaining] supplies very difficult. Improvements made to the airfield. Staffeln 6, 10 and 11 on the field just east of Beugneux, Staffel 4, 400 m east of there. Airplanes housed in part in hangars and tents. Accommodations good in houses and huts. As to fuel, only four barrels of oil were found. Provisioning for the most part from the neighboring village.

Total strength for Jagdgeschwader Freiherr von Richthofen: 51 officers (including doctors and clerks), 523 non-commissioned officers and enlisted personnel, total 574.

Site sketch of the Geschwader's airfields.

Good visibility. Combat Flights: 93. Enemy air activity brisk at times in the afternoon.

2 June   Numerous enemy bombing squadrons made an appearance, especially in the afternoon hours. Ten successful air combats.

Aircraft Downed:

11.55 a.m., a Bréguet by Lt Udet (Jasta 4) as 25th.

5.20 p.m., a Spad-2 by Lt Janzen (Jasta 6) as 10th.

5.35 p.m., a Spad-2 by Lt Kirschstein (Jasta 6) as 17th victory.

5.45 p.m., a Spad-2 by Lt Steinhäuser (Jasta 11) as 8th victory.

5.45 p.m., a Spad-2 by Hptm Reinhard, as 15th.

5.45 p.m., a Spad-1 by Lt Löwenhardt (Jasta 10) as 25th.

6.20 p.m., a Bréguet by Lt Maushake (Jasta 4) forced to land on the other side, recognized [as a victory].

8.30 p.m., a Spad-2 by Hptm Reinhard, as 16th.

9.00 p.m., a Spad-2 by Hptm Reinhard, as 17th.

9.00 p.m., a Bréguet by Lt Kirschstein (Jasta 6) as 18th victory.

Casualty: Lt Heidenreich (Jasta 6) did not return from a front-line patrol.

The Staffeln are still not finished moving.

Telegram from Kogenluft: Lt Löwenhardt, leader of Jasta 10, was awarded the Order *Pour le Mérite*.

---

[1] Lt Skowronski is listed as detailed to Jasta 6 upon joining JG I on 24 April 1918.
[2] Killed in action over Soissons.
[3] Taken prisoner after landing at a French airfield.

Clear weather. Combat Flights: 77. Enemy air activity brisk between [the] Aisne [River] and the large forest near Villers-Cotterêts during the evening hours.

3 June The enemy airmen were very cautious. Five successful air combats.

12.50 p.m., a Spad-1 by Lt Skowronski (Jasta 6) as 2nd.

6.30 p.m., a Spad by Lt Löwenhardt (Jasta 10) as 26th.

7.30 p.m., a Bréguet by Lt Kirschstein (Jasta 6) as 19th victory.

7.30 p.m., a Bréguet by Lt Bretschneider (Jasta 6) as 4th victory.

7.35 p.m., a Bréguet by Lt Kirschstein (Jasta 6) as 20th victory.

Move completed. The Geschwader's new airdrome. Deployment of the fighter pilots.

Clear weather. Combat Flights: 75. Almost no enemy air activity in the morning, moderate activity in the afternoon and evening.

4 June No particular combat engagements. Preparations were made for a systematic attack in lieu of the war of movement.

Towards evening, brisk enemy air activity above and on the other side of the lines. The enemy infantry-support pilots were very active.

Four Aircraft Downed:

5.25 p.m., a Spad-2 by Hptm Reinhard, as 18th.

5.25 p.m., a Spad-2 by Lt Wolfram Freiherr von Richthofen (Jasta 11) as 1st.

6.45 p.m., a Spad-1 by Lt Drekmann (Jasta 4) as 3rd.

8.40 p.m., a Spad-2 by Oblt von Wedel (Jasta 11) as 5th.

Clear visibility. Combat Flights: 55. Enemy air activity brisk towards evening.

5 June Kofl. Order: from 9.30 a.m. on, air supremacy in the Attichy–Villers-Cotterêts–Troësnes–Nouvron sector is to be secured by Jagdgeschwadern I and III. The Army Group François will attack from the Autrêches–Nouvron line, the Army Group Wichura from the Longpont–Corcy line. All captive balloons are to be shot down or forced to descend.

Aircraft Downed:

7.45 a.m., a balloon by Lt d. R. Grassmann (Jasta 10) as 1st.

11.20 a.m., a balloon by Lt Friedrichs (Jasta 10) as 8th.

11.35 a.m., a Spad-1 by Lt Kirschstein (Jasta 6) as 21st.

11.37 a.m., a Spad-1 by Lt Udet (Jasta 4) as 26th.

5.35 p.m., a Bréguet by Lt Kirschstein (Jasta 6) as 22nd.

5.35 p.m., a Bréguet by Lt Richard Wenzl (Jasta 6) as 4th.

6.45 p.m., a Spad by Lt Löwenhardt (Jasta 10) as 27th.

6.45 p.m., a Spad by Lt Heldmann (Jasta10) as 6th.

8.25 p.m., a Spad by Lt Kirschstein (Jasta 6) as 23rd.

8.25 p.m., a Spad by Lt Janzen (Jasta 6) as 12th.

8.10 p.m., a balloon by Lt Friedrichs (Jasta 10) as 7th.

Clear weather. Combat Flights: 63. Enemy air activity held to moderate limits, and picked up between 5.00 and 6.00 in the afternoon.

6 June Between 10.00 and 11.00 in the morning, three enemy bombing squadrons coming from the Marne break through and systematically bomb the

Fère-en-Tardenois region. The squadrons were reported much too late. It is absolutely essential that balloon observers report such bombing squadrons already assembling on the other side of the lines. Only by doing so is successful opposition possible. Corresponding proposition was made to Kofl. 7. Otherwise, moderate enemy flight operations during the entire day.

Aircraft Downed:

7.25 a.m., a balloon by Lt Friedrichs (Jasta 10) as 9th.

7.50 a.m., a balloon by Lt Otto (Jasta 10) as 1st.

11.40 a.m., a Spad-1 by Lt Udet (Jasta 4) as 27th.

Casualties: Lt Otto (Jasta 10) severely wounded in the right arm by ground machine gun following a successful attack on a captive balloon.

Good visibility, slightly cloudy. Combat Flights: 78. Enemy air activity low.

7 June Situation unchanged. Enemy very cautious.

Successes:

7.00 a.m., a Spad-1 by Lt Udet (Jasta 4) as 28th.

7.05 a.m., a Spad by Lt Janzen (Jasta 6) as 13th.

7.10 a.m., a Spad by Lt Kirschstein (Jasta 6) as 24th.

Lt Schröder (Jasta 10) is ordered to Fl. Abt. (A) 206 (official letter).

Slight haze, cloudless. Combat Flights: 58. Enemy air activity: none on this side, moderate on the other side.

8 June Assaults on the right flank of the Army Group Conta repulsed. Order for supporting the attack by the 18th Army.

Successes:

7.10 a.m., a balloon by Lt Friedrichs (Jasta 10) as 10th.

Slight haze, cloudless. Combat Flights: 44. Enemy air activity in the evening hours only on the other side of the lines at high altitude.

9 June Attack by the 18th Army.[1] Together with Jagdgeschwader III, the Geschwader undertook the protection of the 18th Army's flank in the Noyon–Compiègne–Vic sur Aisne sector. Attack went well.

Enemy air activity brisk on the right flank in the morning. Towards evening, no flight operations on account of haze and heavy clouds.

Aircraft Downed:

9.00 a.m., a Spad by Lt Steinhäuser (Jasta 11) as 9th.

9.00 a.m., a Spad by Oblt von Wedel (Jasta 11) as 6th.

9.00 a.m., a Spad by Hptm Reinhard, as 19th.

12.20 p.m., a Spad by Lt Steinhäuser (Jasta 11) as 10th.

12.20 p.m., a Spad by Lt Wolfram Freiherr von Richthofen (Jasta 11) as 2nd.

4.30 p.m., a Bréguet by Lt Friedrichs (Jasta 10) as 11th.

Casualty: Lt Janzen (Jasta 6) did not return from a front-line patrol.

On 9 June, the Geschwader scored its 400th air victory.

Heavily overcast, hazy. Combat Flights: 66. Enemy air activity low on the right flank of the 7th Army and on the left flank of the 18th Army.

10 June Tactical Situation: continuation of the attack by the 18th Army.

---

[1] Operation 'Gneisenau', between Montdidier and Noyon (Battle of the Matz).

Pursuit area of the Geschwader is both sides of the Oise River south of Noyon. No enemy air activity on account of unfavorable weather conditions.
Successes:

4.35 p.m., a balloon by Vfw Gabriel (Jasta 11) as 4th.

Acting Staffel Command: Lt Kirschstein assumes acting command of the Staffel.[1]

Heavily overcast, rain at times, good ground visibility. Combat Flights: 9. No enemy air activity.

11 June   With low clouds, no special occurrences. Attack order for 12 June. Very hazy in the morning, visibility good in the afternoon. Combat Flights: 17. No enemy air activity.

12 June

Aircraft Downed:

Spad-2 by Hptm Reinhard, as 20th victory.

Report concerning practical experiences. Slightly cloudy, hazy. Combat Flights: 55. No enemy air activity.

13 June

Aircraft Downed:

5.45 a.m., a Spad-1 by Lt Drekmann (Jasta 4) as 4th.

5.45 a.m., a Spad-1 by Lt Udet (Jasta 4) as 29th.

6.30 a.m., a Spad by Lt Bretschneider (Jasta 6) as 5th.

4.05 p.m., a Spad-1 by Vfw Gabriel (Jasta 11) as 5th.

Lt Esser was transferred to Armee Flugpark 17 as technical officer. Slightly cloudy, hazy. Combat Flights: 62. Enemy air activity moderate all day long.

14 June   No particular combat engagements.

Successes:

8.00 a.m., a Spad-1 by Lt Udet (Jasta 4) as 30th.

9.00 a.m., a balloon by Lt Kirschstein (Jasta 6) as 25th.

9.15 a.m., a Spad by Lt Kirschstein (Jasta 6) as 26th.

Radio telegraph reports of mass deployment of enemy aircraft.

Casualty: Vfw Degen (Jasta 6) did not return from a flight.

Hazy. Combat Flights: 63. Enemy air activity: none in the morning, moderate in the afternoon.

15 June   No special occurrences. Cloudy, hazy. Combat Flights: 137. Enemy air activity brisk particularly towards noon, otherwise moderate.

16 June

Aircraft Downed:

6.45 a.m., a balloon by Offz Stellv Aue (Jasta 10) as 7th victory.

7.00 a.m., a balloon by Lt Friedrichs (Jasta 10) as 12th.

10.00 a.m., a balloon by Vfw Gabriel (Jasta 11) as 6th victory.

Transfers: Lt Otto is placed at the disposal of Id. Flieg. in accordance with Kogenluft No. 177789 Fl. I of 16 June. Lt d. R. Stoy (Jasta 10) is placed at the disposal of Id. Flieg. according to Kogenluft No. 177723 Fl. I of 16 June.

Slightly cloudy in the morning, good visibility, hazy in the afternoon, some

---

[1] Jasta 6.

rain, good visibility towards evening. Combat Flights: 47.

17 June   No particular combat engagements.

Lt d. R. Lehmann transferred to the Geschwader in conformity with Kogenluft No. 177739 Fl. I, and is detailed to Jasta 6. Lt d. R. Nöldecke (Jastaschule I) transferred to the Geschwader and detailed to Jasta 6.

Good visibility. Combat Flights: 11. No enemy air activity.

18 June   Lt Udet assumes acting command of the Geschwader for the commander who is on leave. Good visibility in the morning, hazy in the afternoon. Combat Flights: 67. No enemy air activity.

19 June   No special occurrences. Lt Löwenhardt assumes acting command of the Geschwader for the commander who is on leave. Rain, clearing up at times. No enemy air activity.

20 June   No special occurrences. Aircraft Downed: 7.10 p.m., a Bréguet by Lt Paul Wenzel (Jasta 6) as 5th. Rain. Combat Flights: 15. No enemy air activity.

21 June   No special occurrences. Rain, clearing up at times. Combat Flights: 15. No enemy air activity.

22 June   8.45 [p.m.] by Lt Löwenhardt (Jasta 10) as 28th victory. Poor visibility. Combat Flights: 10. Enemy air activity low.

23 June

Aircraft Downed:

> 9.45 a.m., a Spad by Lt Heldmann (Jasta 10) as 7th.
>
> 9.45 a.m., a Spad by Sgt Schumacher (Jasta 10) as 1st.
>
> 9.45 a.m., a Spad by Lt Friedrichs (Jasta 10) as 13th.
>
> 12.10 p.m., a Bréguet by Lt Udet (Jasta 4) as 31st.
>
> 8.15 p.m., a Bréguet by Lt Udet (Jasta 4) as 32nd.

Good visibility. Combat Flights: 61. Enemy air activity low.

24 June

Aircraft Downed:

> 9.45 a.m., a Bréguet by Lt Kirschstein (Jasta 6) as 27th.
>
> 10.00 a.m., a Bréguet by Lt Udet (Jasta 4) as 33rd.

Regarding offensive engagements by a uniform air defense for the Army Groups' Front (see enclosure 140). Hazy, cloudy. Combat Flights: 19. Enemy air activity low.

25 June   No special occurrences.

Aircraft Downed:

> 6.45 p.m., a Spad by Lt Udet (Jasta 4) as 34th.
>
> 6.45 p.m., a Spad by Lt Udet (Jasta 4) as 35th.
>
> 8.40 p.m., a balloon by Lt Friedrichs (Jasta 10) as 14th.

Order concerning deployment of the fighter- and ground-support forces. Visibility: hazy. No enemy air activity in the morning, brisk activity in the evening.

26 June

Aircraft Downed:

> 8.25 p.m., a balloon by Sgt Schumacher (Jasta 10) as 2nd victory.

Transfers: Lt Graf von Hohenau transferred to the Geschwader in conformity with Kogenluft No. 178069 Fl. I of 20 June 1918 and detailed to Jasta

11. Sgt Schumacher was transferred to Jasta 10 in conformity with Kogenluft No. 178072 Fl. I of 23 June 1918.

Casualty: Lt Steinhäuser (Jasta 11) crashed fatally following air combat around 8.00 a.m.

Good visibility. Combat Flights: 37. Enemy air activity low.

27 June

Aircraft Downed:

9.00 a.m., a Spad by Lt Friedrichs (Jasta 10) as 15th.

9.15 a.m., a Spad by Lt Löwenhardt (Jasta 10) as 29th.

1.00 p.m., a Spad by Lt Friedrichs (Jasta 10) as 16th.

8.00 p.m., a balloon by Lt Drekmann (Jasta 4) as 5th.

Cloudy, hazy. Combat Flights: 73. Enemy air activity low.

28 June   Powerful enemy attack south-west of Soissons. The French put considerable aerial forces into action in this sector. The combat action subsided towards evening.

Aircraft Downed:

8.20 a.m., a Spad by Lt Löwenhardt (Jasta 10) as 30th.

8.30 a.m., a Spad by Lt Friedrichs (Jasta 10) as 17th.

9.00 a.m., a Spad by Lt Mohnicke (Jasta 11) as 9th.

9.05 a.m., a Spad by Lt Mohnicke (Jasta 11) as 8th.[1]

9.45 a.m., a Spad by Lt Maushake (Jasta 4) as 2nd.

9.50 a.m., a Spad by Lt Meyer (Jasta 4) as 2nd.

9.50 a.m., a Spad by Lt Drekmann (Jasta 4) as 6th.

12.30 p.m., a Spad by Vfw Hemer (Jasta 6) as 11th.

12.30 p.m., a Spad-2 by Lt Löwenhardt (Jasta 10) as 31st.

Award: the Order *Pour le Mérite* was awarded to Lt d. R. Kirschstein (Jasta 6).

Transfer: Lt Schäfer is transferred to Jasta 10 as officer for special duty by order of Kogenluft 178186 Fl. I of 26 June 1918.[2]

Burial: The burial of Lt Steinhäuser (Jasta 11) took place at 5.00 p.m. in the military cemetery in Beugneux.

Good visibility, somewhat hazy in the afternoon. Combat Flights: 86. Enemy air activity brisk in the morning, low in the afternoon.

29 June   No particular combat engagements. Order concerning deployment of fighter forces.

Lt Udet (leader, Jasta 4) received a direct anti-aircraft hit to his airplane which then crashed, badly damaged. Lt Udet landed safe and sound behind our own infantry lines by jumping out at an altitude of 500 m using a parachute.

Good visibility, somewhat cloudy towards evening. Combat Flights: 44. Almost no enemy air activity in the morning, low activity in the afternoon.

30 June

Aircraft Downed:

10.40 a.m., a balloon by Lt Friedrichs (Jasta 10) as 18th victory.

---

[1] Victories have been arranged here according to time. In the original text, the victory at 9.05 a.m. was confirmed first, and thus recorded as 8th.

[2] Technical Officer of Jasta 10. He remained with Jasta 10 until the end of the war.

11.05 a.m., a balloon by Lt Grassmann (Jasta 10) as 2nd.

3.50 p.m., a balloon by Sgt Schumacher (Jasta 10) as 3rd victory.

3.55 p.m., a balloon by Lt Friedrichs (Jasta 10) as 19th victory.

8.00 [p.m.,] a Spad by Lt Löwenhardt (Jasta 10) as 32nd victory.

Lt Udet (Jasta 4) a Spad as 36th victory.[1]

Casualties: Lt Hofmann (Jasta 11) shot down in flames during air combat around 8.00 p.m. Lt Feige (Jasta 10) did not return from a front-line patrol.[2]

Transfers: Lt d. R. Rolff and Lt d. R. von Dorrien (Jastaschule I) transferred to the Geschwader. Lt Rolff detailed to Jasta 6, Lt von Dorrien detailed to Jasta 11.

Departure: Lt Skowronski (Jasta 6) transferred to Armee Flugpark 3 in conformity with Kogenluft 3584 Fl. I (personnel) of 28 June 1918.

Aircraft Downed:

9.30 a.m., a Sopwith by Lt Gabriel (Jasta 11) as 7th victory. 300th air victory of Jasta 11.

Good visibility. Combat Flights: 57. Enemy air activity low.

As to accuracy: Airdrome, 30 June 1918. Signed: Bodenschatz, Oberleutnant

Beugneux

1 July No special occurrences.

Aircraft Downed:

10.30 a.m., a balloon by Sgt Schumacher (Jasta 10) as 4th.

10.45 a.m., a Bréguet by Lt Udet (Jasta 4) as 37th.

8.55 p.m., a Spad by Lt Udet (Jasta 4) as 38th.

Departure: Lt Skowronski transferred to Armee Flugpark 3.

Total strength for Jagdgeschwader I: 49 officers, 545 non-commissioned officers and enlisted personnel, including men posted.

Good visibility. Combat Flights: 45. Enemy air activity low in the morning, picking up in the evening, brisk on the other side.

2 July No special occurrences.

Aircraft Downed:

8.10 a.m., a Nieuport by Lt Löwenhardt (Jasta 10) as 33rd victory.

8.15 a.m., a Nieuport by Lt Löwenhardt (Jasta 10) as 34th victory.

8.15 a.m., a Nieuport by Lt Udet (Jasta 4) as 39th.

8.20 a.m., a Nieuport by Lt Friedrichs (Jasta 10) as 20th victory.

Detailed: Lt d. R. Rolff and Lt d. R. von Dorrien transferred from Jastaschule I. The first detailed to Jasta 6, the latter to Jasta 11.

Good visibility, somewhat hazy towards evening. Combat Flights: 15. Enemy air activity low.

3 July No special occurrences.

Aircraft Downed:

8.00 a.m., a Spad by Vfw Hemer (Jasta 10) as 12th.[3]

---

[1] Shot down at 8.00 p.m.
[2] Killed in action near Nauroy.
[3] This should be Jasta 6.

8.20 a.m., a Bréguet by Lt Drekmann (Jasta 4) as 7th.

8.25 a.m., a Spad by Lt Drekmann (Jasta 4) as 8th.

8.25 a.m., a Spad by Lt Udet (Jasta 4) as 40th.

7.10 p.m., a Spad by Lt Nöldecke (Jasta 6) as 1st victory.

Casualty: According to Kogenluft's radio message of 3 July 1918, the commander of Jagdgeschwader No. I, Hauptmann Reinhard, crashed fatally during a test flight at Berlin-Adlershof on 3 July 1918.

Good visibility without exception. Combat Flights: 42. Enemy air activity brisk in the morning, low in the afternoon.

4 July No special occurrences.

Transfer: Lt d. R. Laumann (Jasta 10) placed at the disposal of Id. Flieg. in conformity with Kogenluft 178416.

Good visibility. Combat Flights: 20. No enemy air activity in the morning, low in the afternoon.

5 July No special occurrences.

Telegram of condolence from (Kofl.) Kogenluft of Kofl. 7,[1] dated 5 July 1918, on the death of the commander, Hauptmann Reinhard. Letter of condolence from Kofl. 2, Major Haehnelt, 5 July, on the death of the commander, Hauptmann Reinhard.

The flying units were deployed to decide matters on the ground.

Poor visibility. Combat Flights: 34. Enemy air activity low in the morning, no activity in the afternoon.

6 July No special occurrences. Kofl. Operating Order No. 8. Cloudy and ground haze. Combat Flights: 33. Enemy air activity low.

7 July No special occurrences. Order for the air defense reporting service. Hazy in the morning, good visibility in the evening. Combat Flights: 36. Enemy air activity low in the morning, no activity in the afternoon, picking up towards evening.

8 July No special occurrences.

Aircraft Downed:

12.30 p.m., a Nieuport by Lt Friedrichs (Jasta 10) as 21st victory.

Telegram of condolence on the death of the commander, Hauptmann Reinhard, from Major Freiherr von Richthofen, dated 8 July.

In conformity with Kogenluft 178654 of 6 July 1918, Oblt Göring is appointed commander of Jagdgeschwader I.

Good visibility in the morning, extremely hazy in the afternoon. Combat Flights: 41. Enemy air activity low.

9 July No special occurrences. Activity report for the time period from 1 May to 30 June 1918, inclusive. Good visibility, rain at times. Combat Flights: 17. Almost no enemy air activity.

10 July No special occurrences.

Detailed: Lt Groos is transferred to the Geschwader from Jastaschule II and detailed to Jasta 11. Gefr Möller transferred to Jagdgeschwader I from

---

[1] Telegram was from the Commanding General of the Air Service, General Ernst von Hoeppner.

Jastaschule II and detailed to Jasta 10. Vfw Schaffen of Jastaschule II is transferred to Jagdgeschwader I and detailed to Jasta 10.

Order: Uffz Biewers and Gefr Nitsche, both Jasta 10, are ordered to Park 7. Good visibility. Combat Flights: 23. Enemy air activity low.

11 July No special occurrences. Kofl. Operating Order No. 10.

Order: Lt von Puttkammer (Jasta 4) ordered to Park 7.

Detailed: Lt Markgraf is transferred to Jagdgeschwader I from Jastaschule II and detailed to Jasta 6. Good visibility. Combat Flights: 23. Enemy air activity: low.

12 July No special occurrences.

Transfers: Uffz Biewers and Gefr Nitsche (Jasta 10) are transferred to Park [7] as pilots for C-type aircraft.

Good visibility. Combat Flights: 13. Enemy air activity low in the'morning, no activity in the afternoon.

13 July No special occurrences. Hazy. Combat Flights: 29. Enemy air activity very low.

14 July No special occurrences. Oblt Göring has assumed command of the Geschwader as of today.

Aircraft Downed:

8.15 [a.m.] a Bréguet by Lt Löwenhardt (Jasta 10) as 35th victory.

Ground haze in the morning hours, later on low clouds, rain. Combat Flights: 41. Enemy air activity low.

15 July Attack by the 7th Army.[1] The Geschwader's deployment directed towards the numerous enemy aviation forces appearing in the Marne valley. Enemy flight operations moderate in the morning. In the afternoon, superior enemy squadron operations at all altitudes, above all, appearances by strong squadrons of English single-seaters. Individual Staffeln of the Geschwader joined together into a half-Geschwader formation. Closest possible collaboration with Jagdgeschwader III.

Aircraft Downed:

10.45 a.m., a balloon by Lt Paul Wenzel (Jasta 6) as 6th.

1.07 p.m., a Sopwith Camel by Lt Löwenhardt (Jasta 10) as 36th victory.

4.40 p.m., a Spad by Lt Meyer (Jasta 4) as 3rd.

Casualty: Lt Friedrichs (Jasta 10) crashed in flames (dead).

Good visibility. Combat Flights: 99. Enemy air activity: activity picking up.

16 July Continuation of the 7th Army's attack. The Staffeln deployed in half-Geschwader formation in the attack sector.

Aircraft Downed:

5.25, a Spad by Lt Bretschneider (Jasta 6) as 6th.

5.30, a Sopwith Camel by Vfw Hemer (Jasta 6) as 13th.

5.35, a Sopwith Camel by Vfw Hemer (Jasta 6) as 14th.

1.55 p.m., a Spad by Gefr Möller (Jasta 10) as 1st.

6.20, a Spad by Lt Löwenhardt (Jasta 10) as 37th.

---

[1] The Second Battle of the Marne, 15 July to 5 August, 1918, beginning with the Fourth Battle of Champagne (15-18 July).

Casualties: Lt Markgraf (Jasta 6) crashed fatally near Magneux. Lt Kirschstein (Jasta 6) died in hospital following the crash near Magneux. At 7.45 [p.m.], at an altitude of 1,200 m, Lt Bender's machine (Jasta 4) began to burn as a result of the spontaneous combustion of his phosphorus ammunition. Lt Bender jumped out with a parachute at an altitude of 1,200 m and landed uninjured on the Geschwader's airfield. Machine totally destroyed.

Visibility good. Combat Flights: 50. Enemy air activity brisk in the morning, no activity in the afternoon.

17 July No special occurrences. Counterattack by the French. Report concerning the combat situation in the air during the days of the attack from 15 July on.

Aircraft Downed:

  10.45 a.m., a Bréguet by Lt Maushake (Jasta 4) as 2nd.
  10.50 a.m., a Bréguet by Lt Koepsch (Jasta 4) as 3rd.
  10.35 a.m., a Bréguet by Lt Paul Wenzel (Jasta 6) as 7th.
  10.35 a.m., a Bréguet by Lt Matzdorf (Jasta 6) as 1st.
  10.40 a.m., a Bréguet by Lt Rolff (Jasta 6) as 1st.

Hazy. Combat Flights: 55. Enemy air activity low.

18 July Following an intense artillery barrage, attack by strong French forces between the Aisne and the Marne [Rivers]. Massive deployment of enemy squadrons in the morning hours until 10.00 a.m. Relatively quiet in the afternoon hours. Towards evening, enemy air activity picked up again. Deployment of the Geschwader in Staffeln and half-Geschwader formation. Closest possible cooperation with Jagdgeschwader III. The enemy suffered heavy losses in the air.

Preparations were made for changing airdromes due to our forward lines withdrawing by several kilometers. A new airdrome just north and east of the Monthussart Farm, two km north-east of Braisne, was scouted out. Move made during the night.

Aircraft Downed:

  6.20 a.m., a Spad by Lt Löwenhardt (Jasta 10) as 38th.
  6.29 a.m., a Spad by Vfw Schumacher (Jasta 10) as 5th.[1]
  7.35 a.m., a Spad by Lt Heldmann (Jasta 10) as 8th.
  8.15 a.m., a Spad by Oblt Göring, Commander, as 22nd.[2]
  8.30 a.m., a Spad by Oblt von Wedel (Jasta 11) as 7th.
  9.15 a.m., a Bréguet by Vfw Hemer (Jasta 6) as 15th.
  9.25 a.m., a DH 9 by Lt Maushake (Jasta 4) as 3rd.
  9.30 a.m., a Sopwith by Lt Meyer (Jasta 4) as 4th.
  9.50 a.m., a Spad by Vfw Gabriel (Jasta 11) as 8th.
  10.00 a.m., a Spad by Vfw Gabriel (Jasta 11) as 9th.
  10.22 a.m., a Bréguet by Vfw Gabriel (Jasta 11) as 10th.
  2.30 p.m., a Spad by Lt Löwenhardt (Jasta 10) as 39th.
  3.30 p.m., a Spad biplane by Vfw Gabriel (Jasta 11) as 11th.

---

[1] Rank should be Sergeant (Feldwebel).
[2] Only victory scored by Oblt Göring while commander of JG I.

Casualties: Lt Bretschneider-Bodemer (Jasta 6) crashed in flames near Grand Rozoy (dead). Gefr Möller (Jasta 10) did not return from a front-line patrol.[1]

Burial: The burial of Lt Friedrichs took place from the Field Hospital 28, Beugneux, at 5.00 p.m. on 17 July 1918.

Hazy. Combat Flights: 47. Enemy air activity brisk.

Monthussart Farm

19 July   Enemy divisional attacks, German air activity was vastly lower than on the previous day. The Geschwader deployed in Staffeln.

Aircraft Downed:

    11.30 a.m., a Spad by Lt Löwenhardt (Jasta 10) as 40th.

    3.30 p.m., a Spad by Lt Maushake (Jasta 4) as 4th.

    8.50 p.m., a Spad by Lt Löwenhardt (Jasta 10) as 41st.

Detailed: By order of Kogenluft 178961, Lt Freiherr von Richthofen (Lothar) is transferred to the Geschwader and assigned as leader of Jasta 11.

Appointed: Lt Paul Wenzel is appointed to acting leadership of Jasta 6.

The entire move to Monthussart Farm made without any hold-ups. The new field set up. Pilots quartered in Braisne (Staffeln 4, 10, and 11) and Courcelles (Staffel 6). Quarters for non-commissioned officers and enlisted personnel at the farm. Machines are housed in tents.

Cloudy (poor). Combat Flights: 49. No enemy air activity.

20 July   Powerful French divisional attack; German counterattack.

Enemy air activity picked up only in the evening. In the early hours of the afternoon, several Staffeln intervened in the ground conflict, the focal point of which was in the Hartennes region, in particular. Jasta 10 attacked tanks, enemy gun batteries, and troop concentrations; Jasta 11 attacked columns and a captive balloon on the north-east edge of Villers–Collerêts forest. In the evening, Jasta 10 subsequently attacked a firing gun battery.

Aircraft Downed:

    8.30 a.m., a DH 9 by Lt Drekmann (Jasta 4) as 9th.

    8.35 a.m., a balloon by Lt Paul Wenzel (Jasta 6) as 8th victory.

At 6.00 p.m. the burials of Lt Bretschneider-Bodemer, Lt Markgraf, and Lt Kirschstein, leader of Jasta 6, took place at the military cemetery in Courcelles.

Allocation of the airdromes in case of a pull-back of the Front.

Cloudy, poor. Combat Flights: 56. Enemy air activity moderate.

21 July   The offensive continues bitterly on. Only towards evening did the enemy appear with superior aerial forces. Geschwader deployed in Staffeln. Deployment of enemy aviation forces (see enclosure 150).

Aircraft Downed:

    8.15 p.m., a Sopwith by Oblt von Wedel (Jasta 11) as 8th.

    8.15 p.m., a Sopwith by Lt Wolfram Freiherr von Richthofen (Jasta 11) as 3rd.

    8.15 p.m., a Sopwith by Lt Löwenhardt (Jasta 10) as 42nd.

---

[1] Killed in action near Chaudun.

Detailed: Flieger Blümener is transferred to Jagdgeschwader I and detailed to Jasta 6. Uffz Reimers is transferred to Jagdgeschwader I and detailed to Jasta 6.

Good. Combat Flights: 29. Enemy air activity brisk, powerful squadrons at all altitudes.

22 July   The offensive took its bitter course. Only towards evening did heavier enemy air activity commence.

Aircraft Downed:

4.20 p.m., a Spad by Lt Richard Wenzl (Jasta 6) as 4th.

4.20 p.m., a Spad by Vfw Hemer (Jasta 6) as 16th.

7.10 p.m., a DH 9 by Lt Koepsch (Jasta 4) as 4th.

8.30 p.m., a Sopwith by Lt Löwenhardt (Jasta 10) as 43rd victory.

Detailed: Lt Reinhardt is transferred to Jagdgeschwader I and detailed to Jasta 4.

Casualty: Lt Nöldecke (Jasta 6) slightly injured, remains with the unit.

Instructions for the deployment of the aviation units. Designation of radio telegraphic take-off order.

Good visibility. Combat Flights: 78. Enemy air activity low, brisk in the evening.

23 July   No particular combat engagements. Flight operations low. Telegram of condolence from Id. Flieg. for Hauptmann Reinhard.

Departure: Lt von Puttkammer (Jasta 4) is transferred to Park 7 for use on C-type aircraft.

Heavily overcast, poor visibility. No enemy air activity.

24 July   No special occurrences.

Casualty: Vfw Schumacher (Jasta 10) badly wounded, was delivered to the Bavarian Field Hospital 7 in Courcelles.[1]

Enemy bombing raid on the rear areas. Deployment involves Rittmeister von Braun and Oblt Loerzer.[2]

Good in part. Combat Flights: 62. No enemy air activity.

25 July   No special occurrences.

Aircraft Downed:

7.30 [p.m.] a Spad by Lt Drekmann (Jasta 4) as 10th.

7.50 [p.m.] a Sopwith by Lt Lothar Freiherr von Richthofen (Jasta 11) as 30th victory.

8.30 p.m., a Spad by Lt Just (Jasta 11) as 3rd.

8.50 p.m., a Spad by Lt Löwenhardt (Jasta 10) as 44th.

As of today, the Jagdgeschwader Freiherr von Richthofen No. I has scored its 500th air victory.

Casualties: Lt Graf von Hohenau (Jasta 11) wounded at 7.45 p.m., following air combat, was delivered to Field Hospital 103, Grugny, and died on the evening of 26 July.[3] Lt von Dorrien (Jasta 11) wounded by machine gun during

---

[1] Rank should be Sergeant (Feldwebel).

[2] Rittmeister Konstantin von Braun, leader of Jagdgruppe 5, and Hauptmann Bruno Loerzer, leader of Jagdgeschwader III.

[3] Lt von Hohenau is listed in the casualty lists as 'Freiherr' (Baron), and not 'Graf' (Count).

air combat (a shot through the left foot).

Clouds and ground haze. Combat Flights: 59. Enemy air activity picking up in the evening.

26 July No special occurrences.

Substitutions: Lt Lothar Freiherr von Richthofen assumes acting command of the Geschwader for the duration of Oblt Göring's leave. Oblt von Wedel assumes the acting command of Jasta 11 until further notice.

Rain. Combat Flights: 4. No enemy air activity.

27 July No special occurrences.

Transfers: Lt Festler (Jastaschule II) is transferred to the Geschwader in conformity with Kogenluft 179228 Fl. I of 25 July 1918, and is detailed to Jasta 11. Lt Mentz (Jastaschule I) is transferred to the Geschwader in conformity with Kogenluft 179272 of 25 July and detailed to Jasta 11.

Rain. No enemy air activity.

28 July No special occurrences.

Aircraft Downed:

3.10 p.m., a Spad by Lt Löwenhardt (Jasta 10) as 45th victory.

7.50 p.m., a Sopwith by Lt Grassmann (Jasta 10) as 3rd.

Radio message from His Excellency von Hoeppner: congratulatory telegram on 500 air victories.

Visibility good, hazy towards evening. Combat Flights: 54. Enemy air activity low, picking up towards evening.

29 July Advance detail to Puisieux Farm.

Aircraft Downed:

12.10 p.m., a Bréguet by Lt Paul Wenzel (Jasta 6) as 9th.

12.15 p.m., a Bréguet by Oblt von Wedel (Jasta 11) as 9th.

7.30 p.m., a Spad by Lt Löwenhardt (Jasta 10) as 46th.

Transfers: Sgt Jagla (Jasta 11) is relieved of duty as fighter pilot in conformity with Kogenluft 179220 of 26 July 1918, and is transferred to Park 7 for duty as a pilot of C-type aircraft. Lt d. R. Krayer (Jastaschule II), Lt d. R. Maletsky (Jastaschule),[1] Uffz Strecker (Jastaschule II) were transferred to the Geschwader and detailed to Jasta 10.

Illness: Lt von Winterfeld and Lt von Conta (Jasta 4 and Jasta 11) are in the hospital on account of illness.

Order concerning the pullback and reconnaissance by the flying units during the taking of the Vesle position (see enclosure 155a). Order concerning the withdrawal of the units of the Army High Command.

Moderate visibility. Combat Flights: 87. Enemy air activity brisk at times.

Puisieux Farm

30 July No special occurrences.

Aircraft Downed:

3.10 p.m., a Sopwith by Lt Löwenhardt (Jasta 10) as 47th victory.

---

[1] The Jastaschule from which Lt Maletsky was transferred was not specified, but was Jastaschule II.

6.45 p.m., a Spad by Lt Drekmann (Jasta 4) as 11th.

8.10 p.m., a Sopwith by Lt Löwenhardt (Jasta 10) as 48th victory.

Departure: Lt d. R. Brocke (Jasta 6) is placed at the disposal of Id. Flieg. in conformity with Kogenluft 179220 of 27 July 1918.

Added to Strength: Lt d. R. Laumann is transferred back to Jasta 10 according to Kogenluft Order 179244 of 27 July 1918. Lt von Köckeritz (Jastaschule I) is transferred to the Geschwader in conformity with Kogenluft 179335 Fl. I of 27 July 1918 and detailed to Jasta 11.

Casualties: Lt Drekmann (Jasta 4) did not return from a front-line patrol.[1] Lt von Raffay (Jasta 6) transported to hospital as a result of an accident (broken bone, left foot).

Radio message from Major Freiherr von Richthofen: 'Sincere congratulations on the proud number of 500 air victories. The Fliers' Father'.[2]

Visibility good. Combat Flights: 38. Enemy air activity low.

31 July No special occurrences.

Aircraft Downed:

6.40 p.m., a Nieuport by Lt Rolff (Jasta 6) as 2nd.

Activity report for the time period from 1 to 31 July 1918, inclusive (see enclosure 157).

Lt Krayer (Jasta 10) is transferred to Jasta 6.

Total ration strength for JG I: 46 officers (including doctors and clerks), 495 non-commissioned officers and enlisted personnel (including men posted).

Organization and allocation of the flying units following capture of the Blücher position on 3 August 1918.

Visibility: hazy. Combat Flights: 45. Enemy air activity low.

As to accuracy: Airdrome, 31 July 1918. Signed: Bodenschatz, Oberleutnant

1 Aug

Aircraft Downed:

9.10 a.m., a Nieuport by Vfw Hemer (Jasta 6) as 17th.

9.15 a.m., a Nieuport by Lt Richard Wenzl (Jasta 6) as 5th.

9.30 a.m., a Nieuport by Lt Jessen (Jasta 4) as 1st.

9.30 a.m., a Nieuport by Lt Koepsch (Jasta 4) as 5th.

9.30 a.m., a Nieuport by Lt Udet (Jasta 4) as 41st.

9.40 a.m., a Nieuport by Vfw Hemer (Jasta 6) as 18th.

12.15 p.m., a Bréguet by Lt Udet (Jasta 4) as 42nd.

1.05 p.m., a Spad by Lt Groos (Jasta 11) as 7th.

1.10 p.m., a Spad by Lt Lothar Freiherr von Richthofen (Jasta 11) as 31st victory.

7.30 p.m., a Spad by Lt Udet (Jasta 4) as 43rd.

8.25 p.m., a Spad by Lt Lothar Freiherr von Richthofen (Jasta 11) as 32nd victory.

Order: Lt d. R. Krayer (Jasta 6) is ordered to Jasta 45.[3] Vfw Schaffen (Jasta

---

[1] Killed in action over Grand Rozoy.

[2] An affectionate nickname given to Major von Richthofen by the pilots of JG I.

[3] See also entry for 13 Sep 1918.

10) is ordered to Armee Flugpark.[1]

Casualties: Lt Lehmann (Jasta 10) did not return from a front-line patrol.[2] Lt Paul Wenzel (Jasta 6) slightly wounded, remains with the unit.

Order: Lt Wolfram Freiherr von Richthofen (Jasta 11) ordered to Asch on 30 July for the armorers' course.

Visibility: hazy. Combat Flights: 80. Enemy air activity low, moderate in the afternoon.

2 Aug No special occurrences.

Gefr Henschler was transferred to the Geschwader from Jastaschule I in conformity with Kogenluft 179481 Fl. I of 30 July 1918.

Rain. Combat Flights: 3. No enemy air activity.

3 Aug No special occurrences.

Added to Strength: Lt Adomeit (Jastaschule I) transferred to the Geschwader, is detailed to Jasta 10. Lt d. R. Kraut (Jastaschule I) transferred to the Geschwader, is detailed to Jasta 4.

Visibility good, rain at times. Combat Flights: 21. Enemy air activity very low.

4 Aug No special occurrences.

Aircraft Downed:

8.00 p.m., a Spad by Lt Jessen (Jasta 4) as 2nd.

8.05 p.m., a Spad by Lt Udet (Jasta 4) as 44th.

Casualty: Uffz Strecker (Jasta 10) crashed during a test flight, is in the hospital.

Visibility good, rain at times. Combat Flights: 11. No enemy air activity.

5 Aug Advance detail to the 2nd Army. Scouting out and construction of an airfield. Rain. Combat Flights: 6. No enemy air activity.

6 Aug No special occurrences. Report concerning the experience gained during the last battles of the retreat, see enclosure 158.

Added to Strength: According to order of Kogenluft 176915 Fl. I of 3 August, Lt von der Wense and Uffz Martens are transferred to the Geschwader from Jastaschule I and detailed to Jasta 6 and 11.

Good visibility. Combat Flights: 18. No enemy air activity.

7 Aug No particular combat engagements. Heavily overcast, hazy visibility. Combat Flights: 48. No enemy air activity.

8 Aug As a result of a day of heavy fighting with the 2nd Army, the Geschwader deployed in this Army's sector.[3] The Staffeln used the airdrome in the area of Peronne as an intermediate landing field. Superior enemy flight operations at all altitudes.

Aircraft Downed:

12.45 p.m., a Sopwith Camel by Lt Löwenhardt (Jasta 10) as 49th.

5.30 p.m., an SE 5 by Lt Udet (Jasta 4) as 45th.

5.30 p.m., a Sopwith by Lt Lothar von Richthofen (Jasta 11) as 33rd.

---

[1] Armee Flugpark 4.
[2] Taken prisoner.
[3] Attack by the British Fourth Army under General Henry Rawlinson and the French First Army under Général Debeney east of Amiens (Battle of Amiens).

5.30 p.m., a Sopwith by Lt Löwenhardt (Jasta 10) as 50th.

5.45 p.m., an SE 5 by Lt Lothar von Richthofen (Jasta 11) as 34th.

6.30 p.m., 2 SE 5s Lt Udet (Jasta 4) one as 46th and one as 47th.[1]

6.30 p.m., a Bristol by Lt Grassmann (Jasta 10) as 4th.

6.50 p.m., a Sopwith by Lt Löwenhardt (Jasta 10) as 51st.

6.50 p.m., an SE 5 by Lt Lothar Freiherr von Richthofen (Jasta 11) as 35th.

7.00 p.m., a DH 12 by Vfw Hemer (Jasta 6) as 19th.

7.30 p.m., a two-seater by Uffz Reimers (Jasta 6) as 1st.

7.40 p.m., a two-seater by Lt Richard Wenzl (Jasta 6) as 6th.[2]

The Geschwader returned to Puisieux Farm in the evening.

Concerning the air defense radio telegraph system.

Good visibility, slightly cloudy. Combat Flights: 49. Enemy air activity: superior enemy air activity at all altitudes.

9 Aug   As on 8 August 1918.

Aircraft Downed:

7.25 a.m., a Sopwith by Lt Heldmann (Jasta 10) as 9th.

7.30 a.m., a DH 9 by Lt Lothar von Richthofen (Jasta 11) as 36th.

7.35 a.m., a Sopwith by Lt Just (Jasta 11) as 4th.

7.40 a.m., a Sopwith by Oblt Löwenhardt[3] (Jasta 10) as 52nd.

8.00 a.m., a DH 9 by Lt Paul Wenzel (Jasta 6) as 10th.

8.00 a.m., a DH 9 by Uffz Reimers (Jasta 6) as 2nd.

4.20 p.m., a DH 9 by Lt Maushake (Jasta 4) as 6th.

4.25 p.m., a Sopwith by Lt Udet (Jasta 4) as 48th.

6.40 p.m., a DH 9 by Lt Lothar Freiherr von Richthofen (Jasta 11) as 37th.

6.55 p.m., a Sopwith by Oblt Löwenhardt (Jasta 10) as 53rd.

9.20 p.m., a Sopwith by Lt Udet (Jasta 4) as 49th.

Casualties: Vfw Hemer (Jasta 6) slightly wounded in air combat, remains with the unit. Lt Reinhardt (Jasta 4) did not return from a flight; according to a telephone message, he is in the military hospital at Tincourt, slightly wounded on both feet.

Slightly cloudy. Combat Flights: 107. Superior enemy air activity.

Puisieux Farm — Ennemain–Falvy Road

10 Aug   Move to the 2nd Army; to Ennemain airdrome by truck. The transports were all directed to the advance landing fields on both sides of the Ennemain–Falvy Road. Fields were unprepared and poor. Despite great difficulties, flight operations could be maintained to some extent.

Aircraft Downed:

11.20 a.m., a Sopwith by Lt Udet (Jasta 4) as 50th.

12.15 p.m., an SE 5 by Lt von Köckeritz (Jasta 11) as 1st.

3.50 p.m., an RE 8 by Lt Maushake (Jasta 4) as 7th.

7.45 p.m., a Sopwith by Lt Udet (Jasta 4) as 51st.

---

[1] Udet's 47th victory was a Sopwith Camel, downed at 8.40 p.m.

[2] DH 9.

[3] Note promotion to Oberleutnant as of 9 August 1918.

Casualty: 12.15 p.m., following the downing of an SE 5 in air combat,[1] Oblt Löwenhardt collided with Lt Wentz (Jasta 11) and crashed.

Added to Strength: Lt d. R. Wolff is transferred to the Geschwader in conformity with Kogenluft 179687 and is detailed to Jasta 6.

Staffel Command: Lt d. R. Heldmann (Jasta 10) assumes the acting command of Jasta 10.

Good visibility. Combat Flights: 62. Enemy air activity moderate, more cautious than in the previous days.

Advance Landing Field on the Ennemain–Falvy Road. From Noon: Bernes
11 Aug Scouting of an airdrome north-east of Bernes. Moved there in the afternoon. Field very large. After getting rid of a few trenches, holes, etc., field very good. Quartering of airplane pilots and enlisted personnel in English corrugated huts, the machines in tents.

Aircraft Downed:

9.30 a.m., a DH 12 by Lt Lothar von Richthofen (Jasta 11) as 38th.

10.00 a.m., a DH 12 by Lt Udet (Jasta 4) as 52nd.

6.55 p.m., a Sopwith by Lt Grassmann (Jasta 10) as 5th.

7.00 p.m., a Sopwith by Lt Heldmann (Jasta 10) as 10th.

Casualties: Lt Paul Wenzel wounded in air combat, delivered to the hospital in St Quentin. Lt von der Wense (Jasta 6) did not return from a flight (dead). Lt Festler (Jasta 11) did not return from a flight (dead).

Weather: hazy. Combat Flights: 51. Enemy air activity brisk.

Bernes
12 Aug Tactical deployment in conjunction with Jagdgruppe Greim in Hervilly. Jagdgruppe Thuy was posted from the 1st Army as well.[2]

Aircraft Downed:

9.30 a.m., a Sopwith by Lt Wolfram Freiherr von Richthofen (Jasta 11) as 5th.

9.35 a.m., a Sopwith by Lt Just (Jasta 11) as 5th.

9.35 a.m., a Sopwith by Lt Lothar Freiherr von Richthofen (Jasta 11) as 39th.

9.50 a.m., a Sopwith by Lt Lothar Freiherr von Richthofen (Jasta 11) as 40th.

11.30 a.m., an SE 5 by Lt Udet (Jasta 4) as 53rd.

Radio message from His Excellency von Hoeppner on the hero's death of Oblt Löwenhardt (see enclosure 160). Radio message No. 555 from the Army Group of the German Crown Prince (see enclosure 161).

Hazy visibility. Combat Flights: 31. Enemy air activity: moderate enemy flight operations.

13 Aug Due to the heavy losses of the last few days, the Geschwader was condensed to one Staffel. Close cooperation with Jagdgeschwader III and Jagdgruppe Greim.

Casualty: Lt Lothar Freiherr von Richthofen, slightly wounded in the thigh during air combat.

---

[1] This was Löwenhardt's fifty-fourth victory.
[2] Jagdgruppe Greim was commanded by Oblt Robert Greim (JGr 10); Jagdgruppe Thuy was under the command of Lt Emil Thuy (JGr 7).

Aircraft Downed:

A Bréguet by Lt Koepsch (Jasta 4) as 6th victory.

Hazy visibility. Combat Flights: 36. Enemy air activity very brisk.

14 Aug   No special occurrences.

Aircraft Downed:

7.00 p.m., a Bristol by Lt Udet (Jasta 4) as 54th.

Transfers: Oblt Grosch and Vfw Lechner transferred to the Geschwader from Jastaschule[1] in conformity with Kogenluft 179807 Fl. I of 9 August and were detailed to Jasta 4 and Jasta 6. In accordance with Kogenluft Order 179969 of 13 August, Lt d. R. Laumann (Jasta 66) is appointed leader of Jasta 10.

Acting Command: Lt Udet (Jasta 4) assumes acting command of the Geschwader, Lt Mohnicke (Jasta 11) the acting command of Jasta 11.

Good visibility at times. Combat Flights: 55. Enemy air activity held to moderate limits.

15 Aug   No special occurrences.

Aircraft Downed:

5.15 p.m., a Sopwith Camel by Lt Udet (Jasta 4) as 55th.

Transfers: Lt d. R. Schibilsky transferred to the Geschwader from Jastaschule II in conformity with Kogenluft 179851, and was detailed to Jasta 10. Transferred from Jastaschule I to the Geschwader by order of Kogenluft 179974 of 14 August: Lt Schliewen to Jasta 6, and Lt Freiherr von Barnekow to Jasta 11.

Burial: The burial of Lt Festler (Jasta 11) took place in the afternoon from the Bernes airfield to the St Quentin military cemetery.

Visibility: hazy. Combat Flights: 47. No enemy air activity in the morning, moderate activity in the afternoon.

16 Aug   Due to heavy enemy attacks near the 18th Army, the pursuit area was extended as far as Roye.

Aircraft Downed:

10.40 a.m., a Spad by Lt Udet (Jasta 4) as 56th.

12.30 p.m., a Sopwith Camel by Lt Rolff (Jasta 6) as 3rd.

Transfer: Uffz Klamt was transferred to the Geschwader in conformity with Kogenluft 179877 of 12 August, and detailed to Jasta 10.

Casualty: Vfw Lechner (Jasta 6) slightly injured during a test flight, and is in the St Quentin field hospital.

Good visibility. Combat Flights: 57. Enemy air activity brisk.

17 Aug   As on 16 August 1918.

Transfer: Lt Kohlbach (Jasta 50) was transferred to the Geschwader in conformity with Kogenluft 179824 of 15 August, and is detailed to Jasta 10.

Visibility good, cloudy. Combat Flights: 17. Enemy air activity low in the morning, no activity in the afternoon.

18 Aug   As on 16 August 1918.

Transfers: By order of Kogenluft 180113 Fl. I of 17 August, pilot Flieger Rhode (Jastaschule II) is transferred to the Geschwader and detailed to Jasta 4. Lt von Raczek (Jastaschule II) was transferred to the Geschwader in

---

[1] No Jastaschule number given; but Jastaschule I.

conformity with Kogenluft 179730 of 17 August, and detailed to Jasta 11.

Good visibility. Combat Flights: 4. Enemy air activity very low.

19 Aug   No special occurrences.

Aircraft Downed:

8.42 a.m., an SE 5 by Lt Laumann (Jasta 10) as 25th.

9.00 a.m., an SE 5 by Lt Heldmann (Jasta 10) as 11th.

9.00 a.m., a Sopwith by Offz Stellv Aue (Jasta 10) as 8th.

9.50 a.m., a Sopwith Camel by Lt Matzdorf (Jasta 6) as 2nd victory.

Casualty: 9.50 a.m., Lt Rolff (Jasta 6) crashed fatally with a Fokker Parasol[1] near the Bernes sugar factory. Airplane broke apart at an altitude of 300 m. The Fokker Parasol was banned by Geschwader order.

Visibility good. Combat Flights: 38. Enemy air activity brisk in the morning, no activity in the afternoon.

20 Aug   No special occurrences. Secret: Deployment of aviation units of the 2nd Army. Secret: Ground radio traffic of the flying service.

Departure: In conformity with Kogenluft No. 179930 Fl. I of 18 August, Vfw Schaffen (Jasta 10) is transferred to Park 4.

Moderate visibility. Combat Flights: 2. Enemy air activity very low.

21 Aug   Powerful attack by the English near the 17th Army.[2] The Geschwader deployed in the attack zone between Arras and Albert. Intermediate landing field at Epinoy north of Cambrai with Jagdgruppe Schleich.[3] Returned to home field in the afternoon.

Aircraft Downed:

7.00 p.m., an SE 5 by Lt Udet (Jasta 4) as 57th.

7.20 p.m., a Sopwith by Lt Udet (Jasta 4) as 58th.

Departure: In conformity with Kogenluft 179977 of 18 August, Vfw Schumacher (Jasta 10) is placed at the disposal of Id. Flieg.[4]

Visibility moderate. Combat Flights: 71. Enemy air activity: strong showing by single-seaters at times.

22 Aug   Enemy assault on the right flank of the 2nd Army. The Geschwader deployed in the attack zone north of the Somme.

Aircraft Downed:

8.40 a.m., a Sopwith Camel by Lt Udet (Jasta 4) as 59th.

12.45 p.m., an SE 5 by Lt Laumann (Jasta 10) as 26th.

12.30 p.m., an SE 5 by Lt Udet (Jasta 4) as 60th.

5.45 p.m., an SE 5 by Lt Kohlbach (Jasta 10) as 3rd.

5.45 p.m., an SE 5 by Lt Laumann (Jasta 10) as 27th.

Geschwader Command: Oblt Göring has resumed command of the Geschwader.

Leave and Staffel Command: Lt d. R. Udet (Jasta 4) is granted four weeks' leave to Munich. Lt d. R. Koepsch (Jasta 4) assumes acting command of Jasta

---

[1] Fokker E V monoplane.

[2] The British Third Army under Field Marshal Julian Byng, Second Battle of the Somme, 8 August – 4 September 1918.

[3] Commanded by Oblt Eduard von Schleich (JGr 8).

[4] Rank should be Sergeant (Feldwebel).

4 as of 22 August.

Added to Strength: In conformity with Kogenluft 180180 of 20 August, Lt d. R. Gussmann (FEA 5) is transferred to the Geschwader and detailed to Jasta 11.

Departure: Pilot Vfw Gabriel (Jasta 11) is ordered to Armee Flugpark 2.

Burial: The burial of Lt Rolff (Jasta 6) took place at 5.00 p.m., from the Bernes airfield to the military cemetery at St Quentin.

Visibility: mostly hazy. Combat Flights: 37. Enemy air activity was brisk in the early hours of the morning, and later kept to moderate limits.

23 Aug   No special occurrences.

Casualty: Lt von Barnekow (Jasta 11) slightly wounded in the left and right thigh by splinters following air combat, remains with the unit.

Poor visibility. Combat Flights: 23. Enemy air activity brisk in the morning hours, moderate later, no activity towards evening.

24 Aug   No special occurrences.

Casualty: Oblt Grosch (Jasta 4) wounded by a shot in the arm during air combat and made an emergency landing near Guise.

Funeral: The funeral of Oblt Löwenhardt took place at 1.00 p.m. from the airfield to Roisel (body conveyed home).

Cloudy, good visibility. Combat Flights: 9. Enemy air activity brisk, action by enemy single-seater fighters.

25 Aug   No special occurrences.

Leave: Fw Lt Schubert assumes the duties of adjutant for the duration of Oblt Bodenschatz's leave.

Visibility: hazy. Combat Flights: 59. Enemy air activity brisk in the morning, no activity in the afternoon.

26 Aug   No special occurrences.

From today on, Lt Wolfram Freiherr von Richthofen assumes the acting command of Jasta 11. Lt Groos assumes the duties of the special duty officer for Jasta 11 as of today. Lt Meyer assumes the duties of the special duty officer for Jasta 4.

Transfers: Lt d. R. Fischer and Uffz Derflinger were transferred to the Geschwader from Jastaschule I in conformity with Kogenluft 180291 Fl. I of 23 August. The former was detailed to Jasta 4, the latter to Jasta 10.

Good visibility. Combat Flights: 39. Enemy air activity very low.

27 Aug   Powerful attack by the English near the 2nd Army. The Geschwader attacked infantry, cavalry and gun-battery positions near Foucaucourt with good results. The batteries ceased firing.

Casualty: Lt Wolff (Jasta 6) severely wounded during an emergency landing west of Nesle, delivered to the Auxiliary Hospital in Rouy.

Low clouds, rain. Combat Flights: 68. Enemy air activity low.

28 Aug   Continuation of enemy assaults in the sector of the [2nd] Army.

Order: Lt Mohnicke (Jasta 11) and Lt d. R. Heldmann (Jasta 10) were ordered to Breslau as representatives of the Geschwader at Oblt Löwenhardt's funeral.

Added to Strength: Transferred to the Geschwader from Jastaschule I, in conformity with Kogenluft 180361 Fl. I of 25 August, and detailed as follows: Lt d. R. Hildebrandt to Jasta 4; Lt d. R. Schulte-Frohlinde to Jasta 11.

Transfer: Lt d. R. Hirschfeld (Jasta 4) is transferred to Jasta 81 in conformity with Kogenluft 180383 Fl. I of 25 August.

New Airdrome: An advance detail, consisting of telephonists, was sent off to the new field between Busigny and Escaufourt.

Good visibility, heavily overcast, rain towards evening. Combat Flights: 5. No enemy air activity.

29 Aug Day of a major battle with the 9th Army.[1] The 18th Army placed its fighter forces at its [9th Army's] disposal. The Jagdgeschwader extends its fighter cover to the sector of the 18th Army in the region of Noyon.

Advance detail to the new field (Busigny).

Visibility: hazy, cloudy. Combat Flights: 78. Enemy air activity moderate in the afternoon, very low in the evening.

Bernes, Busigny–Escaufourt
30 Aug Move completed. Each Staffel has left behind a rear detachment with a strength of six men each. Quarters and airfields good. Aircraft hangars for every two D-type aircraft on hand from the flying unit domiciled here earlier, in fact: Jasta 4, three hangars; Jasta 6, four hangars; Jasta 10, two hangars; Jasta 11, three hangars. Size of the Busigny landing field 300 x 400, size of the Escaufourt landing field 300 x 300. Sites of the Staffeln: Jastas 4 and 10 north-west of Escaufourt, Jastas 6 and 11 north of Busigny. Geschwader Staff in Busigny.

Aircraft Downed:

9.55 a.m., a Sopwith Camel by Lt Laumann (Jasta 10) as 28th.

9.55 a.m., a Sopwith Camel by Offz Stellv Aue (Jasta 10) as 9th.

Departure: Lt Förster (Jasta 11) is transferred to Jastaschule I as instructor in conformity with Kogenluft 180507 Fl. I of 29 August.

In conformity with Kogenluft 180509 Fl. I of 29 August, Lt d. R. Reinhardt (Jasta 4), Lt d. R. von Raffay, Lt Paul Wenzel, Vfw Lechner (all Jasta 6), Uffz Strecker [Jasta 10] and Lt Lothar Freiherr von Richthofen (Jasta 11) were placed at the disposal of Id. Flieg.

Visibility good, partially cloudy. Combat Flights: 60. Enemy air activity picked up for a time in the morning hours, in the afternoon a few bombing squadrons, one of which was pushed back to the Front.

31 Aug During front-line patrols, ground targets along the Roman road were strafed.

Aircraft Downed:

4.20 p.m., an SE 5 by Lt Koepsch (Jasta 4) as 7th.

7.45 p.m., a Sopwith Dolphin by Oblt von Wedel (Jasta 11) as 10th.

7.45 p.m., a Sopwith Camel by Lt Schulte-Frohlinde (Jasta 11) as 1st.

Staffel Command: Oblt von Wedel (Jasta 11) assumes the acting command of Jasta 11 from today on.

Total ration strength for JG I: 51 officers (including doctors and clerks), 519 non-commissioned officers and enlisted personnel (including men posted).

Medical Services: By order of Army Doctor of the Second Army, Medical

---

[1] Battle of Noyon.

Officer Fisser is ordered to the Geschwader from Armee Flugpark 2.

Good visibility. Combat Flights: 29. Enemy air activity low.

As to accuracy: Airdrome, 31 Aug 1918. Signed: Bodenschatz, Oberleutnant

Busigny–Escaufourt

1 Sept   No special occurrences.

Added to Strength: Lt Neckel was transferred to the Geschwader in conformity with Kofl. 2, and appointed leader of Jasta 6.

Low-lying cloud cover in the morning, rain, clearing in the afternoon. Combat Flights: 75. Enemy air activity low in the morning, several squadrons in the rear areas during the afternoon, very brisk activity in the evening hours.

2 Sept   No special occurrences.

Aircraft Downed:

9.55 a.m., an armor-plated infantry-support airplane by Oblt von Wedel (Jasta 11) as 11th victory.[1]

Order: Oblt Göring was ordered to Army Group Headquarters today for discussion purposes.

Geschwader Leadership: As of today, Oblt von Wedel (Jasta 11) assumes the acting command of the Geschwader.

Visibility moderate, heavily overcast. Combat Flights: 42. Enemy air activity brisk only in the evening hours.

3 Sept   Activity report from 1 to 31 August, inclusive. Letter from General of the Infantry, von Eberhardt, Army High Command 7.

Visibility good. Combat Flights: 39. Enemy air activity low all day, picking up only in the evening hours.

4 Sept   Geschwader Leadership: Oblt Göring resumes command of the Geschwader.

Transfer: Lt Förster (Jasta 11) is transferred to Jastaschule I as instructor in conformity with Kogenluft 180517 Fl. I of 29 August.

Casualty: Uffz Reimers (Jasta 6) did not return from a front-line patrol.[2]

Medical Services: As of today, Medical Officer Fisser assumes the unit medical duties with the Geschwader and emergency first-aid duties on the airfields. Infirmary services for Staffeln 11 and 6 take place at 9.00 a.m. in Busigny, Belowstrasse 23; for Staffeln 10 and 4 in Escaufourt at 10.00 a.m. in the back of the local infirmary.

Aircraft Downed:

5.15 p.m., a balloon by Lt Just (Jasta 11) as 6th.

11.00 a.m., a Sopwith Camel by Lt Richard Wenzl (Jasta 6) as 7th victory.

Good visibility. Combat Flights: 31. Enemy air activity brisk in the morning, also brisk in the evening hours only in the Cambrai–Arras region.

5 Sept   Today is quiet with the northern and southern 2nd Army. The enemy has put a few feelers out across the Somme using only very weak forces. In the area to the north, the enemy lies on the other side of the Moislains–

---

[1] Believed to be an RE 8 brought down near Le Catelet.

[2] Killed in action near Ligny–St Flochel.

Manancourt Canal. In the morning hours, enemy reconnaissance squadrons at low altitude penetrated as far as Vermand.

Aircraft Downed:

3.25 p.m., a balloon by Lt Richard Wenzl (Jasta 6) as 8th.

3.25 p.m., a balloon by Lt Schliewen (Jasta 6) as 1st.

7.00 p.m., an SE 5 by Lt Koepsch (Jasta 4) as 8th.

Casualty: Lt von Winterfeld (Jasta 4) plunged to his death from his burning airplane in the region of Avesnes le Sec (shot down).

Visibility good. Combat Flights: 62. In the morning hours, enemy air activity was brisk between Bapaume and Arras, in the evening only brisk in the Cambrai region.

6 Sept   8.00 a.m., the enemy crossed the Somme with great masses of infantry. We took up the Siegfried position.[1] Near the 17th Army, the line runs from Palluel along the canal.

Aircraft Downed:

9.45 a.m., a Sopwith Dolphin by Lt Wolfram Freiherr von Richthofen (Jasta 11) as 5th victory.

10.45 a.m., a Sopwith Camel by Lt Maushake (Jasta 4) as 7th victory.

Transfer: By Geschwader Order No. 106, numeral 3, from 8 September[2] the ordering of Fw Lt Schubert (Jasta 6) to the staff of the Geschwader as technical officer is to be considered a transfer.

Variable cloudiness, good visibility. Combat Flights: 54. Enemy air activity low, picking up somewhat only in the evening hours.

7 Sept   No special occurrences.

Order: Lt Hücking, Air Defense Officer South, was ordered to the Geschwader and posted permanently to the staff.

Aircraft Downed:

1.00 p.m., an SE 5 by Lt Schulte-Frohlinde (Jasta 11) as 2nd.

7.40 p.m., an SE 5 by Lt Wolfram Freiherr von Richthofen (Jasta 11) as 6th.

7.45 p.m., an SE 5 by Lt Wolfram Freiherr von Richthofen (Jasta 11) as 7th.

7.45 p.m., an SE 5 by Oblt von Wedel (Jasta 11) as 12th.

Visibility: somewhat hazy. Combat Flights: 40. Enemy air activity brisk till noon, no activity in the afternoon, picking up in the evening hours.

8 Sept   In conformity with Kofl.'s order, the Geschwader deployed for forcible reconnaissance.

Casualty: Gefr Blümener (Jasta 6) plunged to his death with a parachute following air combat.

Transfer: Lt Mohnicke (Jasta 11) is placed at the disposal of Id. Flieg. for Section A, in conformity with Kogenluft 180381 Fl. I of 7 September.

Staffel Command: In conformity with Kogenluft 180911 Fl. I of 7 September, Oblt von Wedel (Jasta 11) is assigned as leader of Jasta 11.

---

[1] The German term for the Hindenburg Line, the battle for which began on 20 September 1918.

[2] In the original book, the date is given as 8.1 (8 January), and was most likely a typographical error. It has been changed to read '8 September', which would make Fw Lt Schubert's transfer effective two days after the original order was issued.

Visibility good. Combat Flights: 20. No enemy air activity.

9 Sept   Forcible reconnaissance in accordance with Kofl.'s order.

Transfers: Uffz Derflinger (Jasta 10) was transferred to Jasta 4 as of today. In conformity with Kogenluft 180682 Fl. I of 4 September, Lt d. R. Schmidt (FEA 6) was transferred to the Geschwader and detailed to Jasta 6.

Variable cloudiness in the morning, good visibility. Heavily overcast in the afternoon, rain at times. Combat Flights: 34. No enemy air activity during the day, low activity towards evening.

10 Sept   No special occurrences.

Burial: At 3.30 p.m., the funeral service for the fallen Lt von Winterfeld took place in Escaufourt. Following the service, the body was conveyed home by train.

Variable cloudiness, rain at times. Combat Flights: 12. Enemy air activity quite low.

11 Sept   No special occurrences.

Added To Strength: In conformity with Kogenluft 130954 Fl. I of 8 September, Lt d. R. Baehren and Uffz Hennig (Jastaschule I) were transferred to the Geschwader and detailed as follows: Lt d. R. Baehren to Jasta 10, Uffz Hennig to Jasta 10.

Departure: Lt von Conta was placed at the disposal of Id. Flieg. and from there was transferred out to the Observers' School at Jüterborg.

Rain in the morning, variable cloudiness in the afternoon, clearing in the evening. Combat Flights: 27. No enemy air activity in the afternoon, activity very low in the evening.

12 Sept   No special occurrences.

In conformity with Kogenluft 180873 Fl. I of 10 September, Oblt Grosch (Jasta 4) was placed at the disposal of Id. Flieg.

Burial: The burial of Gefr Blümener who fell in air combat on 8 September, took place today at 6.00 p.m. at the Busigny cemetery.

Cloudy, rain at times. Combat Flights: 4. No enemy air activity.

13 Sept   No special occurrences.

Transfer: Lt d. R. Krayer (Jasta 6) is transferred to Jasta 45 in conformity with Kogenluft 181038 Fl. I of 12 September.

Visibility good, variable cloudiness. Combat Flights: 16. Enemy air activity low.

14 Sept   No particular combat engagements.

Transfer: In conformity with Kogenluft 181087 Fl. I of 13 September, Lt d. R. von Dorrien (Jasta 11) is placed at the disposal of Id. Flieg.

Confidential: Radio telegraph traffic in the Air Defense Service Ia/d. Operation is secret in accordance with No. 888.

Good visibility. Combat Flights: 40. Enemy air activity brisk in the morning, low in the afternoon.

15 Sept   No special occurrences.

Aircraft Downed:

    12.35 p.m., a Bristol Fighter by Lt Neckel (Jasta 6) as 25th.

    12.55 p.m., a Sopwith Camel by Lt Kohlbach (Jasta 10) as 4th.

Concerning the move: Telegrams from Kofl. 2 Ia of 15 Sep 1918, [at] 12.30 p.m. and 2.30 p.m. According to order, everything was held in readiness for loading. The aircraft were dismantled. An advance detail was sent out to Montmédy-Metz.

Good visibility. Combat Flights: 40. Enemy air activity very brisk in the afternoon hours, reconnaissance and bombing squadrons far this side of the lines.

16 Sept No special occurrences. The Geschwader commander, Staffel leaders, and technical officers arrived in Metz-Frescaty by air. The Geschwader is ready to entrain and is awaiting the order to leave.

Transfer: Lt Groos (Jasta 11) is transferred to Jastaschule II as technical officer in conformity with Kogenluft 181217 Fl. I of 16 September.

Good visibility, cloudy at times. Enemy air activity brisk.

17 Sept As on previous day. Frescaty airfield ordered for JG I, placed tactically under the command of Army Section C. Enemy air activity brisk.

18 Sept As on previous day.

Aircraft Downed:

An American DH by Lt Neckel (Jasta 6) as 26th. Enemy air activity brisk.

19 Sept Telegram from Kofl. 2, Ia No. 1909, concerning the move.

Aircraft Downed:

4.00 p.m., a Bristol Fighter by Lt Schulte-Frohlinde (Jasta 11) as 3rd.

In conformity with Kogenluft 181232 Fl. I of 18 September, Lt Meyer (Jasta 4) is transferred to Jastaschule II as instructor.

Low-lying clouds, strong wind gusts. Combat Flights: 25. Enemy air activity low.

Metz, Busigny, Escaufourt

20 Sept Advance detail in Metz-Frescaty. Geschwader still with the 2nd Army, ready for entraining.

Promotion: Vfw Hemer (Jasta 6) was promoted to Leutnant der Reserve.

Added to Strength: Lt d. R. Block from Jastaschule I is transferred to the Geschwader in conformity with Kogenluft 181327 Fl. I of 19 September and is detailed to Jasta 6.

Lt d. R. Wolff (Jasta 6) is placed at the disposal of Id. Flieg. in conformity with Kogenluft 181219 Fl. I of 19 September.

Good visibility, intermittently cloudy. Combat Flights: 49. Enemy air activity low all day long.

21 Sept Geschwader order concerning moving the aircraft by air. One group of the mechanics dispatched by way of the ground.

Transfers: In conformity with Kogenluft 181298 Fl. I of 20 September, Lt d. R. Adomeit (Jasta 10) is transferred to Jasta 62 with the 1st Army. Lt Noltenius (Jasta 27) is transferred to the Geschwader in conformity with Kogenluft 181290 Fl. I of 20 September, and detailed to Jasta 6.

Good visibility. Combat Flights: 20. Enemy air activity low all day long.

22, 23, and 24 Sept Airplanes and advance detail have arrived in Metz-Frescaty. The rest of the Geschwader with the 2nd Army, ready to entrain. Installation of the telephone system in Fort Württemberg. Pilots' quarters in the city of Metz. Airplanes housed in hangars.

Heavily overcast, moderate visibility. Combat Flights: 40. Enemy air activity brisk.

25 Sept With enemy flight operations extremely low, orientation flights by the individual Staffeln with Army Section C and the 19th Army.

Aircraft Downed:

A balloon by Lt Grassmann (Jasta 10) as 6th victory.

Rainy, visibility poor. Enemy air activity brisk.

26 Sept Heavy artillery fire near Army Section C, French attack near the 3rd and 5th Armies. JG II stood at the disposal of the 5th Army. Pursuit region of the Geschwader as far as Verdun. Enemy bombing squadrons which attacked Metz were fought successfully.

Aircraft Downed:

4.15 p.m., a DH 4 by Lt von Gluszewski (Jasta 4).[1]

5.10 p.m., a DH 4 by Oblt Udet (Jasta 4) as 61st.

5.15 p.m., a DH 4 by Oblt Udet (Jasta 4) as 62nd.

5.15 p.m., a DH 4 by Lt Kraut (Jasta 4) as 1st.

Cloudy at times, good visibility. Combat Flights: 20. Enemy air activity low in the morning, brisk in the afternoon, frequent appearance of bombing squadrons.

27 Sept A relatively quiet day with Army Section C. Little air activity. The Geschwader entrained with the 2nd Army. Heavily overcast, light rain. Enemy air activity low.

Metz

28 Sept No special occurrences. The fighter forces of Army Section C deployed. Army order concerning distribution and deployment of the flying units. [Weather] as on previous day. Enemy air activity low.

29 Sept No special occurrences. The train transport arrived. Officers quartered in Ulmenhof, St Privat and Elizabeth Streets in Monteningen, enlisted personnel in Fort Württemberg. Airplanes housed partly in hangars, partly in tents.

Transfer: Oblt Zander was transferred to the Geschwader as officer posted for special duty, in conformity with Kogenluft No. 181475 Fl. I of 26 September, and detailed to Jasta 11.

Award: Lt Mohnicke,[2] Oblt von Wedel (Jasta 11), Lt Laumann (Jasta 10), were awarded the Knight's Cross with Swords of the Hohenzollern House Order.

[Weather] as on previous day. Enemy air activity low.

30 Sept No air activity.

Added to Strength: Vfw Niemz (Jastaschule II) was transferred to the Geschwader in conformity with Kogenluft 181600 Fl. I and detailed to Jasta 11.

Order: Pilots Uffz Martens (Jasta 11) and Uffz Derflinger (Jasta 10)[3] were ordered to Armee Flugpark C.

---

[1] Second victory.
[2] Posted to Id. Flieg. on 8 September 1918.
[3] Should be Jasta 4.

Activity report for the time period from 17 to 30 September, inclusive. Total ration strength for JG I: 53 officers (including doctors and clerks), 473 non-commissioned officers and enlisted personnel (including men posted).

Heavily overcast, rain at times. No enemy air activity.

For accuracy:

By Order: (signed) Bodenschatz   (signed) Göring
Oberleutnant   Oberleutnant and Geschwader Commander

Metz

1 Oct With little enemy air activity, our own flight operations moderate. Deployment of the fighter forces, Army Section C, No. Ia 16304.

Added to Strength: In conformity with Kogenluft No. 181624 Fl. I of 29 September, Lt d. R. Geppert of Jastaschule II was transferred to the Geschwader and detailed to Jasta 4.

In conformity with Kogenluft No. 25579 A. of 30 September, Fw Lt Schubert (Jasta 6) promoted to Saxon Leutnant der Landswehr of the Fliegertruppe 2 in accordance with His Majesty's Decree of 22 September. Public notices sent.

Cloudy, light rain, visibility poor. Combat Flights: 75. Enemy air activity very brisk in the evening hours.

2 Oct Low enemy air activity. Kofl. Order No. Ia 16329 (see enclosure) could not be carried out due to unfavorable weather conditions.

Installation of the telephone system ran into great difficulties. The necessary lines to the air defense officers were missing. Reports concerning enemy flight operations in Army Section C therefore impossible.

Medical Services: Infirmary service takes place at 9.00 a.m. daily in the sick-bay of Armee Flugpark C, Fort Württemberg.

One group of the reserve airplanes is housed at the alternate airfield in Avril, north of Briey. Hangars for 17 airplanes are available there. A detail consisting of one non-commissioned officer and seven men assembled to guard them.

Heavily overcast, hazy. Combat Flights: 42. Enemy air activity brisk in the evening hours.

3 Oct The Geschwader ready for deployment with the 5th Army. Due to unfavorable weather conditions and low fighting activity on both sides of the Meuse, deployment not necessary. Almost no flight operations with Army Section C. Additional orders concerning distribution and deployment of the flying units. Army order concerning aviation forces.

Heavy fog, light north-west wind, clearing up in the afternoon. Combat Flights: 23. Enemy air activity low during the day, picking up only in the evening hours.

Metz, Frescaty

4 Oct Geschwader deployed in the sector of the 5th Army.

Successes: 11.30 a.m., a Spad by Offz Stellv Aue (Jasta 10) as 10th victory.

Transfers: Lt d. R. Riehm was transferred to the Geschwader staff as technical officer in conformity with Kogenluft No. 181719 Fl. I of 3 October.

Lt Koepsch (Jasta 4) was sworn in by Kofl. C as magistrative officer.

Casualty: Lt Schibilsky [Jasta 10] did not return from a front-line patrol.[1]

Heavily overcast. Combat Flights: 41. Enemy air activity brisk at times in the sector of the 5th Army, no activity in Army Section C.

5 Oct   Geschwader stood at the disposal of the 5th Army, no flight operations there.

Transfers: Lt d. R. Riehm was transferred to the Geschwader staff as technical officer in conformity with Kogenluft No. 181719 Fl. I of 3 October.[2]

Fog, clearing later. Combat Flights: 62. No enemy flight operations.

6 Oct   No special occurrences.

Aircraft Downed: At 11.15 a.m., Lt Noltenius shot down a captive balloon in the southern tip of Puvenelle Forest.

Rain at times. Combat Flights: 24. Enemy air activity low.

7 Oct   With light enemy flight operations, few fighter patrols. Order of the Army Group Gallwitz for moving the Geschwader to the 5th Army. Scouting of the airdrome at Marville.

Poor visibility, haze, rain. Combat Flights: 7. No enemy air activity.

8 Oct   The Geschwader moved to the 5th Army. Two motor columns stood at our disposal. The Geschwader still deployed in the sector of Army Section C where enemy flight operations were light. Move completed without difficulties. Reserve machines kept back in Metz for the time being.

Clear. Combat Flights: 34. Enemy air activity low.

Marville

9 Oct   The ground transport arrived without any particular delays. In the course of the morning, the Staffeln arrived by air.

Enemy air activity moderate during the day on both sides of the Meuse, picking up towards evening. A powerful enemy bombing squadron forcibly broke through.

Quarters for officers and enlisted personnel in well-constructed huts, machines in hangars. Airfield sufficient for a Jagdgeschwader, very good in an east-west direction. The communications center set up.

Fog in the morning, clear in the afternoon. Combat Flights: 52. Enemy air activity picking up towards evening.

10 Oct   Despite favorable weather conditions, only occasional appearances by strong enemy squadrons of single-seaters.

Successes:

12.00 p.m., a Spad by Vfw Niemz (Jasta 11) as 3rd.

3.00 p.m., Lt Noltenius (Jasta 6) shoots down a Spad as 15th.

4.50 p.m., a Spad by Lt Heldmann (Jasta 10) as 12th.

4.50 p.m., a Spad by Lt Grassmann (Jasta 10) as 7th.

4.50 p.m., a Spad by Lt Kohlbach (Jasta 10) as 5th.

Transfers: Uffz Martens (Jasta 11) and Uffz Derflinger transferred to Jasta 64 in conformity with Kogenluft 181864 Fl. I. In conformity with Kogenluft 153/9. 18 IIc of 26 September, Lt d. R. Dorrien (Jasta 11) was transferred to FEA 5.

---

[1] Taken prisoner.
[2] Duplication of entry from 4 October 1918.

Lt Kohlbach (Jasta 10) jumped using a parachute following air combat and landed smoothly near Lihou.[1]

Jagdgruppe 1 in Preutin and Lancres were placed under tactical command of the Jagdgeschwader.

Work on the telephone system.

Clear. Combat Flights: 69. Enemy air activity: powerful squadrons of single-seaters from time to time.

11 Oct No special occurrences.

Transfers: In conformity with Kogenluft 181940 Fl. I of 7 October, Lt d. R. Rieth and Lt Meise (Jastaschule II) are transferred to the Geschwader, and detailed as follows: Lt d. R. Rieth, Jasta 6; Lt Meise, Jasta 10.

Fog, hazy. No enemy air activity.

12 Oct No special occurrences.

Transfer: In conformity with Kogenluft No. 182053 Fl. I, Lt d. R. Kirst (Jastaschule II) is transferred to the Geschwader and detailed to Jasta 10.

Slightly cloudy, hazy visibility. Combat Flights: 34. No enemy air activity.

13 Oct No special occurrences. Low-lying clouds, unbroken cloud cover, precipitation at times. Combat Flights: 4. No enemy air activity.

14 Oct No special occurrences.

Transfers: In conformity with Kogenluft No. 1, 182116 Fl. I of 13 October, transferred to the Geschwader from Jastaschule II and detailed as follows: Lt Suck to Jasta 4, Lt Sienz to Jasta 10.

Low-lying clouds, poor visibility. Combat Flights: 2. No enemy air activity.

15 Oct No special occurrences. In conformity with Kogenluft No. 1 of 12 October, Lt d. L. II Schubert (JG I staff) is placed at the disposal of Id. Flieg. Rain. No enemy air activity.

16 Oct No special occurrences. Assigning of alternate airfields. Fog, rain.

17 Oct No activity in the air. Drills, roll-calls for strengthening discipline. Scouting of alternate airfields in the Buzenol and Etalle region. Cloudy.

18 Oct Despite good visibility, no brisk activity. Casualty: Lt Baehren (Jasta 10) did not return from a front-line patrol. Fog, hazy. Combat Flights: 60. No enemy air activity.

19 Oct No special occurrences. Hazy. Combat Flights: 12. No enemy air activity.

20 Oct No flying activity. Rain.

Transfers: Transferred are: Lt Noltenius (Jasta 6) to Jasta 11, Lt Richard Wenzl (Jasta 11) to Jasta 4,[1] Lt Koepsch (Jasta 4) to Jasta 11.

21 Oct Despite good weather, conspicuously low enemy air activity. Variable cloudiness, poor visibility, clearing towards evening. Combat Flights: 46. Enemy air activity low.

22 Oct During fighter patrols, the north edge of Brieulles was strafed with machine guns.

Transfer: In conformity with Kogenluft [Orders] of 20 October, transferred

---

[1] Collided with, or was rammed by, an American Spad of the 147th Aero Squadron.
[2] Should be Jasta 6.

to the Geschwader were: Lt Held (Jastaschule II) with No. 182360, detailed to Jasta 4; Lt Gilles (Jastaschule II) with No. 182320, detailed to Jasta 10.

Replacement: During the absence of Oblt Göring and Lt Udet, Oblt von Wedel assumes acting command of the Geschwader, and Lt Maushake assumes acting command of Jasta 4.

Hazy, clearing towards evening. Combat Flights: 63. Enemy air activity low.

23 Oct

Aircraft Downed:

   12.55 p.m., Lt Noltenius (Jasta 11) a balloon as 16th.

   4.05 p.m., Lt Noltenius (Jasta 11) a Spad as 17th.

   4.15 p.m., Lt Neckel (Jasta 6) an AR as 27th.[1]

   5.35 p.m., Lt Noltenius (Jasta 11) a balloon as 18th.

Slightly cloudy, hazy, clearing towards evening. Combat Flights: 68. Enemy air activity: none in the morning, brisk towards evening.

24 Oct   No special occurrences. Poor visibility. Combat Flights: 47. No enemy air activity.

25 Oct   No special occurrences. In conformity with Kogenluft Order Fl. I No. 182249 of 23 October, Uffz Henschler (JG I) ordered and transferred to Jasta 66. Poor visibility. Combat Flights: 6. No enemy air activity.

26 Oct   Transfer: Lt d. R. Bahlmann and Flieger Flassbeck (Jastaschule II) were transferred to the Geschwader with Order No. 182430 Fl. I, and detailed to Jasta 4. Rain in the morning, clearing in the afternoon. Combat Flights: 25. Enemy air activity low.

27 Oct   No special occurrences.

Award: Lt d. R. Arthur Laumann (Jasta 10) was awarded the order *Pour le Mérite*.

Slightly cloudy, hazy. Combat Flights: 62. Enemy air activity low. At 4.30 p.m., an enemy bombing squadron of about 30 aircraft was cruising on the other side of the lines, but withdrew amidst heavy pursuit action.

28 Oct   No special occurrences.

Aircraft Downed:

   5.00 p.m., a balloon by Lt Noltenius (Jasta 11) as 19th.

Transfer: In conformity with Kogenluft Fl. I. of 26 October, Lt d. R. Rödiger was transferred to the Geschwader from Jastaschule II with Order No. 182510 and detailed to Jasta 6.

Hazy. Combat Flights: 24. No enemy air activity until 4.00 p.m., enemy fighters this side and other side of the lines, moderate activity by single-seater fighters in the meantime.

29 Oct   No special occurrences.

Successes:

   11.00 a.m., a Spad by Lt Richard Wenzl (Jasta 6) as 9th.

   4.25 p.m., a Spad by Lt Schliewen (Jasta 6) as 2nd.

   4.30 p.m., a Spad by Lt Rieth (Jasta 6) as 1st.

   4.55 p.m., a Spad by Lt Grassmann (Jasta 10) as 8th.

---

[1] Dorand AR2.

Casualty: Lt Fischer (Jasta 6) did not return from a front-line patrol.[1]

Hazy in the morning, good visibility in the afternoon. Combat Flights: 71. Enemy air activity in the morning mostly just activity by single-seater fighters on other side of and over the lines. Between 1.45 and 2.45 p.m., forcible breakthrough by enemy bombing and reconnaissance squadrons.

30 Oct The pursuit region was extended as far as the Aisne River. With the 3rd Army, enemy flight operations held to moderate limits.

Aircraft Downed:

4.45 p.m., a Spad by Lt Neckel (Jasta 6) as 28th.

5.00 p.m., a Spad by Lt Heldmann (Jasta 10) as 13th.

5.35 p.m., a Sopwith Camel by Lt Grassmann (Jasta 10) as 9th.

Misty in the morning, clearing in the afternoon. Combat Flights: 52. No enemy air activity in the morning; in the afternoon, only moderate activity in the sector of the 3rd Army as well. Enemy flight operations by individual flights of single-seater fighters and fighter pilots spotted on the other side, activity picking up in the evening hours.

31 Oct No special occurrences. Ten-day transport of sick troops (see enclosure 176).[2]

Aircraft Downed:

12.50 p.m., a Spad-2 by Lt Neckel (Jasta 6) as 29th.

Total ration strength of JG I: 63 officers including doctors and clerks, 484 non-commissioned officers and enlisted men.

Hazy, clearing in the afternoon. Combat Flights: 46. Enemy air activity picked up only in the afternoon hours, and was otherwise limited to reconnaissance and fighter activity over and on the other side of the lines.

1 Nov No flight operations on account of fog. Scouting for an airdrome near the 3rd Army.

Promotion: In accordance with Army HQ [Order] of 10 October, Lt Schäfer (Jasta 10) is promoted to Oberleutnant (Kogenluft No. 25530 A. 1 of 25 October).

Poor visibility.

2 Nov No flight operations on account of fog. Scouting for an airdrome in the region of Tellancourt. Tents transported from Metz to the alternate airfield at Tellancourt. Hazy in the morning, rain in the afternoon.

3 Nov Increasing enemy air activity in the afternoon hours in connection with the heavy fighting near the Army Groups Argonne and Meuse-West.[3]

Brisk squadron activity, especially between 3.00 and 4.00 p.m. Successfully combated by numerous take-offs. Reports concerning enemy flight operations came in only rarely because the air defense officers were in retreat.

Successes:

2.55 p.m., a Spad by Lt Richard Wenzl (Jasta 6) as 10th.

2.55 p.m., a Spad by Lt Richard Wenzl (Jasta 6) as 11th.

3.15 p.m., a DH 9 by Lt Noltenius (Jasta 11) as 20th.

---

[1] Killed in action near Montfaucon.

[2] Evidently the influenza epidemic of 1918 was sweeping through JG I as well.

[3] Battle of Le Chesne and Buzancy.

3.50 p.m., a Spad by Lt von Köckeritz (Jasta 11) as 3rd.

4.05 p.m., an AR by Lt Gussmann (Jasta 11) as 5th.

4.45 p.m., a Spad by Lt Hildebrandt (Jasta 4) as 1st.

4.50 p.m., a Spad by Lt Geppert (Jasta 4) as 1st.

4.50 p.m., a Spad by Lt Reinhardt (Jasta 4) as 1st.

Casualty: Lt Maushake (Jasta 4) severely wounded in air combat.

Mostly fine, cloudy at times. Combat Flights: 56. In the morning, enemy air activity mostly just individual fighters and reconnaissance planes over and on the other side of the lines. In the afternoon and evening hours, particularly brisk activity by fighters and bombing squadrons.

4 Nov   Continuation of the powerful American assault west of the Meuse.[1] The Geschwader on heightened take-off readiness, since Jagdgeschwader II and Jasta 67 are on the move. Deployment in Staffel formation over the battlefield. Expansion of the pursuit region as far as Tannay east of Le Chesne (3rd Army). Cover flight by Jasta 10 for the Schlachtstaffel attack on Beaufort.

Successes:

2.50 p.m., Lt Koepsch (Jasta 4) a DH 9 as 9th.

4.45 p.m., Vfw Niemz (Jasta 11) as 4th.[2]

4.50 p.m., Lt Noltenius (Jasta 4)[3] a DH 9 as 21st.

5.00 p.m., Lt Schulte-Frohlinde (Jasta 11) as 4th.[4]

Mostly cloudless skies, good visibility. Combat Flights: 64. Enemy air activity: just a few fighter pilots in the morning hours; between 11.30 and 12.30 p.m., heavy single-seater action at all altitudes, particularly in the region of Le Chesne. In the afternoon hours, powerful enemy bombing squadrons protected by single-seaters, even on this side.

5 Nov   Focal point of the fighting in the Sivry region and the Staffeln now deployed in this sector.

Successes:

10.10 a.m., Lt Richard Wenzl (Jasta 6) a DH 9 as 12th.[5]

10.30 a.m., Lt Wolfram von Richthofen (Jasta 11) a DH 9 as 8th.[6]

10.35 a.m., Oblt von Wedel (Jasta 11) a Spad as 13th.

10.35 a.m., Lt Heldmann (Jasta 10) as 14th.[7]

10.35 a.m., Lt Bahlmann (Jasta 4) a DH 4 as 1st.

Casualty: Lt Kirst (Jasta 10) crashed fatally following air combat.[8]

Good in the morning, rain in the afternoon. Combat Flights: 41. Enemy air activity: brisk single-seater activity in the morning, no air activity in the afternoon.

6 Nov   New Front of the Army and order for deployment of the pursuit forces

---

[1] Battle of the Sambre.

[2] No type given; aircraft was a Spad.

[3] This should be Jasta 11.

[4] No type given; aircraft was either a DH 4 or DH 9.

[5] Aircraft listed as a Spad in *Above The Lines*, op. cit

[6] This was the last victory scored by a member of the von Richthofen family.

[7] No type given; aircraft was a Spad.

[8] Last casualty of JG I.

(see enclosure 180). Enemy air activity picking up only towards noon. Geschwader deployed in the region of Dun, where the enemy has advanced across the Meuse. Support of the Schlachtstaffeln which attacked the Meuse bridges between Dun and Sivry.

Successes:

11.30 a.m., a Spad by Lt Neckel (Jasta 6) as 30th victory.

11.30 a.m., a Spad by Lt Grassmann (Jasta 10) as 10th victory.

11.30 a.m., a Spad by Lt Heldmann (Jasta 10) as 15th victory.

Beginning of the move to Tellancourt.

Rain in the morning, clearing in the afternoon. Combat Flights: 45. Enemy air activity moderate in general.

Tellancourt

7 Nov Heavy fighting on the east bank of the Meuse in the Dun region. Enemy advanced further to the east. Marville airdrome must be evacuated. Move to Tellancourt with the help of the [Geschwader's] own trucks. Airfield on the west edge of town. Condition poor, bumpy, little grass cover. Quarters very mediocre. Fog and rain.

8 Nov The airdrome and quarters established. Hazy, low clouds.

9 Nov With unfavorable weather conditions, no special occurrences. Preparations for the retreat. Cloudy.

10 Nov To Darmstadt by order of the Commander of Aviation of the 5th Army, aircraft by way of the air, valuable material by way of the ground. Two columns of eight trucks each left for FEA 9. Tents, a few unusable machines, and small supplies of materials left in Tellancourt. Enlisted personnel were transported in part on the trucks. One group set off on foot for the ordered railway station. Concerns about provisions were met to an adequate degree.

11 Nov Armistice. Geschwader flight to Darmstadt under unfavorable weather conditions. Hazy.

The Geschwader has achieved 644 air victories since its founding. Casualties due to enemy action amounted to: 56 officers and pilots, six enlisted men dead; 52 officers and pilots, seven enlisted men wounded.

signed: Hermann Göring,
Oberleutnant and Geschwader Commander

APPENDIX: REVISED ACCOUNT OF 21 APRIL 1918

But how had it happened?

Oberleutnant Fabian's report did not prove to be totally correct. The Baron had already been fatally hit in the air, and his machine therefore heavily damaged upon landing. Photographs later proved this conclusively.

It was not possible to clarify completely the circumstances of his death during the war. However, the last commander of the Jagdgeschwader Freiherr von Richthofen, at that time Oberleutnant Göring, now Reichs Marshal and Commander-in-Chief of the Luftwaffe, did not give up in his search for the true reason for Richthofen's fatal crash. He contacted numerous English pilots who, to the best of their beliefs, held the view that Captain A. Roy Brown had fired the fatal shot in air combat. However, after further careful research, this conclusion was no longer supported. Following detailed letters from England, Canada, and Australia, the dispute between air victory and ground defense, which arose so often during the war, had to be submitted to a renewed investigation. After two decades, strict scientific research has now ruled in favor of the ground defense. Rittmeister Freiherr von Richthofen fell, undefeated, after gaining eighty victories. The map on next page shows the combat area in which Richthofen's final flight found its tragic conclusion.

With his machine guns blazing, Richthofen flew over the Front at an altitude of scarcely three hundred meters, in pursuit of two fleeing opponents. Just behind the Front, he came into heavy machine-gun ground fire from two companies who laid a barrage of bullets between the opponents, a barrage directed at the pursuer who was forced to fly into it. Recognizing the danger, Richthofen made a sharp turn to avoid the bursts of fire.

It was too late. A shot to the heart from the right shoulder put an end to his heroic life.

This account has been confirmed by an artillery observer of the 10th Company of the Foot Artillery, Regiment No. 6; by gunners of the English 24th Machine Gun Company (numeral 2 on the diagram); of the Lewis gun battery (numeral 3 on the diagram); by gunners of the Australian 108th howitzer battery (numeral 5 on the diagram); and by gunners of Section 11 of the 'F' anti-aircraft battery (the Royal Garrison Artillery), who were on the Bray–Corbie road, completely independent of one another. No other airmen were over this sector of the combat area during this hour.

Several days after Richthofen's crash, one of those fleeing Canadian pilots came to the crash site with his squadron commander. They thanked the ground defense crews for the help they had given them, for the pilots had been defenseless against their pursuer due to the jamming of their machine guns.

This is the historical truth which can no longer be assailed from either side.

Richthofen fell fighting for a new victory, undefeated in the element in which he had so often risked his life for his fighting comrades on the ground. They were witnesses to his last flight into eternity.

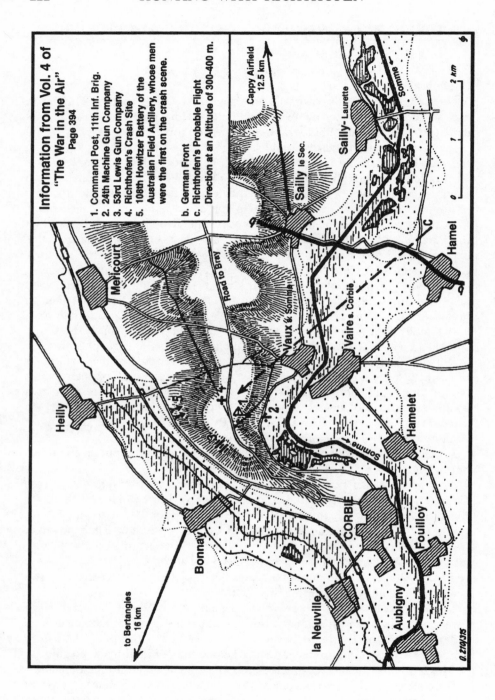

Information from Vol. 4 of "The War in the Air"
Page 394

1. Command Post, 11th Inf. Brig.
2. 24th Machine Gun Company
3. 53rd Lewis Gun Company
4. Richthofen's Crash Site
5. 108th Howitzer Battery of the Australian Field Artillery, whose men were the first on the crash scene.

b. German Front
c. Richthofen's Probable Flight Direction at an Altitude of 300-400 m.

Cappy Airfield
12.5 km

Sailly le Sec.

Sailly-Laurette

Somme

2 km

0   1

Mericourt

Road to Bray

Vaux s. Somme

Vaire s. Corbie

Hamel

Heilly

Hamelet

Somme

CORBIE

Fouilloy

Bonnay

la Neuville

Aubigny

to Bertangles
16 km

0.216/375